A Guide to the Family Law Act 1996

A Guide to the Family Law Act 1996

Maryly La Follette
Solicitor, Partner in Charles Russell
Robert Purdie, LLB (Wales)
Of the Middle Temple, Barrister

Butterworths
London, Edinburgh, Dublin
1996

United Kingdom	Butterworths a Division of Reed Elsevier (UK) Ltd, Halsbury House, 35 Chancery Lane, LONDON WC2A 1EL and 4 Hill Street, EDINBURGH EH2 3JZ
Australia	Butterworths, SYDNEY, MELBOURNE, BRISBANE, ADELAIDE, PERTH, CANBERRA and HOBART
Canada	Butterworth Canada Ltd, TORONTO and VANCOUVER
Ireland	Butterworth (Ireland) Ltd, DUBLIN
Malaysia	Malayan Law Journal Sdn Bhd, KUALA LUMPUR
New Zealand	Butterworths of New Zealand Ltd, WELLINGTON and AUCKLAND
Singapore	Reed Elsevier (Singapore) Pte Ltd, SINGAPORE
South Africa	Butterworths Publishers Pty Ltd, DURBAN
USA	Michie, CHARLOTTESVILLE, Virginia

A CIP catalogue record for this book is available from the British Library.

ISBN 0 406 08160 3

Printed and bound in Great Britain by Clays Ltd, St Ives plc

Lord Chancellor: 'Ah, my Lords, it is indeed painful to have to sit on a woolsack which is stuffed with such thorns as these !'.

WS Gilbert, Iolanthe, Act 1

Contents

Table of Statutes

References in this Table to *Statutes* are to Halsbury's Statutes of England (Fourth Edition) showing the volume and page at which the annotated text of the Act may be found.

Table of Cases

S

T

V

W

Tenancies

1.14 The lack of a discretionary power to transfer tenancies between former cohabitants (where there are no children of the relationship) has been remedied.[1] This is an important development which enables a long term solution to housing problems to follow on the short term relief provided by an injunction or occupation order. The power to order compensation where a tenancy is transferred enables the court to achieve a balanced solution to what is often a difficult jurisdiction to exercise.

1 This overcomes problems that were highlighted by *Wiseman v Simpson* [1988] 1 All ER 245, [1988] 1 WLR 35, CA and *J v J (A Minor: Property Transfer)* [1993] 2 FLR 56.

PROCEDURE

1.15 The Lord Chancellor has extensive rule-making powers to prescribe the relevant procedures outlined in the Act.

CONCLUSION

1.16 Part II of the Act is as yet uncharted water and it is difficult, in the absence of the subordinate legislation, to see whether it will work in practice. Inevitably the cost of divorce (as opposed to ancillary matters) may rise as a result of all the potential applications in connection with the procedure. Part IV has been the result of a great deal of careful thought and informed debate. It follows the developments of CA 1989 by introducing the concept of 'significant harm' into the criteria to be considered in determining non-molestation and occupation applications. Furthermore, it strengthens the development of an interventionist 'Family Court' by enabling the courts to make certain orders of their own motion and by providing a consistent series of remedies available at each level of court. During the Second Reading of the Family Homes and Domestic Violence Bill, Lord Meston said[1] that 'the Bill is surely right to take the focus away from proof of misconduct and replace it with a more pragmatic focus on the need for housing and protection and on the balance of harm as between the adults and children who may be involved'. Inevitably, once the Act comes into force difficult questions of interpretation will have to be decided by the appellate courts.

1 Family Homes and Domestic Violence Bill, HL 2R, 23 February 1995, col 1262.

2 Divorce and separation: definitions relating to Parts II and III

INTRODUCTION

2.1 Part II of the 1996 Act introduces new terminology including (i) divorce order (s 2(1)(a)),[1] (ii) divorce proceedings (s 20),[2] (iii) separation order (s 2(1)(b)),[3] (iv) separation proceedings (s 20),[4] (v) marital proceedings (s 20),[5] (vi) order preventing divorce (s 10(2)),[6] (vii) period for reflection and consideration (s 7),[7] (viii) statement of marital breakdown (s 6(1))[8] and (ix) information meeting (s 8(6)(a), (b)).[9]

1 See para 3.4.
2 See paras 3.4–3.7.
3 See para 3.4.
4 See paras 3.4–3.7.
5 See para 2.3.
6 See paras 2.4, 4.10–4.20.
7 See paras 2.5, 3.18–3.22.
8 See paras 2.6, 3.13, 3.14.
9 See paras 2.7, 3.23–3.27.

THE DEFINITIONS

Divorce proceedings and separation proceedings

2.2 Section 20(3)(a) states that there are 'separation proceedings' if an application for a separation order has been made under s 3 by reference to the statement and not withdrawn. Section 20(3)(b) defines 'divorce proceedings' as those made by an application for a divorce order under s 3 by reference to the statement and not withdrawn.

Marital proceedings

2.3 Section 20(4) defines 'marital proceedings' as being both divorce proceedings and separation proceedings at any time when no application by reference to the statement, either for a divorce order or for a separation order, is outstanding.

Order preventing divorce

2.4 If an application for a divorce order has been made by one of the parties to a marriage, the court may, on the application of the other party, order that the marriage is not to be dissolved.[1]

1 'The involvement of the court in the process is a recognition that marriage is not simply a private contract. Marriage is a public commitment in which society has a stake . . . ' (The Lord Bishop of Oxford, HL 2R, 30 November 1995, col 735.)

Period for reflection and consideration

2.5 Section 7(1) defines the period for reflection and consideration as that period (nine months) which must pass in cases where a statement has been made to give the parties a chance to reflect on whether the marriage can be saved and to have an opportunity to effect a reconciliation and to consider what arrangements should be made for the future.[1]

1 'The details of the process, . . . the year which must be set aside for reflection and consideration, for example, signify clearly that it is not just a private arrangement. Marriage will remain what it was: a commitment for life, made in public with legal consequences.' (The Lord Bishop of Oxford, HL 2R, 30 November 1995, col 735.)

Statement of marital breakdown

2.6 The shorthand term for this document is a 'statement'. Section 6(1) defines the statement as being that made under s 5(1)(a): one or both of the parties to the marriage will state that the maker of the statement (or each of them) believes that the marriage has broken down. The statement must comply with the requirements of s 6.[1]

1 'The statement of breakdown of marriage is not a petition to the court. It comes very near to being an instruction to the judge to set in process the machinery which will inevitably lead to divorce. Its grounds cannot be challenged and it does not have to be proved to be sound. It expresses merely the unexamined opinion of interested parties to what is always a complex matter.' (Lord Craigmyle HL 2R, 30 November 1995, col 719.)

Information meeting

2.7 Section 8(6) defines an 'information meeting' as a meeting organised in accordance with prescribed provisions for the purpose of providing relevant information to the party or parties attending about matters which may arise in connection with the provisions of Part II and Part III. It is also an opportunity for the party or parties to meet with a marriage guidance counsellor and be encouraged to attend such a meeting.

3 Marital proceedings

INTRODUCTION

3.1 Part I of the 1996 Act introduces the principles upon which the provisions in respect of divorce, separation and legal aid in connection with mediation, contained in Parts II and III, are based. The previous provisions[1] relating to the ground for divorce or separation and the corresponding procedure are all repealed. The Lord Chancellor, Lord Mackay told the House of Lords on Second Reading that—

> 'I should like to begin this important debate by reaffirming my commitment and that of the Government to marriage . . . this government will not do anything to undermine it.'

He stated that there was a ' . . . need for greater emphasis on and support for marriage.'[2] Part I sets out the principles and Part II purports to provide the statutory code to give effect to those principles.

1 Contained in the Matrimonial Causes Act 1973.
2 HL 2R, 30 November 1995, col 700.

3.2 It is intended that the 1996 Act will provide the statutory basis for the following principles. First, the institution of marriage is to be supported (s 1(a)). Secondly, the parties to a marriage who believe that their marriage may have broken down, although the question of whether this is irretrievable remains open, are to be encouraged to take all practical steps that they believe are suitable to determine if the marriage can be saved (s 1(b)). Marriage counselling or other steps which might achieve a reconciliation are to be encouraged and supported.[1]

1 See paras 3.38–3.41.

IRRETRIEVABLE BREAKDOWN

3.3 Irretrievable breakdown remains the ground for divorce (s 1(c)). The provisions of MCA 1973 relating to the production of evidence of breakdown through accusations of adultery, behaviour, desertion or separation are eliminated. The evidence provided may not in any way establish what may have been the cause of the irretrievable breakdown and the court is to proceed on the provisional basis that the marriage has broken down irretrievably. Having recognised that a marriage has broken down irretrievably, statutory provisions then provide a framework within which the end of the marriage can be accomplished—

(a) with minimum distress to the parties and to any children;
(b) with questions dealt with in a manner designed to promote as good a continuing relationship between the parties and any children as is possible in the circumstances; and
(c) without unreasonable costs being incurred.

(S 1(c)(i)–(iii)).

Any risk to one of the parties of violence should be removed or diminished so far as that is practicably possible to achieve (s 1(d)).

CIRCUMSTANCES IN WHICH ORDERS ARE MADE

3.4 Either one or both of the parties may make an application to the court for a divorce order or a separation order (s 3(1)). A divorce order under s 2(1)(a) is a single order dissolving a marriage and replaces the present two stage process of decrees nisi and absolute. A separation order under s 2(1)(b) provides for the separation of parties to a marriage, and remains in force while the marriage continues or until cancelled by the court on the joint application of the parties (s 2(3)). Divorce and separation orders come into force as soon as they are made (s 2(2)). The court shall make the order applied for if (but only if)—

- (a) the marriage has broken down irretrievably (s 3(1)(a));
- (b) the requirements with regard to information meetings as set out in s 8 are satisfied (s 3(1)(b));
- (c) the requirements with regard to arrangements for the future as set out in s 9 are satisfied (s 3(1)(c)); and
- (d) the application has not been withdrawn (s 3(1)(d)).

A divorce order may not be made if there is an order preventing divorce in accordance with the provisions of s 10 (s 3(2)).[1]

---

1 See paras 4.10–4.20.

3.5 If there are applications before the court both for a divorce order and a separation order in respect of the same marriage, the court shall proceed as though it were only considering a divorce order unless: (a) there is an order preventing divorce; (b) at this time the court makes an order preventing divorce; (c) a statement has been made within one year of marriage (s 3(3)); or (d) the period for reflection and consideration has been extended by six months (s 7(6) or (13)).

3.6 No divorce order shall be made in cases where a statement is made before the first anniversary of the marriage (s 7(6)). The party to the marriage making a statement must attend an information meeting not less than three months prior to making the statement (s 8(2)). Thus it would seem that a party may attend an information meeting the day after the marriage and be able to make a statement a year later! It would appear that there is no designation as to the maximum period of time which would be allowed to pass before invalidating the attendance at an information meeting in relation to the making of a statement.

3.7 Fourteen days after the statement is filed there follows a nine month minimum period of reflection and consideration (s 7(3)). This minimum period must expire before an application for a divorce order can be made. In effect this means that no marriage will be dissolved until at least 15 months have elapsed from the date of the marriage (s 7(1)). This is somewhat surprising and the 1996 Act does not give the court the power to abridge time. Lord Irvine of Lairg commented as follows—

> 'Let me give an example from the recent experience of a solicitor who is a distinguished family law specialist. A man who was separated from his wife more than 10 years ago was diagnosed in February this year as dying from cancer. He and his wife had not divorced; neither of them had seen any need to do so. He was living with his new partner. She

became pregnant. He wanted, so far as he could, to provide for her and their child after his death. His lawful wife was entirely supportive. She too was living with another. The lawful husband had substantial pension policies. Within a few months he was able to obtain a divorce from his wife with her full agreement and the co-operation of the courts. The divorce was in June of this year. He died in September. His new wife now has the benefit of a widow's pension under his occupational scheme, to the great benefit not just of herself but of their child too. I should be astonished if the noble and learned Lord could think other than that the courts should be given flexibility to grant divorces in less than a year in exceptional circumstances.'

(HL 2R, 30 November 1995, col 707).

CONVERSION OF A SEPARATION ORDER INTO A DIVORCE ORDER

3.8 A separation order which is made prior to the second anniversary of the marriage may not be converted into a divorce order until after that anniversary (s 4(1)). Therefore if the proceedings are begun by way of a separation rather than a divorce, the time requirements for obtaining a divorce order are at least three months longer. Furthermore, a separation order may not be converted into a divorce order under s 4 if—

- (a) at any time an order preventing divorce is in force under s 10 (s 4(2)(a)); or
- (b) there is a child of the family (for definition see s 24(1)) who is under 16 when the application under this section is made (ss 4(2)(b), 4(4)(a)) or the application is made by one party and the other party applies to the court for time for further reflection (ss 4(2)(b), 4(4)(b)).

Subsection 4 does not apply if—

- (i) at the time when the application under this section is made, there is an occupation order or a non-molestation order in force in favour of the applicant, or of a child of the family, made against the other party (s 4(5)(a)); or
- (ii) the court is satisfied that delaying the making of a divorce order would be significantly detrimental to the welfare of any child of the family.

Sub-s (4) ceases to apply either at the end of the period of six months beginning with the end of the period for reflection and consideration by reference to which the separation order was made, or if earlier, on there ceasing to be any children of the family to whom sub-s (4)(a) applied (s 4(5)(b)).

MARITAL BREAKDOWN

3.9 A marriage has broken down irretrievably if four criteria are satisfied (s 5(1)). The criteria are purely procedural in nature and any reference to matters set out in MCA 1973, s 1(2)(a)–(e) has disappeared. The Lord Chancellor hopes that the elimination of fault will enable the parties to a divorce to dissolve the marriage with a minimum of distress and in a manner designed to promote as good a continuing relationship as possible in the circumstances.[1] He believes that allegations by one party against the other lead to feelings of bitterness and resentment in the other party which in turn could result in damage to children. Therefore, the establishment of marriage breakdown now takes on the neutral tones of procedure as follows. A marriage has broken down irretrievably if (but only if)—

(a) a statement has been made by one (or both) of the parties that the maker of the statement (or each of them) believes that the marriage has broken down (s 5(1)(a));[2]
(b) the statement complies with the requirements of s 6 (s 5(1)(b));[3]
(c) the period for reflection and consideration fixed by s 7 has ended (s 5(1)(c));[4] and
(d) the application under s 3 is accompanied by a declaration by the party making the application that—
    (i) having reflected on the breakdown, and
    (ii) having considered the requirements of the Part as to the parties' arrangements for the future (s 5(1)(d)(i), (ii)),

the applicant believes that the marriage cannot be saved. The statement of marital breakdown and the application for a divorce order do not have to be made by the same party (s 5(2)).

1 'How can it be said that a requirement to make allegations of fault provides the law with an underlying moral base when in fact to commit a wrong—such as adultery—actually means that you can be divorced in less than six months and so be free to marry again?' (HL 2R, 30 November 1995, col 701.)

2 See paras 3.13, 3.14.

3 The requirements of s 6 are fulfilled when one or both parties make a statement of marital breakdown in accordance with the rules made under s 12. The Lord Chancellor is going to make the rules rather than the Family Proceedings Rules Committee.

4 The requirements of s 7 are fulfilled at the end of the period for reflection and consideration.

3.10 An application may not be made under s 3 by reference to a particular statement if (a) the parties have jointly given notice withdrawing the statement or (b) the specified period has passed since the end of the period for reflection and consideration (s 5(3)). The 'specified period' is a period of one year since the end of the period for reflection and consideration (s 5(3)(b)). The effect of this provision would be to end the marital breakdown procedure after a minimum period of 21 months after the start of the period for reflection and consideration in cases where there are no children under the age of 16 and after a minimum period of 27 months in cases where there are children under the relevant age.

3.11 The conclusion of divorce proceedings merely by the passing of time is a significant departure from the current position and one to which practitioners must pay careful attention. Under MCA 1973 a petition for divorce remains alive indefinitely. If circumstances have changed during the period between lodging the petition and serving the documents, then amendments can be made without leave of the court or the consent of the other party. If circumstances have remained the same, even if several years have passed, the proceedings are alive and can be progressed.[1] To terminate proceedings by reference to a petition the petitioner must file a notice of discontinuance before the petition is served on any person (FPR 1991, r 2.8). Once a petition has been served it cannot be withdrawn and can only be dismissed. The leave of the court is required to make a decree nisi absolute if more than one year has elapsed from the date on which application for decree absolute can first be made.[2] If the parties become reconciled after a decree nisi or a decree of judicial separation then the application is for an order that the decree be rescinded and the petition dismissed.

1 It may be that a supplemental petition may be necessary, and for this leave is required.

2 See *Court v Court* [1982] Fam 105, [1982] 2 All ER 531, *Savage v Savage* [1982] Fam 100, [1982] 3 All ER 49.

3.12 FLA 1996 contains provisions for interrupting the passage of time under the specified period. An application may not be made under s 3 by reference to a particular statement if (a) the parties have jointly given notice (in accordance with rules of court) withdrawing the statement or (b) the specified period has passed since the end of the period for reflection and consideration (s 5(3)). Any period during which an order preventing divorce under s 10 is in force will not count towards the specified period (s 5(4)). The specified period is a period of one year since the end of the period for reflection and consideration (s 5(3)(b)), and may be modified if, before the end of that period, the parties jointly give notice to the court that they are attempting a reconciliation but require additional time (s 5(5)). The specified period stops running on the day on which the notice is received by the court (s 5(6)(a)); but resumes running on the day on which either of the parties gives notice to the court that the attempted reconciliation has been unsuccessful (s 5(6)(b)). This is another crucial time period which practitioners must monitor carefully. It would be advisable for practitioners to record each case by reference to the crucial dates which apply. If the specified period is interrupted by a continuous period of more than 18 months, any application by either of the parties for a divorce order or for a separation order must be by reference to a new statement received by the court at any time after the end of the 18 months (s 5(7)). The Lord Chancellor may by order amend sub-s (3)(b) by varying the length of the specified period (s 5(8)). The effect of the 18 months provision is that the parties must recommence proceedings.

Statement of marital breakdown

3.13 The statement specified under s 5(1)(a) is known by its full title as a statement of marital breakdown but will generally be referred to simply as 'a statement' (s 6(1)). Section 6 details the form and content of a statement, with particular reference to s 12. The content of a statement will vary to some degree depending upon whether it is lodged by one party or by both parties. If a statement is lodged by one party only, then it must also state that that party is aware of the purpose of the period for reflection and consideration as described in s 7 and that that party wishes to make arrangements for the future (s 6(2)(a), (b)). If the statement is lodged by both parties, then it must also state that each of them is aware of the purpose of the period for reflection and consideration (described in s 7) and that they wish to make arrangements for the future (s 6(3)(a), (b)).

3.14 A statement made at a time when the circumstances of the case include any of those mentioned in s 6(7) is ineffective for the purposes of Part II. The circumstances are—

(a) that a statement has previously been made with respect to the marriage and it is, or will become, possible—
  (i) for an application for a divorce order, or
  (ii) for an application for a separation order,
  to be made by reference to the previous statement (s 6(7)(a));
(b) that such an application has been made in relation to the marriage and has not been withdrawn (s 6(7)(b));
(c) that a separation order is in force (s 6(7)(c)).

This would prevent a multiplicity of proceedings.

LORD CHANCELLOR'S RULES

Statements

3.15 The precise nature of the statement will be contained in rules made by the Lord Chancellor under s 12(1) as to the form, content, manner to be given to the court, service and information to be given to the parties by their respective legal representatives.

Duties of legal representatives

3.16 In addition, there is provision for the Lord Chancellor to make rules governing a person who is the legal representative of a party to a marriage with respect to which a statement has been or is proposed to be made (s 12(2)). The rules may include a requirement that the legal representative inform that party about the availability of marriage support services, mediation and, where there are children of the family, that in relation to the arrangements to be made the parties should consider the child's welfare, wishes and feelings (s 12(2)(a)(i), (ii)). The legal representative may also be required to provide that party with names and addresses of persons qualified to help effect a reconciliation or in connection with mediation (s 12(2)(b)(i), (ii)). The legal representative may also be required to certify that they have complied with the foregoing regulations (s 12(2)(c)(i)–(iii)). It is likely that the requirements of these rules will impose a duty upon the legal representative which is far greater than that currently imposed by the requirement to complete a certificate with regard to reconciliation. Currently, each legal representative is required to complete such a certificate stating whether they have discussed with the petitioner the possibility of reconciliation and whether they have given to the petitioner the names and addresses of persons qualified to help with reconciliation. There is no *duty* actually to do so.

3.17 Section 12(2)(c) would on the surface appear to impose a similar duty upon the legal representative as previously, but it may be that the duty under the 1996 Act will be far heavier. Lord Meston stated that—

> 'Finally on procedural matters, I should like to see a more positive obligation in the rules to be made under clause 11(2) (now s 12(2)). At present, they echo the rather lame obligation upon lawyers in the 1969 Act to certify whether they have discussed reconciliation and certain other matters with their clients. If that is the only obligation, what will happen is what so often happened: the lawyer will simply certify that he has not discussed the question of reconciliation.'[1]

Legal advisors may be obliged to suggest reconciliation and mediation and make referrals to the appropriate people. Practitioners will need to compile a list of names and addresses of qualified people. No doubt each legal representative will want to carry out a careful screening of the counsellors/mediators to whom clients are to be referred. The standard of performance and cost will no doubt vary considerably.

---

1 HL 2R, 30 November 1995, col 771.

PERIOD FOR REFLECTION AND CONSIDERATION

3.18 Before an application for a divorce order or for a separation order may be made by reference to the statement, there must be a period for the parties to (a) reflect on whether the marriage can be saved and to have an opportunity to effect a reconciliation, and (b) consider what arrangements should be made for the future (s 7(1)). This time is to be known as the period for reflection and consideration (s 7(2)). It lasts for nine months beginning with the 14th day after the day on which the statement is received by the court for those couples who do not have children under the age of 16 (s 7(3)). When added to the period between the information meeting and the statement of marital breakdown, the minimum period for divorce is 12 months and 15 days (s 7(3)). If there are children under the age of 16 then the period for reflection and consideration is extended by six months (s 7(11)). The time could be much longer if the information meeting precedes the statement by more than three months.

3.19 Where either the statement has been made by one party, or rules made under s 12 require the court to serve a copy of the statement on the other party, or failure to comply with the rules causes inordinate delay in service, the court may, on the application of that other party, extend the period for reflection and consideration (s 7(4)(a)–(c)). An extension under s 7(4) may be for any period not exceeding the time between (a) the beginning of the period for reflection and consideration; and (b) the time when service is effected (s 7(5)(a), (b)). Simply because the rules are not complied with, it does not mean that the court, on application, would extend the period for reflection and consideration; it will only do so where non-compliance has caused inordinate delay in service. Requirements for service of petitions under MCA 1973 include service by the court. The 1996 Act seems to require service of a statement by the court (s 12(1)(d)). The inordinate delay of service, whether caused by the statement maker or the court may give rise to an extension of time. A statement which is made before the first anniversary of the marriage to which it relates is ineffective for the purposes of any application for a divorce order (s 7(6)). It follows that it is not ineffective for the purposes of an application for a separation order. Therefore, the bar to commencing divorce proceedings within the first year of marriage is preserved unless attendance at an information meeting within the first year of marriage is commencing proceedings.

3.20 If at any time during the period for reflection and consideration, the parties jointly give notice to the court that they are attempting a reconciliation but require additional time (s 7(7)), then the period for reflection and consideration stops running on the day on which the notice is received by the court but resumes running on the day on which either of the parties gives notice to the court that the attempted reconciliation has been unsuccessful (s 7(8)). The interruption of the period for reflection and consideration is not unlimited. If there is an interruption under s 7(8) by a continuous period of more than 18 months, any application by either of the parties for a divorce order or for a separation order must be by reference to a new statement received by the court at any time after the end of the 18 months (s 7(9). It is not known whether the parties are required to attend an information meeting again.[1] Because s 7(3) provides that a statement must be followed by a period for reflection and consideration without limiting the circumstances to original or first statements, it would appear that time starts running again. For practitioners the importance of meeting these procedural deadlines must be stressed, and the scope for professional negligence litigation gives cause for concern. The requirement for a new statement emphasises the need to have clear evidence of the irretrievable breakdown of the marriage. This requirement is similar to that contained in the old provisions of MCA 1973 with regard to a period exceeding six months in relation to s 1(2)(a) and (b).

---

1 The circumstances for exemption from information meetings have not yet been prescribed under s 8(2).

3.21 Where an application for a divorce order is made by one party and (a) the other party applies to the court within the prescribed period for time for further reflection and (b) the arrangements for the future have been made in accordance with s 9, then the period for reflection and consideration is extended by six months (s 7(10), (13)). Therefore, if one party to the marriage applies to the court for further time but the other does not, then the period for reflection and consideration is automatically extended by six months. The scope for a spiteful spouse to make difficulties for the other is worrying and must be of concern to practitioners. Once the party has applied for a divorce order he or she will have to wait for the expiration of the six months period but will not have to make a new application for a divorce order at the end of the period.

3.22 Most importantly, where an application for a divorce order is made s 7(13) also applies if there are children of the family under the age of 16 (s 7(11)). A period of reflection and consideration is thus always at least 15 months in those circumstances. A period for reflection and consideration which has been extended under s 7(13), and which has not otherwise come to an end, comes to an end on there ceasing to be any children of the family under the age of 16 (s 7(11)). Therefore, if the period of reflection and consideration began when the youngest child of the family was aged 15 years and 3 months then there would be no extension of time under s 7(11) as there would be no child of the family to whom that subsection could apply.

ATTENDANCE AT INFORMATION MEETINGS

3.23 An 'information meeting' is a meeting organised, in accordance with prescribed provisions, for the purpose of—

(a) providing relevant information to the party or parties attending about matters which may arise in connection with the provisions of, or made under, Parts II or III. The relevant information must be given in accordance with prescribed provisions; and

(b) giving the party or parties attending the information meeting the opportunity of having a meeting with a marriage counsellor and of encouraging that party or those parties to attend that meeting (s 8(6)(a), (b)).

'Prescribed' means those provisions prescribed by regulations made by the Lord Chancellor (s 8(13)). Therefore, until regulations are published the prescribed circumstances are unknown although invalidity or infirmity of one or both of the parties is likely to be one such circumstance. The need to make an urgent application for an injunction may well be another circumstance, although it is likely that the party would be required to attend an information meeting at a later date. A party making a statement must (except in prescribed circumstances) have attended an information meeting not less than three months before making the statement (s 8(2)).

3.24 Different information meetings must be arranged with respect to different marriages (s 8(3)) and in the case of a statement made by both parties, the parties may attend separate meetings or the same meeting (s 8(4)). Where one party has made a statement, the other party must (except in prescribed circumstances) attend an information meeting before (a) making any application to the court with respect to a child of the family or of a prescribed description relating to property or financial matters or (b) contesting any such application (s 8(5)(a), (b)).

3.25 An information meeting must be conducted by a person who is qualified and appointed in accordance with prescribed provisions and who will have no financial or other interest in any marital proceedings between the parties (s 8(7)). Regulations made under s 8(8) may, in particular, make provision—

(a) about the places and times at which information meetings are to be held;
(b) for written information to be given to persons attending them;
(c) for the giving of information to parties (otherwise than at information meetings) in cases in which the requirement to attend such meetings does not apply;
(d) for information of a prescribed kind to be given only with the approval of the Lord Chancellor or only by a person or by persons approved by him; and
(e) for information to be given, in prescribed circumstances, only with the approval of the Lord Chancellor or only by a person, or by persons, approved by him (s 8(8)(a)–(e)).

3.26 The regulations made under s 8(6) must, in particular, make provision with respect to the giving of information about—

(a) marriage counselling and other marriage support services;
(b) the importance to be attached to the welfare, wishes and feelings of children;
(c) how the parties may acquire a better understanding of the ways in which children can be helped to cope with the breakdown of a marriage;
(d) the nature of the financial questions that may arise on divorce or separation, and services which are available to help the parties;
(e) protection available against violence, and how to obtain support and assistance;
(f) mediation;
(g) the availability to each of the parties of independent legal advice and representation;
(h) the principles of legal aid and where the parties can get advice about obtaining legal aid;
(i) the divorce and separation process (s 8(9)).

3.27 If a meeting with a marriage guidance counsellor under this section is arranged, then it must be held in accordance with prescribed provisions and must be with a person qualified and appointed in accordance with prescribed provisions (s 8(11)). Any person who would not be required to make any contribution towards mediation provided for him under the Legal Aid Act 1988, Part IIIA will not be required to make a contribution towards the cost of a session with a marriage guidance counsellor arranged for him under s 8 (s 8(12)).

ARRANGEMENTS FOR THE FUTURE

3.28 A divorce order can only be made if the provisions of s 9 concerning the parties' arrangements for the future have been fulfilled (s 3(1)(c)).[1] In order to comply with this requirement, one of the following must be produced to the court—

(a) a court order (made by consent or otherwise) dealing with their financial arrangements;
(b) a negotiated agreement as to their financial arrangements;
(c) a declaration by both parties that they have made their financial arrangements;
(d) a declaration by one of the parties (to which no objection has been notified to the court by the other party) that—
  (i) he has no significant assets and does not intend to make an application for financial provision;
  (ii) he believes that the other party has no significant assets and does not intend to make an application for financial provisions; and
  (iii) there are therefore no financial arrangements to be made (s 9(2)).

The requirements of s 11 regarding the welfare of the children must also have been satisfied (s 9(5)).

1 Subject to the exemptions contained in Schedule 1; see Ch 4.

WELFARE OF CHILDREN

3.29 The court must consider whether there are any children of the family to whom s 11 applies and, where there are such children, whether it should exercise any of its powers under CA 1989 with respect to any of them (s 11(1)(a), (b)). Presumably the principles of CA 1989 will prevail, namely that where a court is considering whether or not to make one or more orders under this Act with respect to a child, it shall not make the order or any of the orders unless it considers that doing so would be better for the child than making no order at all (CA 1989, s 1(5)).

3.30 In a case to which s 11 of the 1996 Act applies, and where it appears to the court that the circumstances of the case require it or are likely to require it to exercise its powers under CA 1989 with respect to any such child, it may direct that the divorce order or separation order is not to be made until the court orders otherwise (s 11(2)(a)). Similarly, if the court decides that it is not in a position to exercise the power, or those powers, without giving further consideration to the case and there are exceptional circumstances which make it desirable in the interests of the child that the court should give a direction under s 11, it may direct that the divorce order or separation order is not to be made until the court orders otherwise (s 11(2)(b),(c)).

3.31 The court must treat the interests of the child as paramount when deciding whether the circumstances are as mentioned in s 11(2)(a) (s 11(3)). In making the decision, the court shall also have particular regard to—
(a) the wishes and feelings of the child considered in the light of his age and understanding and the circumstances in which those wishes were expressed;
(b) the conduct of the parties in relation to the upbringing of the child;
(c) the general principle that, in the absence of evidence to the contrary, the welfare of the child will be best served by—
  (i) his having regular contact with those who have parental responsibility for him and with other members of his family; and
  (ii) the maintenance of as good a continuing relationship with his parents as is possible; and
(d) any risk to the child attributable to—
  (i) where the person with whom the child will reside is living or proposes to live;

(ii) any person with whom that person is living or with whom he proposes to live; or

(iii) any other arrangements for his care and upbringing.

(S 11(4)).

Section 11 applies to any child of the family who has not reached the age of 16 at the date when the court considers the case and any child of the family who has reached the age of 16 at that date and in relation to whom the court directs that this section shall apply (s 11(5)(a), (b)).

JURISDICTION AND COMMENCEMENT OF PROCEEDINGS

3.32 The jurisdiction of the court in relation to divorce and separation proceedings is set out in s 19. 'The court's jurisdiction' means—

(a) the jurisdiction of the court under Part II to entertain marital proceedings; and

(b) any other jurisdiction conferred on the court under Part II, or any other enactment, in consequence of the making of a statement (s 19(1)(a), (b)).

The court's jurisdiction is exercisable in very much the same circumstances as those provided by MCA 1973, s 19(2)(a)–(c) as follows—

(i) at least one of the parties was domiciled in England and Wales on the settlement date;

(ii) at least one of the parties was habitually resident in England and Wales throughout the period of one year ending with the statement date (therefore, a party may attend an information meeting when habitually resident for less than a year);

(iii) nullity proceedings are pending in relation to the marriage when the marital proceedings commence.

'Nullity proceedings' means proceedings in respect of which the court has jurisdiction under s 5(3) of DMPA 1973 (s 19(7)). 'Statement date' means the date on which the relevant statement was received by the court (s 19(7)).

3.33 If a separation order is in force or an order preventing divorce has been cancelled, the court continues to have jurisdiction to entertain an application made by reference to the order referred to in s 19(3) and may exercise any other jurisdiction which is conferred on it in consequence of such an application (s 19(4)).

3.34 DMPA 1973 provides for obligatory and discretionary stays of matrimonial proceedings in certain circumstances where there are concurrent proceedings in another jurisdiction.[1] The 1996 Act (Sch 3) amends DMPA 1973 to provide for the changes of terminology brought about by the 1996 Act. In respect of discretionary stays the reference to 'trial or first trial'[2] is replaced so that a stay can be ordered before the marital proceedings are finally determined.[3]

1 See *Rayden and Jackson on Divorce and Family Matters*, Ch 14.

2 *Thyssen-Bornemisza v Thyssen-Bornemisza* [1986] Fam 1, [1985] 1 All ER 328, [1985] 2 WLR 715, CA.

3 DMPA 1973, Sch 1, para 9(1A).

Time when proceedings for divorce or separation begin

3.35 The receipt by the court of a statement is to be treated as the commencement of proceedings (s 20(1)). The proceedings are known as marital proceedings and marital proceedings are also—

(a) separation proceedings if an application for a separation order has been made under s 3 by reference to the statement and not withdrawn (s 20(3)(a));
(b) divorce proceedings if an application for a divorce order has been made under s 3 by reference to the statement and not withdrawn (s 20(3)(b)).

3.36 Marital proceedings are to be treated as being both divorce proceedings and separation proceedings at any time when no application by reference to the statement, either for a divorce order or for a separation order, is outstanding (s 20(4)). Proceedings which are commenced by making an application to convert separation proceedings into divorce proceedings under s 4(3) are marital proceedings and divorce proceedings (s 20(5)). Marital proceedings come to an end on the happening of any of the following events—

(a) the making of a separation order;
(b) the making of a divorce order;
(c) the withdrawal of the statement by a notice given by both parties in the prescribed form in accordance with s 5(3)(a);
(d) at the end of the specified period provided in s 5(3)(b), if no application for a separation order or divorce order set out in s 3 by reference to the statement is outstanding;
(e) the withdrawal of all such applications which are outstanding at the end of that period;
(f) the withdrawal of an application under s 4(3) (s 20(6)(a)–(f)).

3.37 The 1996 Act provides that where a separation order is in force, and, if while the parties to the marriage remain separated, one of them dies intestate as respects any real or personal property, that property devolves as if the other had died before the intestacy occurred (s 21(a), (b)).[1]

1 This is the same as the provisions contained in MCA 1973, s 18(2).

MARRIAGE SUPPORT SERVICES

3.38 The Lord Chancellor may, with the approval of the Treasury, make grants in connection with the provision of marriage support services, research into the causes of marital breakdown and research into ways of preventing marital breakdown (s 22(1)(a)–(c)). Any grant so made may be made subject to such conditions as the Lord Chancellor considers appropriate (s 22(2)). In exercising his power, the Lord Chancellor is to have regard, in particular, to the desirability of services of that kind being available when they are first needed (s 22(3)).

3.39 The Lord Chancellor, or a person appointed by him, may secure the provision of marriage counselling for the parties to a marriage. The provision of marriage guidance counselling will be made in accordance with regulations made by the Lord Chancellor (s 23(1)). Marriage counselling may only be provided under this section at a time when a period for reflection and consideration either is running in relation to the marriage or is interrupted under s 7(8) but not for a continuous period exceeding

18 months (s 23(2)(a), (b)). Marriage counselling may only be provided under this section for persons who would not be required to make any contribution towards the costs of mediation provided for them under Part IIIA of the Legal Aid Act 1988 (s 23(3)). Persons for whom marriage counselling is provided under s 23 are not required to make any contribution towards the cost (s 23(4)).

3.40 Marriage counselling is only to be provided under this section if it appears to the marriage counsellor to be suitable in all the circumstances (s 23(5)). Regulations made by the Lord Chancellor may make provision about the way in which the counselling is to be provided and the circumstances in which the provision of counselling is to be subject to the approval of the Lord Chancellor (s 23(6)(a), (b)). Any contract entered into the purposes of providing marriage counselling must include such provision as the Lord Chancellor may direct (s 23(7)). If the person so appointed under sub-s (1) is the Legal Aid Board, the powers conferred on the Board by or under the Legal Aid Act 1988 shall be exercisable for the purposes of s 23 as they are exercisable for the purposes of the Legal Aid Act 1988 (s 23(8)).

3.41 The Legal Aid Act 1988 is consequentially amended by s 23(9) of the 1996 Act. A new provision 15(3I) is added stating that a person may be refused a Legal Aid Certificate for representation for the purposes of proceedings if the proceedings are marital proceedings within the meaning of the 1996 Act, Part II, and he is being provided with marriage counselling in relation to the marriage.

CONNECTED PROCEEDINGS

3.42 For the purposes of the 1996 Act, Part II, proceedings are connected with marital breakdown if they fall within s 25(2) and, at the time of the proceedings—

- (a) a statement has been received by the court with respect to the marriage and it is or may become possible for an application for a divorce order or a separation order to be made by reference to that statement (s 25(1)(a));
- (b) such an application in relation to the marriage has been made and not withdrawn (s 25(1)(b));
- (c) a divorce order has been made, or a separation order is in force, in relation to the marriage (s 25(1)(c)).

3.43 The proceedings are any under CA 1989, Parts I to V with respect to a child of the family or any proceedings resulting from an application—

- (a) for, or for the cancellation of, an order preventing divorce (s 25(2)(a));
- (b) by either party to the marriage for an order under the 1996 Act, Part IV (s 25(2)(b));
- (c) for the exercise, in relation to a party to the marriage or child of the family, of any of the court's powers under MCA 1973, Part II (s 25(2)(c));
- (d) made otherwise to the court with respect to, or in connection with, any proceedings connected with the breakdown of the marriage (s 25(2)(d)).

Applications made for any s 8 orders under CA 1989 and applications made for ancillary relief under MCA 1973 are connected proceedings for the purposes of the 1996 Act.

RESOLUTION OF DISPUTES

Directions with respect to mediation

3.44 After the court has received a statement, it may give a direction requiring each party to attend a meeting arranged in accordance with that direction (s 13(1)). The purpose of the meeting is to enable an explanation to be given of the facilities available to the parties for mediation in relation to disputes between them and of providing an opportunity for each party to agree to take advantage of those facilities (s 13(1)(a), (b)). The dispute in respect of which the parties may be required by the court to attend a meeting is not limited to finance and includes any dispute with regard to children. A direction may be given at any time, including in the course of proceedings connected with the breakdown of the marriage (s 13(2)).[1] Baroness Young observed that mediation is not conciliation, ' . . . it is quite different. Couples must accept at the outset that the marriage is over before mediation starts. It is a method by which divorce settlements are facilitated. It cannot be compulsory'.[2]

1 Proceedings which are connected with the breakdown of the marriage are set out in s 25, see paras 3.42–3.43.

2 HL 2R, 30 November 1995, col 732.

3.45 A direction may be given on the application of either party or on the initiative of the court (s 13(3)). It may be that the courts will attempt to coerce couples into mediation though it will only have real force in relation to those on legal aid. It is widely thought by experts in the field of mediation that it only works when both parties attend voluntarily, with a desire to resolve disputes in this way and when the couple has already come to terms with the emotional stresses connected with marriage breakdown. Mediation could do much harm to vulnerable women and is suitable for fewer than half the cases. Discovering the true earnings and assets of husbands can prove very difficult, especially in the case of self-employed men with complicated finances. Mediators on performance-related contracts may be urged to engineer 'quick fix deals' against the interests of the most vulnerable. They may not have the expertise to scrutinise complicated and difficult accounts and company and trust arrangements.

3.46 The parties are required to attend the same meeting unless one of them asks, or both of them ask, for separate meetings or the court considers that separate meetings would be more appropriate (s 13(4)(a), (b)). A direction shall specify a person chosen by the court (with that person's agreement) to arrange and conduct the meeting or meetings and require such person as may be specified to produce a report stating whether the parties have complied with the direction and if they have, whether they have agreed to take part in mediation (s 13(5)(a), (b)). Lord Mackay stated that—

> 'It is clear that the children who do best after divorce are the children whose parents co-operate in the discharge of their parental responsibilities and who reach amicable arrangements for the future of their children. . . . I am not intending that mediation should become compulsory—compulsory mediation quite simply does not work, and is a contradiction in terms.'[1]

1 HL 2R, 30 November 1995, col 704.

Adjournments

3.47 The court's power to adjourn any proceedings connected with the breakdown of the marriage includes the power to adjourn for the purpose of allowing the parties to comply with a direction for mediation under s 13 or for the purpose of enabling disputes to be resolved amicably (s 14(1)(a), (b)). In determining whether to adjourn for either purpose, the court shall have regard in particular to the need to protect the interests of any child of the family (s 14(2)). If there is an adjournment of any proceedings connected with the breakdown of the marriage, the period must not exceed the maximum period prescribed by rules of court (s 14(3)). Unless the only purpose of the adjournment is to allow the parties to comply with a direction under s 13, the court must order one or both of them to produce to the court a report as to—

(a) whether they have taken part in a mediation during the adjournment;
(b) whether, as a result, any agreement has been reached between them;
(c) the extent to which any dispute between them has been resolved as a result of any such agreement;
(d) the need for further mediation; and
(e) how likely it is that further mediation will be successful (s 14(4)(a)–(e)).

4 Ancillary relief

INTRODUCTION

4.1 The ancillary relief provisions in the 1996 Act are contained in ss 9,[1] 10 and Sch 2. These contain the procedural steps which must be taken to satisfy the court that proper provision for the parties to the marriage and any children of the family has been made. MCA 1973 continues to provide the framework within which the court will exercise its powers.[2]

1 See para 3.28.
2 MCA 1973, ss 23–25A and 31.

ARRANGEMENTS FOR THE FUTURE

4.2 The requirements as to the parties' arrangements for the future provide that one of the following must be produced to the court—

- (a) a court order (made by consent or otherwise) dealing with their financial arrangements;
- (b) a negotiated agreement as to their financial arrangements;
- (c) a declaration by both parties that they have made their financial arrangements;
- (d) a declaration by one of the parties (to which no objection has been notified to the court by the other party) that—
  - (i) he has no significant assets and does not intend to make an application for financial provision;
  - (ii) he believes that the other party has no significant assets and does not intend to make an application for financial provision; and
  - (iii) there are therefore no financial arrangements to be made.

(S 9(2)(a)–(d)).

Section 9(2)(d) may be considered somewhat similar in practical effect to the financial provision which is made by the petitioner for the respondent being reasonable and fair or the best that can be made in the circumstances.[1] Such a provision has been called a 'Casanova's charter' because the best in the circumstances need not be fair and reasonable.[2]

1 MCA 1973, s 10(3)(b).
2 Quoted by Ms Jean Corston HC 2R, 25 March 1996, col 777.

4.3 Where a Jewish religious marriage has taken place in accordance with the Marriage Act 1949 (s 26(1)(d)) it is possible to obtain a Jewish religious divorce.[1] The court may direct that there must be produced to the court a declaration by both parties that they have taken such steps as are required to obtain a religious divorce (s 9(3)). Such a direction may only be given if the court is satisfied that it is just and reasonable in all the circumstances of the case (s 9(4)(a)), and may be revoked by the court at any time (s 9(4)(b)).

1 Commonly called a 'Get'.

4.4 In determining whether appropriate arrangements for the future have been made, the requirements of s 11 relating to the welfare of the children must have been satisfied (s 9(5)). If the court is satisfied, on an application made by one of the parties after the end of the period for reflection and consideration that the circumstances of the case are those set out in Sch 1, then it may make a divorce order or a separation order even if there is no court order, negotiated agreement or declaration as set out in s 9(2) (s 9(7)).[1]

---

1 See paras 4.5–4.9 for the four exemptions.

The first exemption

4.5 The circumstances referred to are that (s 9(7)(a))—

(a) the requirements of s 11 have been satisfied;

(b) the applicant has, during the period for reflection and consideration, taken such steps as are reasonably practicable to try to reach a financial agreement; and

(c) the applicant has made an application to the court for financial relief and has complied with all requirements of the court in relation to proceedings for financial relief but—

 (i) the other party has delayed in complying with requirements of the court or has otherwise been obstructive; or

 (ii) for reasons which are beyond the control of the applicant, or of the other party, the court has been prevented from obtaining the information which it requires to determine the financial position of the parties.

(Sch 1, para 1(a), (b), (c)(i), (ii)).

The second exemption

4.6 The circumstances referred to are that (s 9(7)(b))—

(a) the requirements of s 11 have been satisfied;

(b) the applicant has, during the period for reflection and consideration, taken such steps as are reasonably practicable to try to reach agreement about the parties' financial arrangements;

(c) because of—

 (i) the ill health or disability of the applicant, the other party or a child of the family (whether physical or mental), or

 (ii) an injury suffered by the applicant, the other party or a child of the family,

 the applicant has not been able to reach agreement with the other party about those arrangements and is unlikely to be able to do so in the foreseeable future; and

(d) a delay in making the order applied for under s 3—

 (i) would be significantly detrimental to the welfare of any child of the family; or

 (ii) would be seriously prejudicial to the applicant.

(Sch 1, para 2).

The third exemption

4.7 The circumstances referred to are that (s 9(7)(c))—

(a) the requirements of s 11 have been satisfied;
(b) the applicant has found it impossible to contact the other party; and
(c) as a result, it has been impossible for the applicant to reach agreement with the other party about their financial arrangements.

(Sch 1, para 3).

The fourth exemption

4.8 The circumstances referred to are that (s 9(7)(d))—

(a) the requirements of s 11 have been satisfied;
(b) an occupation order or a non-molestation order is in force in favour of the applicant or a child of the family, made against the other party;
(c) the applicant has, during the period for reflection and consideration, taken such steps as are reasonably practicable to try to reach agreement about the parties' financial arrangements;
(d) the applicant has not been able to reach agreement with the other party about those arrangements and is unlikely to be able to do so in the foreseeable future; and
(e) a delay in making the order applied for under s 3—
 (i) would be significantly detrimental to the welfare of any child of the family; or
 (ii) would be seriously prejudicial to the applicant.

(Sch 1, para 4(a)–(e)).

4.9 If the parties' arrangements for the future include a division of pension assets or rights under MCA 1973, s 25B, or the Family Law (Scotland) Act 1985, s 10, any declaration under s 9(2)(c) or (d) must be a statutory declaration (s 9(8)).[1]

1 See the Statutory Declarations Act 1835.

HARDSHIP: ORDERS PREVENTING DIVORCE

4.10 If an application for a divorce order has been made by one of the parties to a marriage, the court may, on the application of the other party, order that the marriage should not be dissolved (s 10(1)). Such an order is designated as an order preventing divorce, and it may be made only if the court is satisfied—

(a) that the dissolution of the marriage would result in substantial financial or other hardship to the other party or to a child of the family (s 10(2)(a)); and
(b) that it would be wrong in all the circumstances (including the conduct of the parties and the interests of any child of the family), for the marriage to be dissolved (s 10(2)(b)).

In deciding whether it would be wrong to dissolve the marriage, the court should consider the broad public interest and pay great regard to whether a marriage which has become an empty shell should be preserved.[1] Hardship includes the loss of a chance to obtain a future benefit (as well as the loss of any existing benefit) (s 10(6)). Existing benefits could be, for example, an interest under a trust, matrimonial home rights,[2] loss of title or style, etc.

1 *Mathias v Mathias* [1972] Fam 287, [1972] 3 All ER 1, CA. See also *Talbot v Talbot* (1971) 115 Sol Jo 870.
2 See paras 7.2, 7.4.

4.11 If an application for the cancellation of an order preventing divorce is made by one or both of the parties, the court shall cancel the order unless it is satisfied—

(a) that dissolution of the marriage would result in substantial financial or other hardship to the party in whose favour the order was made or to a child of the family (s 10(3)(a)); and

(b) that it would be wrong, in all of the circumstances (including the conduct of the parties and the interests of any child of the family), for the marriage to be dissolved (s 10(3)(b)).

Obviously the court will have regard to any change in circumstances since the making of the order preventing divorce.

4.12 For some guidance as to the application of s 10 of the 1996 Act the case law developed pursuant to MCA 1973, ss 5, 10 and 25(2)(h) will no doubt prove helpful. It should be noted that s 10 of the 1996 Act extends the provisions of MCA 1973, s 5 considerably and the ability of one party to the marriage to block divorce. MCA 1973, s 5 applied only in respect of petitions for divorce which relied on s 1(2)(e), and s 10 applied additionally to petitions which relied on s 1(2)(d). It did not apply to petitions for divorce which relied on adultery, behaviour or desertion. Therefore, it did not apply to all divorces, whereas s 10 of the 1996 Act applies to all marital proceedings in which an application for a divorce order is made pursuant to s 3. Section 10 also applies to any hardship caused to a child of the family and directs that the court take into account the conduct of the parties.

4.13 The financial or other hardship does not have to be grave, merely substantial; therefore the test to be satisfied may be somewhat lower than previously held in connection with applications under MCA 1973, s 5. If the other party to the marriage or a child of the family is likely to suffer substantial or other hardship, the court may make an order preventing divorce. The financial or other hardship of a child has not been considered before when deciding whether to grant a decree of divorce. It is hard to imagine that a child will not suffer substantial hardship of an emotional nature upon the divorce of his parents and quite often the hardship is also financial. However, the court must also be satisfied that it would be wrong in all the circumstances for the marriage to be dissolved (s 10(2)(b)). The interests of the child of the family are surely best served in a stable home with one parent rather than in an unhappy household.[1] No doubt there will be a good deal of litigation to establish the meaning of this provision and the extent to which divorces will not be granted in relation to the hardship caused to a child.

1 This is always a matter of degree.

4.14 The court is directed to have regard to the conduct of the parties as part of the circumstances in deciding whether to make an order preventing divorce or whether to cancel such an order (s 10(2)(3)). There is no qualifying direction that this conduct need be that which would be 'inequitable to disregard', as in MCA 1973, s 25(2)(g). It has been established in case law that all the circumstances of the case included the parties' conduct and that the conduct of the parties to which the court must have regard in deciding whether or not it would be wrong to dissolve the marriage was not confined to, but included, misconduct in the sense of the old matrimonial offences.[1]

1 *Brickell v Brickell* [1974] Fam 31 (per Davies LJ), [1973] 3 All ER 508, CA.

4.15 It is reasonable to believe that the main, though not the only, purpose of orders preventing divorce is to protect wives, especially those who have reached middle age, from losing the security, especially the financial security, of being married and the chance of the benefits which a continuation of the married state would bring them, eg, widow's pension rights on their husband's predeceasing them at not too remote a date.[1] This consideration may be substantially addressed by virtue of ss 16 and 17. At present, if there are insufficient assets available to compensate a wife for loss of widow's pension rights, then either she must forego such provision or there must be no decree of divorce: the pension after the husband's death is lost unless the rules of a particular scheme permit a divorced wife to receive a dependant's pension and that wife is indeed a dependent (in receipt of maintenance). The 'ear-marking' provisions of the Pensions Act 1995 (s 166) do not address the situation after the death of the person in receipt of a pension. However, in respect of lump sums, there will be provision for the payee to attach the death in service benefits under the Inheritance (Provision for Family and Dependants) Act 1975. Payments under 'ear-marking' continue only during the life of the person entitled to the pension.

1 *Mathias v Mathias* (see para 4.10).

4.16 If the term 'substantial' is less onerous than the term 'grave' the existing case law defining 'grave' will not be of much assistance except in indicating the maximum level of hardship that needs to be established. The approach taken is to define 'grave' as being just that[1] and if it is necessary to say more than that, it could be termed 'important' or 'very serious'.[2] It has been held that the loss to a wife of her widow's army and state pensions was not such a loss as would constitute grave financial hardship, and that the court had to pay regard to the public interest in dissolving marriages which had become an empty shell.[3] The loss of pension rights is not a bar for divorce if the loss of these rights can in some way be mitigated. This can include compensation from public funds. It has been held that the availability of supplementary benefit was a relevant factor to be considered when determining whether, if divorced, a wife would suffer grave financial hardship.[4]

1 *Talbot v Talbot* (1971) 115 Sol Jo 870.
2 *Reiterbund v Reiterbund* (Megaw J), [1974] 2 All ER 455, [1974] 1 WLR 788; affd [1975] Fam 99, [1975] 1 All ER 280, CA.
3 *Mathias v Mathias* (see para 4.10). The parties were in their early 30s and the wife could take a job.
4 *Reiterbund v Reiterbund* (see note 2 above).

4.17 The loss of widow's pensions rights applies most particularly to cases where the wife is beyond the age when she might reasonably be expected to be able to make provision for herself and the husband cannot compensate from his current resources.[1] Compensation can be provided through insurance.[2]

1 *Julian v Julian* (1972) 116 Sol Jo 763 and *Johnson v Johnson* (1981) 12 Fam 116.
2 *Parker v Parker* (1972) Fam 116, [1972] 1 All ER 410.

4.18 The term 'other hardship' is in many ways much more difficult to define. It must mean something other than financial, and 'substantial' (as with the term 'grave') must be determined by fact and degree. Other hardship could be caused by religious and social objections to divorce which might result in perceived shame and degredation.[1] The test is based on a mixture of subjective and objective viewpoints.

The ordinary sensible man would take the view that there are two aspects of hardship—that which the sufferer from the hardship thinks he is suffering and that which a reasonable bystander with knowledge of all the facts would think he was suffering.[2] Where a party wishes to rely on religious matters or practices the matter should be dealt with in evidence; the court will not take judicial notice of the same.[3]

1 *Banik v Banik* [1973] 3 All ER 45, [1973] 1 WLR 860.
2 *Banik v Banik* [1973] (Lawton LJ) (ibid).
3 *Khan v Khan* (Waterhouse J), [1980] 1 All ER 497, [1980] 1 WLR 355.

4.19 The defence of 'other hardship' is considerably more difficult to establish than that of financial hardship. There do not appear to be reported cases in which a respondent has succeeded using this defence. For example, in a case where the argument was that in a Hindu society divorce would cause a wife and children hardship it was held that it did not add to the hardship which the separation had itself caused.[1] Each case must be judged on its own facts and it should not be taken as a general view that divorce could not cause hardship to any Hindu wife—perhaps one who had not been separated for 12 years prior to the petition for divorce. A similar view was taken in *Rukat*[2] and *Balraj*.[3]

1 *Parghi v Parghi* (1973) 4 Fam Law 82, 117 Sol Jo 582.
2 *Rukat v Rukat* (1975) Fam 63, [1975] 1 All ER 343, CA.
3 *Balraj v Balraj* (1980) 11 Fam Law 110, CA.

4.20 If an order preventing divorce is cancelled, the court may make a divorce order in respect of the marriage only if an application is made under ss 3 or 4(3) after the cancellation (s 10(4)). An order preventing divorce may include conditions which must be satisfied before an application for cancellation may be made under subsection (3) above (s 10(5)).

FINANCIAL PROVISION

4.21 Schedule 2 of the 1996 Act provides that, in the case of divorce or separation, an order about financial provision may be made under MCA 1973 before a divorce order or separation order is made. It also aims to retain (with minor changes) the position under MCA 1973 where marriages are annulled (s 15(2)(a), (b)). Under MCA 1973 (save for a maintenance pending suit and interim maintenance orders) orders for periodical payments, secured periodical payments, lump sum and property adjustment can only be made upon pronouncement of decree nisi and do not become effective until after the making absolute of the decree nisi. The 1996 Act provides for some very limited exceptions to the general principle that financial provision orders will not be made prior to the making of a divorce order or separation order save for interim provision, see para 4.27.

Definitions

4.22 A financial provision order for the purposes of the 1996 Act (Sch 2, para 2, substituting a new MCA 1973, s 21) is an order that—

(a) a party must make in favour of another person such periodical payments, for such term, as may be prescribed;
(b) a party must, to the satisfaction of the court, secure in favour of another person such periodical payments, for such term, as may be specified;
(c) a party must make a payment in favour of another person of such lump sum or sums as may be specified.

A property adjustment order for the purposes of the 1996 Act is an order—
(i) that a party must transfer such of his or her property as may be specified in favour of the other party or a child of the family;
(ii) that a settlement of such property of a party as may be specified must be made, to the satisfaction of the court, for the benefit of the other party and of the children of the family, or either or any of them;
(iii) varying, for the benefit of the parties and of the children of the family, or either or any of them, any marriage settlement;
(iv) extinguishing or reducing the interest of either of the parties under any marriage settlement.

4.23 Subject to MCA 1973, s 40 (Sch 2, para 2 of the 1996 Act, substituting new MCA 1973, s 21(3), (4)), where an order of the court under Part II of the 1996 Act requires a party to make or secure a payment in favour of another person or to transfer property in favour of any person, that payment must be made or secured or that property transferred—
(a) if that other person is the other party to the marriage, to that other party; and
(b) if that other person is a child of the family, according to the terms of the order, to the child or to such other person as may be specified, for the benefit of that child.

References in s 21 to the property of a party are references to any property to which that party is entitled either in possession or in reversion. MCA 1973, s 40 provides that where the court makes an order requiring payments to be made, or property to be transferred, to a party to the marriage, and the court is satisfied that the person in whose favour the order is made is incapable, by reason of mental disorder within the meaning of the Mental Health Act 1959 (now the Mental Health Act 1983), of managing and administering his or her property and affairs, then subject to any order, the court may order the payments to be made, or as the case may be, the property to be transferred, to such persons having charge of that person as the court may direct.

Financial provision orders: divorce and separation

4.24 MCA 1973 is further amended by Sch 2, para 3 of the 1996 Act which introduces a new s 22A. The court may at the appropriate time make one or more financial provision orders in favour of a party to the marriage to which the application relates or any of the children of the family (s 22A(1)(a), (b)). The appropriate time is any time (a) after a statement of marital breakdown has been received by the court and before any application for a divorce order or separation order is made (s 22A(2)(a)); (b) when an application for a divorce order or separation order has been made under s 3 of the 1996 Act and has not been withdrawn (s 22A(2)(b)); (c) when an application for a divorce order has been made under s 4 of the 1996 Act and has not been withdrawn (s 22A(2)(c)); (d) after a divorce order has been made (s 22A(2)(d)); and (e) when a separation order is in force (s 22A(2)(e)).

4.25 The court may make a combined order against the parties on one occasion, separate orders on different occasions, different orders in favour of different children or different orders from time to time in favour of the same child (s 22A(3)). The court may not make, in favour of the same party, more than one periodical payments order[1] or more than one order for payment of a lump sum in relation to any marital proceedings whether in the course of the proceedings or by reference to a divorce order or separation order made in the proceedings (s 22A(3)). If the court is not in a position to make a financial provision order in favour of a party or child of the family, the court may make an interim periodical payments order, an interim order for the payment of a lump sum or a series of such orders, in favour of that party or child (s 22A(4)). This provision will considerably assist the non-earning or low-earning spouse who has always been at a disadvantage in seeking legal advice. In *Flick v Flick*[2] Thorpe LJ held that legal costs were a legitimate and appropriate item for an interim budget.

1 A periodical payments order can be varied upon the application of either party so as to take account of changing circumstances.
2 (24 October 1995 unreported), CA, Civil Division.

4.26 Any order for the payment of a lump sum made under MCA 1973, s 22A may provide for the payment of the lump sum by instalments of such amounts as may be specified in the order, and require the payment of the instalments to be secured.[1] Nothing in MCA 1973, s 22A(5) affects—

(a) the power of the court under s 22A to make an order for the payment of a lump sum (s 22A(6)(a)); or
(b) the provisions of Part II of MCA 1973 as to the beginning of the term specified in any periodical payments order or secured periodical payments order (s 22A(6)(b)).

Where the court makes an order ('the main order') for the payment of a lump sum and directs that payment of that sum, or any part of it, is to be deferred, or is to be paid by instalments, then the court may on or at any time after making the main order, make an order ('the order for interest') for the amount deferred, or the instalments, to carry interest at such rate as may be specified (s 22A(7)(a), (b)). The court shall specify the date upon which interest will commence, (which cannot be earlier than the date of the main order), and it can specify that interest will run until the date when the payment is due (s 22A(8)(a), (b)).

1 Section 22A(5)(a), (b). Practitioners should be acutely aware that a lump sum order which provides for payment by instalments is an extremely dangerous order. The payer can apply to the court at any time to vary the amount of the instalment, the time for payment of the instalments and to have any outstanding instalments terminated altogether. It is far better to obtain an order for a series of lump sums.

Restrictions affecting MCA 1973, s 22A

4.27 No financial provision order, other than an interim order, may be made under MCA 1973, s 22A (inserted by Sch 2, para 3 of the 1996 Act) so as to take effect before the making of a divorce order or separation order in relation to the marriage, unless the court is satisfied that the circumstances of the case are exceptional and that it would be just and reasonable for the order to be made (s 22B(1)). Except in the case of an interim periodical payments order, the court may not make a financial provision order under MCA 1973, s 22A at any time while the period for reflection and consideration is interrupted under s 7(8) of the 1996 Act (s 22B(2)). No financial provision order may be made under MCA 1973, s 22A by reference to the making of a statement of marital breakdown if, by a lapse of the divorce or separation process, it has ceased to be possible for an application to be made by reference to that statement or for an order to be made on such an application (s 22B(3)). No financial provision order may be made under MCA 1973, s 22A after a divorce order has been made, or while a separation order is in force, except in response to an application made before the divorce order or separation order was made (s 22B(4)), or on a subsequent application made with the leave of the court.

Financial provision orders: nullity

4.28 MCA 1973, s 23 is substantially amended and relates now only to granting a decree of nullity of marriage (Sch 2, para 4). MCA 1973 now deals with financial provision orders in s 22A (as added by the 1996 Act).

Property adjustment orders: divorce and separation

4.29 On an application made under MCA 1973 s 23A (inserted by Sch 2, para 5), the court may, at any time mentioned in s 22A(2) of that Act make one or more property adjustment orders (s 23A(1)). If the court makes more than one property adjustment order, whether in the course of the proceedings or by reference to a divorce order or separation order, in favour of the same party to the marriage, each order must fall within a different paragraph of s 21(2) of that Act (s 23A(2)). The court shall exercise its powers under s 23A by making on one occasion all such provision as can be made by way of one or more property adjustment orders in relation to the marriage (s 23A(3)). This can only be done in so far as it is practicable.

Restrictions affecting MCA 1973, s 23A

4.30 No property adjustment order may be made under MCA 1973, s 23A so as to take effect before the making of a divorce order or a separation order in relation to the marriage unless the court is satisfied that the circumstances of the case are exceptional and that it would be just and reasonable for the order to be made (s 23B(1)(a), (b)). The court may not make a property adjustment order at any time while the period for reflection and consideration is interrupted under the 1996 Act s 7(8) (s 23B(2)). No property adjustment order may be made by virtue of the making of a statement of marital breakdown if, by a lapse of the divorce or separation process, it has ceased to be possible for an application to be made by reference to that statement or for an order to be made on such an application (s 23B(3)(a), (b)). No property adjustment order may be made after a divorce order has been made, or while a separation order is in force, except in response to an application made before the divorce order or separation order was made or on a subsequent application made with the leave of the court (s 23B(4)(a), (b)).

Property adjustment orders: nullity of marriage

4.31 MCA 1973, s 24 (as substituted by Sch 2, para 6 of the 1996 Act) now applies only in relation to proceedings for property adjustment orders consequent on the grant of a decree of nullity of marriage. In marital proceedings, for a divorce order or a separation order, applications for property adjustment orders are governed by MCA 1973, ss 23A and 23B (as inserted by Sch 2, para 5).

Duration of a continuing financial provision order

4.32 MCA 1973, s 28(1), is amended by Sch 2, para 7 of the 1996 Act, so that a term specified in the order which is to begin before the making of the order shall begin no earlier—

(a) if an order is made after a statement of marital breakdown is received by the court and before any application for a divorce order or separation order is made, or when an application for a divorce order or separation order is made under s 3, than the day on which the statement of marital breakdown or application for an order is received by the court (s 28(1)(a)(i));

(b) where the order is made after an application for a divorce order was made following cancellation of an order preventing divorce under s 10 of the 1996 Act, than the date of the making of that application (s 28(1)(a)(ii));

(c) where the order is made after an application for a divorce order under s 4 of the 1996 Act than the date of the making of the application for the divorce order (s 28(1)(a)(iii));

(d) in any other case, than the date of the making of the application on which the order is made (s 28(1)(a)(iv)).

Variation following reconciliation

4.33 Where at a time before the making of a divorce order—

(a) an order for the payment of a lump sum has been made under MCA 1973, s 22A in favour of a party ('a paragraph (a) order'),

(b) such an order has been made in favour of a child of the family but the payment has not yet been made, or

(c) a property adjustment order ('paragraph (c) order') has been made under s 23A of the 1973 Act,

the court may, on an application made jointly by the parties to the marriage, vary or discharge the order (MCA 1973, s 31A(1)(a)–(c), as inserted by Sch 2, para 8). Where the court varies or discharges a paragraph (a) order, it may order the repayment of an amount equal to the whole or any part of the lump sum (s 31A(2) of the 1973 Act). If the court has ordered an interim lump sum payment for the purchase of a house, then presumably that property will have to be sold or transferred to the payer of the lump sum. On the other hand, if the interim lump sum order had been made in order to meet an essential and necessary expense and the money was effectively spent, presumably the court would not order the repayment of the lump sum.

4.34 Where the court varies or discharges a paragraph (c) order, it may (if the order has taken effect) order any person to whom the property was transferred to transfer the whole or any part of that property, or the whole or any part of any property appearing to represent that property, in favour of a party to the marriage or to a child of the family (s 31A(3)(a)(i), (ii) of the 1973 Act). Under this provision the court may also vary any settlement to which the order relates in favour of any person or extinguish or reduce any person's interest under that settlement (s 31A(3)(b)). Where the court makes an order under MCA 1973, s 31A(3), it may make such supplemental provision as it thinks appropriate in consequence of any transfer, variation, extinguishment or reduction. The supplemental provision may include a further property adjustment order or an order for the payment of a lump sum (s 31A(4)). The court may not make an order under s 31A(2), (3) or (4) unless it appears to it that there has been a reconciliation between the parties to the marriage (s 31A(6)). The court may also not make an order under s 31A(2), (3) or (4) unless it appears to it that the order will not prejudice the interests of any child of the family or any person who has acquired any right or interest in consequence of the paragraph (c) order and is not a party to the marriage or a child of the family (s 31A(7)(a), (b)).

Division of pension rights

4.35 MCA 1973, s 25B is substantially amended by s 16(2) to provide for the division of pension rights in England and Wales. Pension splitting was a concession made by the government at the last moment to ensure that FLA 1996 was passed. The Lord Chancellor is required to make regulations to govern the way in which pension splitting orders may be made. The exact form of these regulations remains to be seen.

> 'For a long time, it has been possible in principle to take into account the value of pension assets as part of a divorce settlement. In practice, however, that could be done only where there were sufficient other assets to be offset against the pension. Real justice could be achieved only if, in some way, the value of pension assets could be shared in appropriate proportions between the divorcing couples.
>
> In practice, that has not been possible. The result has been that many women who have spent lifetimes bringing up children, looking after a home and sacrificing their careers to their husbands' success have been punished for everything that they have ever done. They have been left without a pension on income support and means-tested benefits, as, in a sense, a burden on the taxpayer—a burden that they never wanted to be.'[1]

If there are sufficient assets outside of the pension, it is possible that the court will seek an alternative to pension splitting as the first option for compensation of the loss of this right upon divorce.

1 Mr Denham HC 2R, 17 June 1996, cols 551–552.

4.36 A new MCA 1973, s 25B(8) provides that where a pension splitting order has been made in accordance with the provisions of s 25B(2)(c), then the pensionholder's rights in their scheme/plan shall be reduced and the other party shall acquire new or increased rights. The benefits shall be created and paid in a manner to be prescribed in rules and regulations to be made at a later date. The court shall not have the power to force trustees of a scheme to take in a new member if those trustees or managers are willing and able to create rights for the recipient party by making a transfer to another scheme and the trustees or managers are willing to accept such a transfer. In addition, the court does not have the power to require managers or trustees to make a transfer to another scheme if the paying scheme is unfunded (unless the trustees or managers are willing to make a transfer payment) or in prescribed circumstances (s 25B(8)(a), (b)).

4.37 No pension adjustment order (dividing the pension rights between the parties) may be made under s 25B(2)(c) of the 1973 Act if the scheme is a scheme of a prescribed type, or in prescribed circumstances, or insofar as it would affect benefits of a prescribed type (s 16(9)(a)–(c)). The Lord Chancellor may make such consequential modifications of any enactment or subordinate legislation as appears to him necessary or expedient to give effect to the provisions of s 25B (s 16(4)(a)(i), (ii), (aa)).

4.38 Section 18 of the 1996 Act amends the DPMCA 1978 by providing that behaviour and desertion will cease to be grounds for an order for financial provision under s 1 of that Act (s 18(1)). This is consistent with the removal of fault in divorce and separation proceedings. In addition, DPMCA 1978, s 7 is amended to enable certain orders for financial provision to be made where parties to a marriage are living apart, irrespective of whether the separation is by agreement or as a result of desertion (s 18(2)).

5 Legal aid for mediation in family matters

SCOPE OF PART III

5.1 Part III of the 1996 Act applies to mediation in disputes relating to family matters and inserts ss 2(3A), 13A, 13B, 13C, 15(3F)–(3H) and 16(11) into the Legal Aid Act 1988 (LAA 1988). 'Family matters' are defined as matters which are governed by English law and in relation to which any question has arisen, or may arise, under MCA 1973, DPMCA 1978, Parts I to V of CA 1989, Parts II and IV of the 1996 Act or any other enactment prescribed (s 13A(2)(a)–(c)). Regulations may restrict this Part to mediation in disputes of any prescribed description and are exercisable only with the consent of the Treasury (s 13A(3), (4)). 'Mediation' is defined as mediation to which Part IIIA of the 1988 Act applies and includes steps taken by a mediator in any case in determining whether to embark on mediation, in preparing for mediation and in making any assessment under Part IIIA (s 2(3A)). 'Mediator' is defined as a person with whom the Legal Aid Board (the Board) contracts for the provision of mediation by any person.

PROVISION AND AVAILABILITY OF MEDIATION

5.2 The Board may secure the provision of mediation under Part IIIA of the 1988 Act (s 13B(1)). If mediation is provided, it is to be available to any person whose financial resources are such as, under regulations, make him eligible for mediation (s 13B(2)). A person is not to be granted mediation in relation to any dispute unless mediation appears to the mediator suitable to the dispute and the parties and all the circumstances (s 13B(3)). Presumably if the Legal Aid Board does not grant a certificate for mediation in reliance on this section because in all the circumstances the case, for example, requires substantial complicated discovery and analysis, then this would not affect the applicant's eligibility for a certificate for proceedings under MCA 1973, ss 22A, 22B, 23, 23A, 23B, 24, 25 and 31A. The grant of mediation under Part IIIA may be amended, withdrawn or revoked. These provisions do not add to the powers that the Board already has in relation to certificates. The Lord Chancellor may give directions from time to time as to the manner in which the Board will exercise its powers (s 13B(4), (5)).

Mediator's code of practice

5.3 Any contract entered into by the Board for the provision of mediation under Part IIIA of the 1988 Act must require the mediator to comply with a code of practice (s 13B(6)). The code must require the mediator to have arrangements designed to ensure that—

(a) parties participate in mediation only if willing and not influenced by fear of violence or other harm;

(b) cases where either party may be influenced by fear of violence or other harm are identified as soon as possible;

(c) the possibility of reconciliation is kept under review throughout mediation; and

(d) each party is informed about the availability of independent legal advice.

(S 13B(7) of the 1988 Act).

Where there are one or more children of the family, the code must also require the mediator to have arrangements designed to ensure that the parties are encouraged to consider the welfare, wishes and feelings of each child, and whether and to what extent each child should be given the opportunity to express his or her wishes and feelings in the mediation (s 13B(8)). In reality there are very few couples who do not already consider the welfare of their children as a first priority and who do not already consider the wishes and feelings of each child. Even having taken into account such considerations, neither party to the marriage may alter their course of action in the knowledge that the children rarely wish their parents to divorce. A contract entered into by the Board for the provision of mediation under Part IIIA must also include such other provision as the Lord Chancellor may from time to time direct (s 13B(9)).

Payment for mediation

5.4 Except as provided by LAA 1988, s 13C, as inserted by s 28 of the 1996 Act, the legally assisted person is not to be required to pay for mediation provided under Part IIIA (s 13C(1)). The legally assisted person is to pay to the Board in respect of the costs of providing mediation, a contribution of such amount as is determined or fixed by or under the regulations and if the total contribution exceeds the Board's liability, the excess shall be repaid to him (s 13C(3), (4)). The statutory charge is to apply to all property recovered or preserved for the legally assisted person as a result of mediation (s 13C(5)(a), (b)). Regulations will be made which describe the circumstances in which property is to be taken to have been or not to have been, recovered or preserved, and the circumstances in which the recovery or preservation is to be taken to be or not to be, the result of any mediation (s 13C(6)(a), (b)).

Mediation and civil legal aid

5.5 A person shall not be granted representation for the purposes of proceedings relating to family matters, unless he has attended a meeting with a mediator. That meeting is to determine whether mediation appears to be suitable to the dispute, the parties and all the circumstances and, in particular, whether mediation could take place without either party being influenced by fear of violence or other harm. If mediation does appear to be suitable, the meeting will also help the person applying for representation to decide whether to apply for mediation instead (s 15(3F)(a)(i), (ii), (b) of the 1988 Act). Mediators should bear in mind particularly the equality of bargaining power between the parties in determining whether in all the circumstances the case is appropriate for mediation. Violence or other harm is often extremely subtle and can be found in the advantage one party may take of the other through superior knowledge and/or professional negotiating skills. Mediators must also be careful to judge how far the parties have disengaged from the marriage, as the most successful mediations are achieved in circumstances where the marriage is entirely dead and the parties do not continue to have commonality of interest in any way.

5.6 Sub-section (3F) does not apply to proceedings under Part IV of the 1996 Act (Family Homes and Domestic Violence), MCA 1973, s 37 (avoidance of transactions intended to prevent or reduce financial relief) or CA 1989, Part IV or V (care and supervision or protection of children) (s 15(3G)). So far as proceedings relate to family matters, the Board, in determining whether it is reasonable that a person should be granted representation under LAA 1988, Part IIIA, must have regard to whether and to what extent recourse to mediation would be a suitable alternative to taking proceedings, and must have regard to the outcome of the meeting held under LAA 1988, s 15(3F) and to any assessment made for the purposes of LAA 1988, s 13B(3).

6 Family homes and domestic violence

DEFINITIONS RELATING TO PART IV

6.1 The FLA 1996, Part IV introduces new terminology including (i) cohabitants,[1] (ii) associated persons,[2] and (iii) relevant child.[3] In addition, ss 62 and 63 provide definitions and interpretation. Other terms such as matrimonial home rights,[4] occupation orders[5] and non-molestation orders[6] are considered at Chs 7–9. The Act imports several definitions from CA 1989, such as 'harm' and 'significant harm'.

1 See paras 6.2–6.7.
2 See paras 6.8–6.26.
3 See paras 6.27–6.28.
4 Section 30; see Ch 7.
5 Section 39; see Ch 8.
6 Section 42(1); see Ch 9.

PARTIES TO APPLICATIONS

Cohabitants and former cohabitants

Cohabitants

6.2 Section 62(1)(a) defines 'cohabitants' as a man and a woman who, although not married to each other, are living together as husband and wife. Section 62(1)(b) provides that 'former cohabitants' is to be read accordingly but does not include cohabitants who have subsequently married each other.[1]

1 It is submitted that a void marriage would be ignored; *de Reneville (otherwise Sheridan) v de Reneville* [1948] P 100, [1948] 1 All ER 56, CA. See para 11.11.

6.3 This represents a substantial change in the law from the provisions of DVMPA 1976, s 2(2), as it introduces the definition of 'former cohabitants'. Previously, while an application could be brought after the termination of a relationship, it was limited to relief in respect of incidents that had occurred before such termination[1] and had to be brought promptly. The new law enables relief to be sought against acts of molestation long after the termination of a relationship.

1 *McLean v Burke* (1980) 3 FLR 70, CA.

6.4 Under DVMPA 1976, s 2(2), the Act applied to 'a man and a woman who are living with each other in the same household as husband and wife'. The change from 'living with each other' to 'living together' is merely an alteration in drafting and does not affect the meaning. The abolition of the requirement of living in the same household may be of more significance. The word 'household' has been held[1] to have an abstract meaning rather than referring to something physical. While there could be two households under one roof, without physical division of the property;[2] in some cases a property could be so small that it was impossible to distinguish two separate households rather than one unhappy household.[3]

1 *Santos v Santos* [1972] Fam 247, [1972] 2 All ER 246, CA.
2 *Hollens v Hollens* (1971) 115 Sol Jo 327.
3 *Adeoso v Adeoso* [1981] 1 All ER 107, [1980] 1 WLR 1535, CA.

6.5 The effect of this change is to remove the need for the applicant to show that there is only one household. There are, nonetheless, problems with proving that a couple are 'living with each other as husband and wife' or, in the case of former cohabitants, have lived with each other as husband and wife. These are problems of degree to be decided on the individual facts of each case, particularly where a relationship lasts for a short time. Could it be said, for example, that a couple who had a 'one-night stand' or a one-week holiday romance had in fact lived with each other as husband and wife? In the case of a 'one-night stand', it would be stretching the facts to say that they had lived with each other as husband and wife; but the longer that a relationship lasts the more likely it is that the test will be satisfied.

6.6 The concept of 'living with each other as husband and wife' involves more than a man and a woman living in the same household, as cohabitation can continue even though the parties are living apart.[1] Thus a couple who only physically live together at weekends may well be within the definition of 'cohabitants' where the intention to live together continues.

1 *Santos v Santos* (see para 6.4 above), and *Fuller (otherwise Penfold) v Fuller* [1973] 2 All ER 650, [1973] 1 WLR 730, CA. See also *Bradshaw v Bradshaw* [1897] P 24 at 26 per Sir Francis Jeune P.

Former cohabitants

6.7 Once cohabitants cease to live with each other as husband and wife they become 'former cohabitants'. The Act removes the some of the difficulties in trying to identify precisely when a relationship has come to an end. Cohabitants who subsequently marry are not within the definition of 'former cohabitants' (s 62(1)(b)),[1] as they have become spouses.

1 See para 6.2.

ASSOCIATED PERSONS

6.8 Section 62(3) lists the categories of persons who are associated with another person for the purposes of the Act, the significance of which needs to be examined in some detail. Cohabitants and former cohabitants are associated persons (s 62(3)(b)), and the meaning of these words has already been considered.[1] Spouses and former spouses, common householders, relatives, engaged couples, parents and those with parental responsibility, and parties to family proceedings are all associated persons, and as such they have the right to bring applications against other persons with whom they are associated.

1 See paras 6.2–6.7.

Spouses and former spouses

6.9 A person is associated with another person if they are or have been married to each other (s 62(3)(a)).

Spouses

6.10 For there to be a subsisting marriage there must be a valid marriage which has not been dissolved, or a voidable marriage that has not been annulled. A party to a void marriage is not a spouse as there never was a marriage.[1] However such persons might well be classed as cohabitants or former cohabitants, common householders[2] or an engaged couple for the purposes of the Act.[3] Parties to a valid polygamous marriage (whether actual or potential) are probably included;[4] the husband would be associated with each of the wives but the wives would not necessarily be associated with each other unless they were common householders.[5] Where there is doubt about the validity or subsistence of a marriage, the court may grant interim relief, pending a proper determination of the issue.[6]

1 *de Reneville (otherwise Sheridan) v de Reneville* (see para 6.2).
2 See paras 6.12–6.13.
3 See paras 6.17–6.18.
4 See *Re Sehota (deceased), Surjit Kaur v Gian Kaur* [1978] 3 All ER 385, [1978] 1 WLR 1506.
5 See paras 6.12–6.13.
6 *Seray-Wurie v Seray-Wurie* [1987] Fam Law 124, CA.

Former spouses

6.11 Parties to a marriage in respect of which a decree absolute of divorce has been pronounced or a divorce order[1] has been made and parties to a voidable marriage that has been annulled are former spouses. Parties to a void marriage that has been annulled are not former spouses because since there never was a marriage they never were spouses; in which case the decree is merely declaratory.[2]

1 See s 2(1)(a).
2 *de Reneville (otherwise Sheridan) v de Reneville* (see para 6.2).

Common householders

6.12 A person is associated with another person if they live or have lived in the same household, otherwise than merely by reason of one of them being the other's employee, tenant, lodger or boarder (s 62(3)(c)). The Law Commission Report[1] indicated that this would include people who live or have lived in the same household other than on a purely commercial basis. Whether persons sharing a house or flat live in one household or several households is a question of fact and degree. Factors to be considered are those such as how they share the outgoings, how they do their shopping, whether they take meals together, have the same living room and the degree to which they share the accommodation. 'Living in the same household' is an abstract concept[2] and it is submitted that 'household' has the same meaning as in matrimonial proceedings. The Law Commission recognised[3] that this might give rise to unfortunate distinctions such as where several friends shared a flat; if they are all joint tenants then they have remedies under the Act; if only one is the tenant who sub-lets to the others, then the Act would not apply between the tenant and the others, but would apply as between the sub-tenants.

1 Law Com No 207, para 3.21.
2 *Santos v Santos* (see para 6.6).
3 Law Com No 207, para 3.22.

6.13 Section 62 has the effect of providing that homosexual couples will be associated persons provided that they share the same household.[1] The word 'merely' in s 62(3)(c) is very important. For example, where parties to a homosexual relationship live or have lived in the same household, and one party is the tenant or owner and the other is a lodger, boarder or sub-tenant, it is submitted that the contractual relationship is not a purely commercial one and they would be associated persons for the purposes of the Act. The Law Commission Report proposed[2] that those who 'have or have had a sexual relationship with each other (whether or not including sexual intercourse)' should be a specific category of associated persons. This was rejected by the Government as presenting the courts with problems of definition and proof.[3] Such a provision would have included homosexual couples.

1 See Proceedings on the Family Homes and Domestic Violence Bill in the Special Public Bill Committee HL, Session 1994–95 No 55. Lord Chancellor, 9 March 1995 at p 6; and, Hale J 15 March 1995 at p 12.
2 Law Com No 207, para 3.26.
3 See the speech of the Lord Chancellor, on the Family Homes and Domestic Violence Bill, HL 2R, 23 February 1995, col 1257.

Relatives

6.14 A person is associated with another person if they are relatives (s 62(3)(d)), which is further defined in s 63(1) (see para 5.16 for the relevant relationships). It is important to note that the provision is very wide-ranging and covers relatives of a person and of his spouse, former spouse, cohabitant or former cohabitant. This is a much needed extension of the law and enables direct protection to be given against molestation from within the family or the family of a partner. In addition, it enables direct protection to be given against molestation from the family of a partner or former partner. Previously it was necessary to bring a civil action for assault; or, where there was an injunction against the other partner, to make an application to commit the third party for aiding and abetting a breach of the injunction.[1]

1 See *Seaward v Paterson* [1897] 1 Ch 545, CA, *Thorne RDC v Bunting (No 2)* [1972] 3 All ER 1084, CA, and *Bawden v Bawden* [1979] QB 419n, [1978] 3 All ER 1216, CA, at 420H–421B and at 1218d, per Goff LJ obiter.

6.15 However, subsequent spouses or cohabitants of the former spouse or former cohabitant of a person are not within the definition of 'relatives'.[1] This may be an unfortunate lacuna as there are instances of (former) spouses or cohabitants molesting the current partner of the person with whom they had a previous relationship. This happens particularly when the marriage or cohabitation is breaking down and one party is seeking to distance himself or herself from the current partner and form a relationship with a new partner. In such cases an indirect remedy may still be required. The courts have made orders in a matrimonial cause[2] on the application of a wife to exclude the husband's new partner from the matrimonial home; but have not, it would seem, granted injunctions restraining molestation in such circumstances. Under the former law, in a matrimonial cause where such a person was a co-respondent or party cited he or she would be associated with the petitioner and respondent,[3] and therefore the remedy of a non-molestation injunction would be available. In marital proceedings[4] only the spouses are parties to the proceedings and so this remedy would not be available. Interlocutory relief is available by means of a tort of nuisance to restrain molestation.[5]

1 See Proceedings on the Family Homes and Domestic Violence Bill in the Special Public Bill Committee HL, Session 1994–95 No 55. Hale J 15 March 1995 at p 22.

2 *Adams v Adams* (1965) 109 Sol Jo 899; *Jones v Jones* [1971] 2 All ER 737, [1971] 1 WLR 396, CA; and *Hense v Hense and Churchill* [1976] CA Transcript 403, CA.

3 By virtue of s 62(3)(g), see para 6.25.

4 Under s 20(2) proceedings for divorce or separation orders are called 'marital proceedings' (also defined as 'family proceedings', see s 63(2)(a)).

5 *Burris v Azadani* [1995] 4 All ER 802, [1995] 1 WLR 1372, CA. An injunction may include an exclusion zone to prevent the defendant going near the plaintiff's residence.

Table of relatives

6.16 The following relatives are associated with a person (s 63(1))—

(a) his or her father, mother, stepfather, stepmother, son, daughter, stepson, stepdaughter, grandmother, grandfather, grandson, or granddaughter;

(b) his or her brother, sister, uncle, aunt, niece or nephew (whether of the full blood or half blood or by affinity);

(c) the father, mother, stepfather, stepmother, son, daughter, stepson, stepdaughter, grandmother, grandfather, grandson, or granddaughter of his or her spouse, former spouse, cohabitant or former cohabitant;

(d) the brother, sister, uncle, aunt, niece or nephew (whether of the full blood or half blood or by affinity) of his or her spouse, former spouse, cohabitant or former cohabitant.

Engaged couples

6.17 A person is associated with another person if they have agreed to marry, whether or not that agreement has been terminated (s 62(3)(e)). This provision was recommended by the Law Commission[1] but initially rejected by the government because of problems of definition and proof.[2] In the Special Public Bill Committee[3] on the Family Homes and Domestic Violence Bill the problem was considered in some detail. At Report stage what is now s 44 was added to overcome these problems and provides that evidence of an engagement must be proved in one of three ways.[4]

1 Law Com No 207, para 3.24.

2 See the speech of the Lord Chancellor on the Family Homes and Domestic Violence Bill. HL 2R, 23 February 1995, col 1257.

3 HL, Session 1994–95 Paper No 55.

4 See paras 6.19–6.21.

6.18 It would seem that an agreement to marry need not be valid in order for the parties to be associated;[1] indeed the very fact that an agreement to marry may be contrary to public policy could give rise to incidents requiring the intervention of the court. The law on this topic consists largely of cases on breach of promise[2] and different considerations may well apply under Part IV of the Act. An agreement to marry undertaken by a person who is already married is void as it is contrary to public policy, unless a decree nisi has been pronounced in respect of the subsisting marriage.[3] An agreement to marry on the death of an existing spouse is void as contrary to public policy.[4] Whether a person can enter into a valid agreement to marry with more than one person at the same time appears to be uncertain. It may be that a subsequent engagement would automatically terminate a prior engagement.[5]

1 See *Shaw v Fitzgerald* [1992] 1 FLR 357, [1992] 1 FCR 162, where it was held that there could be an engagement for the purposes of the Law Reform (Miscellaneous Provisions) Act 1970, s 2 even where one party to the engagement was already married.

2 A cause of action abolished by the Law Reform (Miscellaneous Provisions) Act 1970, s 1. The cause of action survives in Scotland; see Clive & Wilson, *The Law of Husband and Wife in Scotland* (2nd Edn 1982).

3 *Fender v St John-Mildmay* [1938] AC 1, [1937] 3 All ER 402, HL. With the abolition of decree nisi and decree absolute, the divorce order will be the relevant date.

4 *Wilson v Carnley* [1908] 1 KB 729, CA; *Robinson v Smith* [1915] 1 KB 711, CA.

5 Except where the parties had the capacity to enter into a valid actually polygamous marriage.

Evidence in writing

6.19 There must be evidence in writing of the agreement to marry (s 44(1)). This, it is submitted, would be fulfilled by an announcement in a newspaper, relevant correspondence between the parties to the agreement or invitations to an engagement party. More doubtful would be third party documents referring to the engagement, particularly where the fact of the engagement was denied.

Other evidence

6.20 Evidence in writing is not required where there is either (a) the gift of an engagement ring by one to the other in contemplation of their marriage (s 44(2)(a)), or (b) a ceremony entered into by the parties in the presence of at least one person assembled for the purpose of witnessing the ceremony (s 44(2)(b)). The mere gift of an engagement ring does not necessarily constitute an agreement to marry.[1] The gift must signify the agreement, which presupposes that the agreement must pre-date or be simultaneous with the gift. The provision relating to ceremonies, originally introduced in the House of Lords at Report stage[2] of the Family Homes and Domestic Violence Bill and amended on Third Reading,[3] is intended to cover formal ceremonies of betrothal and those couples who have undergone a ceremony of marriage outside the requirements of English law. While it would cover certain void marriages, it is perhaps uncertain whether a marriage that was void because either party was already lawfully married,[4] or because the parties were not respectively male and female,[5] would constitute evidence of an engagement as such persons could not lawfully marry and therefore could not validly agree to do so. Where a marriage is void under the provisions of the Marriage Acts 1949 to 1986 because of failure to observe certain requirements[6] or because it is an invalid polygamous marriage,[7] the ceremony might well be considered sufficient in itself to establish evidence of an agreement to marry.

1 Family Homes and Domestic Violence Bill, HL Report, 25 May 1995, col 1062.
2 Family Homes and Domestic Violence Bill, HL Report, 25 May 1995, col 1062.
3 Family Homes and Domestic Violence Bill, HL 3R, 20 June 1995, col 220.
4 MCA 1973, s 11(b); but see para 6.18 and *Shaw v Fitzgerald* (as above).
5 MCA 1973, s 11(c); see *Corbett v Corbett (otherwise Ashley)* [1971] P 83, [1970] 2 All ER 33.
6 MCA 1973, s 11(a)(i)–(iii).
7 MCA 1973, s 11(d).

6.21 Where an agreement to marry is terminated no application can be made under section 33 (occupation order) or section 42 (non-molestation order) after three years from the date of termination of the agreement. This is consistent with the restriction on bringing proceedings under the Married Women's Property Act 1882 (as extended by the Law Reform (Miscellaneous Provisions) Act 1970, s 2) by formerly engaged couples.

Parents or those with parental responsibility

6.22 A person is associated with another person if, in relation to any child, they are both persons who are parents or who have or have had parental responsibility (s 62(3)(f), (4)).[1] The parents[2] of a child are the mother[3] and father.[4] Other natural persons who have parental responsibility are set out at para 6.23. One consequence of this provision is that a man and a woman who have had a child without marriage, engagement or cohabitation would be associated for the purposes of the Act while their child was a minor.[5]

1 By s 63(1), parental responsibility has the same meaning as in CA 1989, see s 3.
2 Family Law Reform Act 1987 (FLRA 1987), s 1(1).
3 A mother always has parental responsibility; CA 1989, s 2; which can only be lost on the making of an adoption order, see the Adoption Act 1976 (AA 1976), s 39(2).
4 A father has parental responsibility where—
   (a) he was married, or deemed to be married, to the mother at the time of the birth of the child; CA 1989, s 2(1).
   (b) he was not married to the mother at the time of the birth of the child (see FLRA 1987, s 1) but—
      (i) obtains an order for parental responsibility, CA 1989, s 4(1)(a),
      (ii) enters into a parental responsibility agreement, CA 1989, s 4(1)(b), or
      (iii) obtains a residence order, CA 1989, s 12(1).
5 This would enable a rape victim (who had given birth to a child conceived as a result) to obtain an injunction against the perpetrator in summary proceedings.

6.23 In addition the following natural persons have parental responsibility in the following circumstances—

Guardian—

(a) If appointed by the court when no one has parental responsibility, or a parent or guardian with a residence order (CA 1989, s 8(1)) died while the order was in force (CA 1989, s 5(1)).
(b) If appointed by a parent or guardian who died while they had a residence order in their favour (CA 1989, s 5(7)(b)).
(c) If he was appointed by a parent or guardian who died leaving no other parent or guardian with parental responsibility (CA 1989, s 5(7)(a)).

Applicant for emergency protection order (CA 1989, s 44)—

While the emergency protection order is in force (CA 1989, s 44(4)(c))—

Applicant for adoption—

(a) On the making of an adoption order (AA 1976, s 12).
(b) On the making of an interim order (AA 1976, s 25(1)).
(c) By order on an application for an overseas adoption (AA 1976, s 55(1)).

Holder of a residence order—

While the order is in force (CA 1989, s 12(2)).

Holder of an order for custody or care and control—

While the order is in force (CA 1989, Sch 14, para 7).

6.24 A local authority has parental responsibility if there is a care order or an interim care order in force (CA 1989, s 33(3)). An adoption agency has parental responsibility on the making of an order declaring the child free for adoption (AA 1976, s 18(5)). However, a body corporate and another person cannot be associated persons under section 62(3)(f) or (g) (s 62(6) of the 1996 Act). The purpose of this restriction is no doubt to prevent applications for non-molestation injunctions against local authorities and adoption agencies and other bodies corporate.

Parties to family proceedings

6.25 A person is associated with another person if they are parties to the same family proceedings (s 62(3)(g))[1] (other than under Part IV of the 1996 Act). The persons associated under this provision may also be associated under other provisions of s 62(3) but in addition it will cover co-respondents and parties cited in a matrimonial cause[2] and parties to applications under the Human Fertilisation and Embryology Act 1990,[3] s 30.

1 Family proceedings are defined by s 63(1), (2) and follow the definitions contained in CA 1989, s 8(3), (4).
2 Until Part II of the Act is in force, after which only husband and wife can be parties to marital proceedings; see ss 6, 20.
3 See the Family Proceedings Rules 1991, SI 1991/1247, r 4A.3.

Additional provisions relating to adoption

6.26 Where a child has been adopted or has been freed for adoption under certain statutory provisions[1] two persons are associated for the purposes of the Act if one person is a natural parent or natural grandparent (s 62(5)(a)), and the other is the child itself, an adoptive parent or an applicant for an adoption order (s 62(5)(b)(i)) or a person with whom the child has at any time been placed for adoption (s 62(5)(b)(ii)). The purpose of this extension is so that the natural parents cease to be parents once an adoption order is made (AA 1976, ss 12, 39). Furthermore an adoption order is a final order and on the making of the order there will no longer be family proceedings between the natural and adoptive parents.

1 Those mentioned in AA 1976, s 16; which are AA 1976, s 18; Adoption (Scotland) Act 1978, s 18; Adoption (Northern Ireland) Order 1987, SI 1987/2203 (NI 22), arts 17(1), 18(1).

RELEVANT CHILD

6.27 'Child' means a person under the age of 18 years (s 63(1)). A relevant child (s 62(2)) is one within any of the following three categories—

(a) any child who is living with or might reasonably be expected to live with either party to the proceedings,
(b) any child in relation to whom an order under AA 1976 or CA 1989 is in question in the proceedings, and
(c) any other child whose interests the court considers relevant. (s 62(2)(a)–(c))

6.28 This definition is very much wider than any previous law. The DVMPA 1976, s 1(1)(b) referred to 'a child living with the applicant', while the DPMCA 1978, s 16 referred to 'a child of the family'[1]. The widest provision was contained in the Matrimonial Homes Act 1983 (MHA 1983), s 1(3) which referred to the 'needs of any children' but this did not define the term 'children'.

1 Section 88(1) defined child of the family in the same terms as in MCA 1973, s 52(1).

7 Matrimonial home rights

INTRODUCTION

7.1 The 1996 Act, s 30 introduces the concept of matrimonial home rights and replaces the previous concept of rights of occupation which was introduced by MHA 1967. Section 30 is derived from parts of MHA 1983, s 1[1] which consolidated the previous legislation. The purpose of matrimonial home rights is to provide protection for a spouse who would otherwise have no legal right to occupy the matrimonial home. Cohabitants cannot have matrimonial home rights as such rights can only arise as the result of a marriage. It is, however, necessary to mention the position of cohabitants and former cohabitants in relation to certain tenancies[2] and in respect of mortgage possession proceedings.[3]

1 Rights of occupation were introduced by MHA 1967 following *National Provincial Bank v Ainsworth* [1965] AC 1175, [1965] 2 All ER 472, HL. For an account of the background to MHA 1967, see Lord Denning, *The Due Process of Law* (1980) Butterworths, Part Seven 'The deserted wife's equity'. See also App 2, Table 3 for the statutory derivation of MHA 1983.

2 See para 7.8.

3 See paras 7.16–7.18.

DETERMINING MATRIMONIAL HOME RIGHTS

7.2 Where a matrimonial home is owned by two spouses by virtue of the legal estate being vested in them jointly,[1] by virtue either of a contract[2] or by statute,[3] they are each entitled to occupy the property.[4] Where only one spouse has proprietory rights entitling him or her to occupy the matrimonial home, statutory matrimonial home rights are given to the other (s 30). The Act, like its predecessors, uses the term 'dwelling-house', which is defined in s 63(1), (4) as including any building or part of a building which is occupied as a dwelling, and any yard, garden, garage or outhouse belonging to the dwelling and occupied with it. The individual facts of each case will determine what constitutes the matrimonial home. In most cases there will be no difficulty in identifying the property but there may be fine distinctions to be drawn in others.[5] The dwelling-house must be or have been the matrimonial home of the parties (s 30(7)),[6] otherwise there cannot be matrimonial home rights. In determining a person's right to occupy a dwelling house by virtue of an estate or interest, any right to possession conferred on a mortgagee is disregarded (s 54(1)), whether or not the mortgagee is in possession (s 54(2)).

1 It is immaterial whether they are joint tenants or tenants in common.

2 Eg a contractual tenancy or a lease.

3 Eg a statutory tenancy.

4 By virtue of their proprietory right. See also *Gurasz v Gurasz* [1970] P 11 at 17, [1969] 3 All ER 822 at 824, CA for the rights at common law of co-owners of a matrimonial home.

5 See *Kinzler v Kinzler* [1985] Fam Law 26, CA, where on the facts the whole of an hotel constituted the matrimonial home. It is an objective test whether a house is the matrimonial home, *Mackintosh v Mackintosh (also known as Courtney-Mackintosh)* [1986] CA Transcript 262.

6 See *Syed v Syed* (1980) 1 FLR 129.

7.3 Where—

(1) One spouse is entitled to occupy a dwelling-house by virtue of a beneficial estate or interest or contract or by virtue of any enactment giving him the right to remain in occupation (s 30(1)(a));

(2) the other spouse is not so entitled (s 30(1)(b));[1]

(3) the dwelling-house is or has been the matrimonial home of the parties (s 30(7)); and

(4) the marriage subsists (s 30(8));[2]

the spouse without proprietary rights has matrimonial home rights (s 30(2)).

1 Ie has no legal interest in the dwelling-house which forms the matrimonial home. Section 30(9) treats a spouse with only an equitable interest in the property as being not entitled to occupy the dwelling-house, solely for the purpose of determining matrimonial home rights.

2 The rights may be extended beyond the subsistence of the marriage by order under s 33(5) made during the subsistence of the marriage.

7.4 Such rights are—

(1) If in occupation, a right not to be evicted or excluded from the dwelling-house or any part of it by the other spouse except with the leave of the court given by order under s 30 (s 30(2)(a)).[1]

(2) If not in occupation, a right with the leave of the court so given to enter into and occupy the dwelling-house (s 30(2)(b)).[2]

1 Such an order can be made under s 33(3)(f) or (g).

2 Such an order can be made under s 33(3)(b).

EFFECT OF MATRIMONIAL HOME RIGHTS

7.5 If a spouse is entitled to occupy the dwelling-house by virtue of matrimonial home rights any payment, tender or other thing done by that spouse in or towards satisfaction of any liability of the other spouse in respect of rent, mortgage payments[1] or other outgoings in respect of the dwelling-house is as good as if done by the other spouse (s 30(3)),[2] whether or not it is made or done under an order made under s 40.[3] A mortgagee[4] may treat such payments made by one spouse as payments by the other spouse but that does not affect the claim of the paying spouse to assert a beneficial interest in the dwelling-house by virtue of such payments (s 30(5)).[5]

1 By s 63(1) 'mortgage payments' includes any payments which the mortgagor is required to make under the terms of the mortgage to any person.

2 In *Penn v Dunn* [1970] 2 QB 686, [1970] 2 All ER 858, CA, it was held that while rent paid by a wife normally kept a statutory tenancy of the husband in existence, the position was different once an order of possession had been made against the husband. See also *Church Comrs for England v Al-Emarah* [1996] 22 LS Gaz R 27, CA.

3 For the scope of orders under s 40, see Ch 8.

4 By s 63(1) 'mortgage', 'mortgagor' and 'mortgagee' have the same meaning as in the Law of Property Act 1925 (LPA 1925), s 205(1)(xvi).

5 For the circumstances in which a claim to a beneficial interest may arise from mortgage payments see *Lloyds Bank plc v Rosset* [1991] 1 AC 107, [1990] 1 All ER 1111, HL and cases cited therein.

7.6 For the purposes of the Rent (Agriculture) Act 1976 (R(A)A 1976) and the Rent Act 1977 (RA 1977),[1] the occupation of a dwelling-house by one spouse, by virtue of matrimonial home rights, is treated as occupation by the other spouse as the residence of that other spouse (s 30(4)(a)).[2] For the purposes of the Housing Act 1985 (HA 1985) and Part I of the Housing Act 1988 (HA 1988), the occupation of a dwelling-house by one spouse as his only or principal home is treated as occupation by the other spouse as the only or principal home of that other spouse (s 30(4)(b)). The dwelling-house in question must, of course, in either case have been the matrimonial home (s 30(7)).[3] The importance of these provisions is that the tenancy in question is kept in existence.[4]

1 Other than Part V and ss 103–106.
2 See *Griffiths v Renfree* [1989] Fam Law 355, CA
3 See also *Hall v King* [1988] 1 FLR 376, CA.
4 See further para 7.8.

7.7 Where one spouse has matrimonial home rights in respect of a dwelling-house by reason of the interest of the other spouse under a trust, the provisions of s 30(3)–(5) apply in relation to the trustees as they do to the other spouse (s 30(6)).[1] The effect of this provision is that trustees are in the same position as the other spouse.

1 See paras 7.5 and 7.6.

TENANCIES

7.8 In respect of protected or statutory tenancies,[1] secure tenancies[2] and assured tenancies[3] the court has an extended discretion to adjourn possession proceedings, stay or suspend execution of an order, or postpone the date of possession for such periods as it thinks fit.[4] Where such possession proceedings are brought and the tenant's spouse or former spouse has matrimonial home rights and is in occupation of the dwelling-house, then if the tenancy is terminated as a result of those proceedings, the spouse or former spouse has the same rights in relation to the adjournment, stay, suspension of postponement as he or she would have had if those matrimonial home rights were not affected by the termination of the tenancy, provided he or she remains in occupation.[5] This applies only where the landlord is claiming possession on a discretionary ground,[6] and does not apply to assured shorthold tenancies.[7] In respect of secure tenancies and assured tenancies additional provisions apply. Where a former spouse no longer has matrimonial home rights,[8] but has rights in respect of a dwelling-house by order under s 35, or where a cohabitant or former cohabitant has rights in a dwelling house by order under s 36, then so long as the former spouse, cohabitant or former cohabitant remains in occupation, he or she has the same rights in relation to adjournment, stay, suspension or postponement as he or she would have had if the rights conferred by the order[9] were not affected by the termination of the tenancy.[10]

1 Under RA 1977. It also applies to protected occupancies and statutory tenancies under R(A)A 1976.
2 Under HA 1985.
3 Under HA 1988.
4 RA 1977, s 100(1), (2); R(A)A 1976, s 7(2A), (3); HA 1985, s 85(1); and HA 1988, s 9(1)
5 HA 1985, s 85(5); HA 1988, s 9(5). RA 1977, s 100(4A), (4B) and R(A)A 1976, s 7(5A), (5B);

although not specifically amended by the 1996 Act, Sch 8, the provisions of Sch 9, paras 11–13 thereof apply.

6 RA 1977, s 100(5); R(A)A 1976, s 7(1); HA 1985, s 85(1); and HA 1988, s 9(6)(a).

7 HA 1988, s 9(6)(b).

8 This is because such rights ended on divorce without any order under s 33(5).

9 Under s 35 or 36 of the 1996 Act.

10 HA 1985, new s 85(5A); HA 1988, new s 9(5A). Thus an order under s 36 gives protection to cohabitants or former cohabitants that was denied in *Colin Smith Music Ltd v Ridge* [1975] 1 All ER 290, [1975] 1 WLR 463, CA.

MATRIMONIAL HOME RIGHTS AS A CHARGE

7.9 Where during the subsistence of a marriage, one spouse is entitled to occupy a dwelling-house by virtue of a beneficial estate or interest (s 31(1)), the matrimonial home rights of the other spouse are a charge on that estate or interest (s 31(2)). Such charge has the like priority[1] as if it were an equitable interest created at the latest of the following dates (i) the date on which the entitled spouse acquired his interest; (ii) the date of the marriage; or (iii) 1st January 1968.[2] A spouse who is not in occupation has a conditional right which is capable of registration as a charge, but it does not become a complete right to occupy until the leave of the court is obtained under s 30(2)(b).[3] A charge improperly registered where there is no intention to occupy may be set aside.[4] Where the matrimonial home rights of a spouse are a charge on the estate or interest of the other spouse, an order under s 33 has the same effect against persons deriving title under the other spouse, except so far as a contrary intention appears (s 34(1)(a)).[5] An order under s 33 may be made against a person deriving title under the other spouse if the court considers it just and reasonable so to order (s 34(1)(b), (2)).

1 For the priority of equitable interests, see 16 *Halsbury's Laws* (4th edn reissue) paras 759 and 781.

2 This is the date on which the MHA 1967 commenced.

3 *Watts v Waller* [1973] QB 153, [1972] 3 All ER 257, CA.

4 *Barnett v Hassett* [1982] 1 All ER 80, [1981] 1 WLR 1385.

5 See *Kaur v Gill* [1988] Fam 110, [1988] 2 All ER 288, CA, for the position of persons deriving title under the other spouse.

7.10 Where a spouses' matrimonial home rights are a charge on an interest of the other spouse under a trust (s 31(5)). Such charge has the same priority[1] as if it were an equitable interest created[2] on the date when it arises (s 31(6)). Where the matrimonial home rights of a spouse are a charge on the estate or interest of the trustees of the other spouse, an order under s 33 has the same effect against the trustees of the other spouse, except so far as a contrary intention appears (s 34(1)(a)). An order under s 33 may be made against the trustees of the other spouse if the court considers it just and reasonable so to order (s 34(1)(b), (2)).

1 For the priority of equitable interests, see 16 *Halsbury's Laws* (4th edn reissue) paras 759 and 781.

2 Under powers overriding the trust.

7.11 Where the title to the legal estate by virtue of which a spouse is entitled to occupy the matrimonial home (including any legal estate held by trustees for that spouse) is registered under the Land Registration Act 1925 (LRA 1925) (s 31(10) of the 1996 Act), the spouse with matrimonial home rights may register a notice against the title in respect of such rights. Matrimonial home rights are not an overriding interest, even though the spouse is in actual occupation[1] of the dwelling-house. Matrimonial home rights cannot be protected by the registration of a caution (s 31(11)).[2] Where the title to the legal estate by virtue of which a spouse is entitled to occupy the matrimonial home (including any legal estate held by trustees for that spouse) is not registered under LRA 1925, the spouse with matrimonial home rights may register a Class F land charge under the Land Charges Act 1972 (LCA 1972), s 2(7). Matrimonial home rights can only be registered where such rights are a charge on a legal estate (s 31(13)).

1 See LRA 1925, s 70(1)(g).
2 Until 14 February 1983 a caution under LRA 1925, s 54 could be lodged in respect of rights of occupation and the effect of such cautions is preserved by the 1996 Act, Sch 9, para 14.

REGISTRATION OF CHARGE

7.12 An application to register matrimonial home rights as a charge on the legal estate is made in the prescribed manner.[1] Where an order is made under s 33(5), the spouse entitled to the charge may register the charge (Sch 4, para 4(3)(b)); or, if the charge was registered before the date of the order, renew the registration (Sch 4, para 3(3)(a)).

1 Schedule 4, para 4(6) enables rules to be made under LCA 1972, s 16 and LRA 1925, s 144. The rules under MHA 1983 are the Land Registration (Matrimonial Homes) Rules 1990, SI 1990/1360. New rules will have to be made to take account of the changes brought about by Part IV of the Act.

7.13 A spouse may be entitled by virtue of s 31 to a registerable charge in respect of more than one dwelling-house (s 31(10)). Only one such charge may be registered at any one time (Sch 4, para 2). If more than one such charge is registered, the Chief Land Registrar must cancel the registration of the charge first registered (ibid).

CANCELLATION OF REGISTRATION

7.14 Unless an order is made under s 33(5), matrimonial home rights continue only so long as the marriage subsists (s 30(8)(a)); or, for as long as the other spouse is entitled to occupy the dwelling-house, except where those rights are a charge on an estate or interest in the dwelling house (ss 30(8)(b), 31). Where matrimonial home rights have been registered under s 31(10), or under LCA 1972, s 2, the Chief Land Registrar shall, subject to an order under s 33(5),[1] cancel the registration if he is satisfied—

(1) that either spouse is dead, by production of a certificate or other sufficient evidence (Sch 4, para 4(1)(a));
(2) that the marriage has been terminated otherwise than by death, by production of an official copy of a decree or order of a court (Sch 4, para 4(1)(b));[2] or,
(3) that the spouse's matrimonial home rights constituting the charge have been terminated, by production of an order of the court (Sch 4, para 4(1)(c)).[3]

1 See paras 7.12 and 7.15.
2 If the decree or order has not been obtained by a court in England and Wales, it is submitted that the decree or order should comply with the requirements of FLA 1986, Part II.
3 Matrimonial home rights may be terminated under s 33(3)(e).

7.15 However, where there is an order under s 33(5), and after the making of such order the charge was registered or the registration was renewed in accordance with Sch 4, para 4(3), the Chief Land Registrar may not cancel the registration under Sch 4, para 4(1)(a) or (b) by virtue of the death of the entitled-spouse or other termination of the marriage, unless he is also satisfied that the order has ceased to have effect (Sch 4, para 4(2)).

MORTGAGES

Priority

7.16 Where a spouse's matrimonial home rights are a charge on the estate of the other spouse or the trustees of the other spouse, and that estate is the subject of a mortgage, then if after the date of the creation of the mortgage[1] the charge is registered under LCA 1972, s 2, the charge is deemed[2] to be a mortgage subsequent to the first mortgage (s 31(12). This means, in practice, that a mortgagee will not make further advances on a mortgage where a charge in respect of matrimonial home is registered, unless the spouse entitled to the charge agrees in writing that the charge of the mortgagee shall rank in priority to the charge in respect of matrimonial home rights (Sch 4, para 6).

1 'The first mortgage' (s 31(12)).
2 For the purposes of LPA 1925, s 94 (which regulates the right of a mortgagee to make further advances ranking in priority to subsequent mortgages).

Rights of connected persons

7.17 A 'connected person' in relation to a person means the spouse, former spouse, cohabitant or former cohabitant of that person (ss 54(5), 55(4)). Where a person is entitled to occupy a dwelling-house by virtue of an estate or interest, a connected person does not have any greater right[1] than the entitled person to occupy the dwelling-house against the mortgagee (s 54(3)), unless, in the case of matrimonial home rights, those rights are a charge on the estate or interest mortgaged and rank in priority to the mortgage (s 54(4)).[2]

1 By virtue of matrimonial home rights under s 30 or an occupation order under ss 35 or 36.
2 As with the MHA 1983, s 8(1) it would seem that s 54(4) merely clarifies rather than changes the existing law.

Actions by mortgagees

7.18 Where a mortgagee of land which consists of a dwelling house[1] brings an action for the enforcement of his security, and at the relevant time[2] there is either a Class F land charge[3] or a subsisting notice or caution,[4] the mortgagee must serve notice of the action on the person on whose behalf the land charge is registered or the notice or caution is entered if that person is not a party to the action (s 56(1), (2)).[5] A plaintiff mortgagee who has not made an official search must satisfy the court that there are no persons to be served with notice of the action.[6] A connected person (s 55(4))[7] may apply to be made a party to a mortgage possession action, whether or not notice of the action has been served upon him or her. Where a connected person is enabled[8] to meet the mortgagor's liabilities under the mortgage (s 55(3)(a)), and applies to be joined as a party before the action is finally disposed of (s 55(3)(b)), then the connected person is entitled to be joined as a party (s 55(2)) provided the court sees no special reason against his being made a party (s 55(3)(c)), and is satisfied that he may be able to meet the mortgagor's liabilities and obligations as might affect the outcome of the case (s 55(3)(c)(i)), or that the expectation should be considered under the Administration of Justice Act 1970, s 36 (s 55(3)(c)(ii)).[9]

---

1 Or substantially so consists (s 56(1)).

2 Where the mortgagee has made an official search which would disclose a Class F land charge, notice or caution in respect of matrimonial home rights, a certificate of the search has been issued and the action is commenced within the priority period (see LCA 1972, s 11(5), (6)), the 'relevant time' is the date of the certificate. Otherwise the 'relevant time' is the time when the action is commenced, s 56(4).

3 In the case of unregistered land, registered against the person who is the estate owner at the relevant time or any person who, where the estate owner is a trustee, preceded him as trustee during the subsistence of the mortgage.

4 In the case of registered land, a notice under s 31(11), a notice under MHA 1983, s 2(8), or a notice or caution under MHA 1967, s 2(7), the effect of which are preserved by Sch 9, para 14.

5 The notice is in Form N438. The County Court Rules 1981, SI 1981/1687, Ord 6, r 5A(3) requires a mortgagee to state in the particulars of claim whether there is any person upon whom notice of the action is required to be served.

6 *Jenroy (Finance) Ltd v Stephens* (28 June 1989, unreported), Thanet County Court.

7 See para 7.17.

8 Under s 30(3) or (6) (or as applied by s 35(13) or s 36(13)).

9 Section 55(3) in effect confirms *Hastings & Thanet Building Society v Goddard* [1970] 3 All ER 954, [1970] 1 WLR 1544, CA.

8 Occupation orders

INTRODUCTION

8.1 FLA 1996 ss 33-41 introduce occupation orders which replace ouster injunctions and orders regulating the occupation of a matrimonial home or cohabitants' home. Part IV of the 1996 Act gives a wide range of powers to the courts. The extent of the available powers depends in each case upon whether the applicant or the associated respondent (or neither) is entitled to occupy the dwelling-house, whether they are spouses or former spouses, cohabitants or former cohabitants. It also depends on the status of the dwelling-house as the home or intended home of the parties. The factors that the court must consider in determining an application are prescribed and these criteria depend upon the category of the applicant as an 'entitled applicant' (s 33), a 'non-entitled former spouse' (s 35), a 'non-entitled cohabitant or former cohabitant' (s 36), or a case where neither party is entitled (s 37 if spouses and s 38 if cohabitants). The duration of time for which an occupation order may be in force is also dependent upon the category under which the applicant's case is brought. All these matters will now be considered in more detail. The flow chart at App 4, Table 1 provides a quick way of identifying the categories of applicant.

ENTITLEMENT TO APPLY

Entitled applicants and those with matrimonial home rights

8.2 Where a person (the entitled applicant) is entitled to occupy a dwelling-house by virtue of a beneficial estate or interest or contract or by virtue of any enactment giving him the right to remain in occupation, or has matrimonial home rights in the dwelling-house[1] and the dwelling-house is or has been at any time the home of the entitled person and of another person with whom he is associated[2] (the respondent), or was at any time intended by the applicant and the respondent to be their home, then the applicant may apply to the court for orders under s 33(3)–(5) against the respondent (s 33(1)). Although parties to an agreement to marry which has been terminated are associated persons (s 62(3)(e)),[3] no application may be made under s 33 by virtue of s 62(3)(e) more than three years after the agreement to marry has been terminated (s 33(2)), unless the applicant and respondent are also associated under some other provision.[4]

---

1 Thus a spouse is always an 'entitled applicant' because matrimonial home rights are given to a spouse without other rights (s 30).

2 For the meaning of 'associated', see paras 6.8–6.26.

3 See paras 6.17–6.21.

4 For example if they are former cohabitants.

Non-entitled former spouses

8.3 In order to apply under s 35, the applicant must be a former spouse. A former spouse (the respondent) must be entitled to occupy a dwelling-house by virtue of a beneficial estate or interest or contract or by virtue of any enactment giving him the right to remain in occupation and the other former spouse must have no such entitlement.[1] The dwelling-house in question must have been, or have been intended by them to be their matrimonial home. Where these conditions apply, the applicant may apply to the court for an order under s 35 against the respondent (s 35(1), (2)).

1 The matrimonial home rights of a former spouse may continue after the dissolution of the marriage where the court has so ordered during the subsistence of the marriage, s 33(5); in which case an application should be brought under s 33.

Non-entitled cohabitants or former cohabitants

8.4 In order to apply under s 36, the applicant must be a cohabitant or former cohabitant. One cohabitant or former cohabitant (the respondent) must be entitled to occupy a dwelling-house by virtue of a beneficial estate or interest or contract or by virtue of any enactment giving him the right to remain in occupation and the other cohabitant or former cohabitant must have no such entitlement. The dwelling-house in question must be or have been the home in which they lived together as husband and wife, or have been a home in which they intended so to live. Where these conditions apply, the applicant may apply to the court for an order under s 36 against the respondent (s 36(1), (2)).

Neither party entitled

8.5 The court may make occupation orders between spouses, former spouses, cohabitants or former cohabitants where neither party wished to establish a right to occupy the dwelling-house or where one could not be established (ss 37 and 38). These provisions would apply where, for example, the parties were squatters or bare licensees. The Law Commission observed[1] that such cases, although probably rare, were covered by the terms of DVMPA 1976 and the level of protection would be reduced if provision was not made for them.

1 Law Com No 207, para 4.8.

Neither spouse or former spouse entitled

8.6 Where one spouse or former spouse, and the other spouse or former spouse occupy a dwelling-house which is or was their matrimonial home, but neither is entitled to occupy the dwelling-house by virtue of a beneficial estate or interest or contract or by virtue of any enactment giving him the right to remain in occupation, then either party may apply to the court for an order under s 37 (s 37(1), (2)).

Neither cohabitant or former cohabitant entitled

8.7 Where one cohabitant or former cohabitant and the other cohabitant or former cohabitant occupy a dwelling-house which is the home in which they live or have lived together as husband and wife, but neither is entitled to occupy the dwelling-house by virtue of a beneficial estate or interest or contract or by virtue of any enactment giving him the right to remain in occupation, then either party may apply to the court for an order under s 38 (s 38(1), (2)).

RANGE OF ORDERS AVAILABLE

8.8 The orders for which applicants may apply vary according to whether the applicant is an entitled applicant,[1] a non-entitled former spouse, a non-entitled cohabitant or former cohabitant or whether neither party is entitled. Appendix 4, Table 2 shows the range of orders available in respect of each class of applicant. The range of orders is broadly similar to those previously available under DVMPA 1976 and MHA 1983; however, the Act goes further than the previous legislation and clarifies the extent of the powers of the courts.

1 This category includes spouses with matrimonial home rights under s 30.

Entitled applicants and those with matrimonial home rights

8.9 All orders in favour of entitled applicants are discretionary.[1] The following is a list of all the orders that may be made (s 33(3)). An order may—

(1) enforce the applicant's entitlement to remain in occupation as against the respondent;
(2) require the respondent to permit the applicant to enter and remain in the dwelling-house or part of the dwelling-house;
(3) regulate the occupation of the dwelling-house by either or both parties;
(4) where the respondent is entitled under s 33(1)(a)(i), prohibit, suspend or restrict the exercise by him of his right to occupy the dwelling-house;
(5) where the respondent has matrimonial home rights in relation to the dwelling-house and the applicant is the other spouse, restrict or terminate those rights;
(6) require the respondent to leave the dwelling-house or part of the dwelling-house;
(7) exclude the respondent from a defined area in which the dwelling-house is included.

An order may declare that the applicant is entitled under s 33(1)(a)(i), or has matrimonial home rights (s 33(4)). Where the applicant has matrimonial home rights and the respondent is the other spouse, an occupation order, made during the subsistence of the marriage, may provide that those rights are not brought to an end by the death of the other spouse or the termination (otherwise than by death) of the marriage (s 33(5)).

1 Section 33(3) uses the word 'may'. See App 4, Table 2, col 1.

Non-entitled former spouses

8.10 Where the court decides to make an order in favour of a non-entitled former spouse, the order will contain a mandatory provision and may contain further discretionary provisions.

Mandatory provisions

8.11 If the applicant is in occupation, the order must contain a provision giving the applicant the right not to be evicted or excluded from the dwelling-house or any part of it by the respondent for the period specified in the order and prohibiting the respondent from evicting or excluding the applicant during that period. If the applicant is not in occupation, the order must contain a provision giving the applicant the right to enter into and occupy the dwelling-house for the period specified in the order and requiring the respondent to permit the exercise of that right (s 35(3), (4), see App 4, Table 2, col 2).

Discretionary provisions

8.12 In addition, an order may (s 35(5))—

(1) regulate the occupation of the dwelling-house by either or both parties;
(2) prohibit, suspend or restrict the exercise by the respondent of his rights to occupy the dwelling-house;
(3) require the respondent to leave the dwelling-house or part of the dwelling-house;
(4) exclude the respondent from a defined area in which the dwelling-house is included.

(See App 4, Table 2, col 2.)

Non-entitled cohabitants and former cohabitants

8.13 Where the court decides to make an order in favour of a non-entitled cohabitant or former cohabitant, the order will contain a mandatory provision and may contain further discretionary provisions.

Mandatory provisions

8.14 If the applicant is in occupation, the order must contain a provision giving the applicant the right not to be evicted or excluded from the dwelling-house or any part of it by the respondent for the period specified in the order and prohibiting the respondent from evicting or excluding the applicant during that period. If the applicant is not in occupation, the order must contain a provision giving the applicant the right to enter into and occupy the dwelling-house for the period specified in the order and requiring the respondent to permit the exercise of that right (s 36(3), (4), see App 4, Table 2, col 3).

Discretionary provisions

8.15 In addition, an order may (s 36(5))—

(1) regulate the occupation of the dwelling-house by either or both parties;
(2) prohibit, suspend or restrict the exercise by the respondent of his rights to occupy the dwelling-house;
(3) require the respondent to leave the dwelling-house or part of the dwelling-house;
(4) exclude the respondent from a defined area in which the dwelling-house is included.

(See App 4, Table 2, col 3.)

Neither spouse or former spouse entitled

8.16 All orders where neither the spouse or the former spouse is entitled to occupy the dwelling-house are discretionary (s 37(3), see Appendix 4, Table 2, col 4). An order may—

(1) require the respondent to permit the applicant to enter and remain in the dwelling-house or part of the dwelling-house;
(2) regulate the occupation of the dwelling-house by either or both parties;
(3) require the respondent to leave the dwelling-house or part of the dwelling-house;
(4) exclude the respondent from a defined area in which the dwelling-house is included.

Neither cohabitant or former cohabitant entitled

8.17 All orders where neither the cohabitant or the former cohabitant is entitled to occupy the dwelling-house are discretionary (s 38(3), see App 4, Table 2, col 5). An order may—

(1) require the respondent to permit the applicant to enter and remain in the dwelling-house or part of the dwelling-house;
(2) regulate the occupation of the dwelling-house by either or both parties;
(3) require the respondent to leave the dwelling-house or part of the dwelling-house;
(4) exclude the respondent from a defined area in which the dwelling-house is included.

CRITERIA FOR EXERCISE OF POWERS

8.18 The basis on which the courts should decide whether and if so in what manner to exercise their powers to make occupation orders was a matter of much debate in the Special Public Bill Committee.[1] The balance of harm test incorporates concepts from CA 1989, s 31(2), while the question of conduct is specifically mentioned. The test under MHA 1983, s 1(3) required the court to make such order as it thinks 'just and reasonable'; there is no such requirement under the 1996 Act. This may present difficulties to the courts if the application of the balance of harm test appears to produce an unjust result. The statutory factors must be considered by the court and vary according to whether the applicant is an entitled applicant, a non-entitled former spouse, a non-entitled cohabitant or former cohabitant, whether neither spouse or former spouse is entitled, or whether neither cohabitant or former cohabitant is entitled (see App 4, Table 3).

1 Family Homes and Domestic Violence Bill, HL, Session 1994–94 No 55. Conservative Backbenchers in the House of Commons indicated considerable opposition to the provisions that did not differentiate between cohabitants and spouses, as a result of which the Bill was dropped.

Entitled applicants and those with matrimonial home rights

8.19 In deciding whether, and if so in what manner, to exercise its powers under s 33(3) the court shall have regard to all the circumstances (s 33(6), see App 4, Table 3, col 1) including—

(1) the respective housing needs and housing resources of the parties and any relevant child;
(2) the financial resources of the parties;

(3) the likely effect of any order, or of any decision by the court not to exercise its powers, on the health, safety or well-being of the parties and of any relevant child[1]; and
(4) the conduct of the parties in relation to each other and otherwise.

The court must also apply the balance of harm test (s 33(7)). As the 1996 Act does not provide that any one factor is to be given more weight in the decision making process than another, it is for the judge determining the application to give such weight to each factor as seems appropriate on the facts of each individual case.[2] If it appears to the court that the applicant or any relevant child is likely to suffer significant harm[3] attributable to conduct of the respondent if an order containing one or more of the provisions in sub-s (3) is not made, the court shall make an order unless it appears to the court (s 33(7)) that—

(a) the respondent or any relevant child is likely to suffer significant harm if the order is made, and
(b) the harm likely to be suffered by the respondent or child in that event is as great as, or greater than, the harm attributable to conduct of the respondent which is likely to be suffered by the applicant or child if the order is not made.

1 'Health' includes physical or mental health, see s 63(1).
2 *Richards v Richards* (see para 1.6).
3 See para 8.31.

Non-entitled former spouses

Mandatory orders

8.20 In deciding whether, and if so in what manner, to exercise its powers to make a mandatory order under s 35(3) or (4) the court shall have regard to all the circumstances (s 35(6), see App 4, Table 3, col 2) including—

(1) the respective housing needs and housing resources of the parties and any relevant child;
(2) the respective financial resources of the parties;
(3) the likely effect of any order, or of any decision by the court not to exercise its powers, on the health, safety or well-being of the parties and of any relevant child[1];
(4) the conduct of the parties in relation to each other and otherwise;
(5) the length of time that has elapsed since the parties ceased to live together;
(6) the length of time that has elapsed since the marriage was dissolved or annulled;
(7) the existence of any pending proceedings between the parties for an order under MCA 1973, ss 23A, 24[2] for an order under CA 1989, Sch 1, paras 1(2)(d) or (e)[3] or relating to the legal or beneficial ownership of the dwelling-house.[4]

1 'Health' includes physical or mental health, see s 63(1).
2 Property adjustment orders in connection with divorce, judicial separation or nullity (s 35(6)(g)(i)).
3 Orders for financial relief against parents (s 35(6)(g)(ii)).
4 Such proceedings would probably include an application for transfer of tenancy under Sch 7 (s 35(6)(g)(iii)).

Discretionary orders

8.21 The next stage involves the court considering whether to exercise its power to make discretionary orders under s 35(5), and if so, in what manner. This involves repeating part of the previous process (see para 8.20). The court must have regard to all the circumstances as set out in s 35(6)(a)–(e). The court must also apply the balance of harm test (s 35(8)). As the 1996 Act does not provide that any one factor is to be given more weight in the decision making process than another, it is for the judge determining the application to give such weight to each factor as seems appropriate on the facts of each individual case.[1] Where the court decides to make an order under s 35 and it appears to the court that, if the order does not include one of the provisions in s 35(5),[2] the applicant or any relevant child is likely to suffer significant harm attributable to conduct of the respondent (s 35(8)),[3] the court shall include the provision under s 35(5) in the order unless it appears to the court[4] that—

(a) the respondent and any relevant child is likely to suffer significant harm if the provision is included in the order (s 35(8)(a)), and
(b) the harm likely to be suffered by the respondent or child in that event is as great as or greater than the harm attributable to conduct of the respondent which is likely to be suffered by the applicant or child if the order is not made (s 35(8)(b)).

---

1 *Richards v Richards* (see para 1.6).
2 These are set out in paras 8.10–8.12 and see App 4, Table 2, col 2.
3 See para 8.23.
4 Ibid.

Non-entitled cohabitants and former cohabitants

Mandatory orders

8.22 In deciding whether, and if so in what manner, to exercise its powers to make a mandatory order under s 36(3) or (4) the court must have regard to all the circumstances (s 36(6), see App 4, Table 3, col 3) including—

(1) the respective housing needs and housing resources of the parties and any relevant child;
(2) the respective financial resources of the parties;
(3) the likely effect of any order, or of any decision by the court not to exercise its powers, on the health, safety or well-being of the parties and of any relevant child;[1]
(4) the conduct of the parties in relation to each other and otherwise;
(5) the nature of the parties' relationship (s 36(6)(e), subject to s 41);
(6) the length of time during which they have lived together as husband and wife;
(7) whether there are or have been children who are children of both parties or for whom both parties have or have had parental responsibility;
(8) the length of time that has elapsed since the parties ceased to live together;
(9) the existence of any pending proceedings between the parties for an order under CA 1989, Sch 1, paras 1(2)(d) or (e),[2] or relating to the legal or beneficial ownership of the dwelling-house.[3]

In considering the nature of the parties' relationship for the purposes of s 36(6)(e), the court must have regard to the fact that they have not given each other the commitment involved in marriage (s 41).

1 'Health' includes physical or mental health (s 59(1)).
2 Orders for financial relief against parents (s 36(6)(i)(i)).
3 Such proceedings would probably include an application for transfer of tenancy under Sch 7 (s 36(6)(i), (ii)).

Discretionary orders

8.23 The next stage involves the court considering whether to exercise its power to make discretionary orders under s 35(5), and if so, in what manner; this involves repeating part of the previous process. The court shall have regard to all the circumstances as set out in s 36(6)(a)–(e) (see para 8.22). The court must also consider the questions mentioned in s 35(8) (s 36(7)(b)). As the 1996 Act does not provide that any one factor is to be given more weight in the decision making process than another, it is for the judge determining the application to give such weight to each factor as seems appropriate on the facts of each individual case.[1] The court must consider—

(a) whether the applicant or any relevant child is likely to suffer significant harm attributable to conduct of the respondent if a provision under s 35(5) is not included in the order (s 36(8)(a)); and
(b) whether the harm likely to be suffered by the respondent or child if the provision is included is as great or greater than the harm attributable to conduct of the respondent which is likely to be suffered by the applicant or child if the provision is not included (s 36(8)(b)).

There is a significant difference in wording between the provisions of ss 30 and 32 in that under those provisions the court must make an order on the basis of greater harm to the applicant or relevant child if an order is not made. In considering the nature of the parties' relationship for the purposes of s 36(6)(e), the court must have regard to the fact that they have not given each other the commitment involved in marriage (s 41).

1 *Richards v Richards* (see para 1.6).

Neither spouse entitled

8.24 In deciding whether, and if so in what manner, to exercise its powers under s 37(3) the court shall have regard to all the circumstances as set out in s 33(6), (7) (see para 8.19 and App 4, Table 3, col 4).

Neither cohabitant or former cohabitant entitled

8.25 In deciding whether to exercise its powers under s 38(3) the court shall have regard to all the circumstances of the case (s 38(4), see App 4, Table 3, col 5), including—

(1) the respective housing needs and housing resources of the parties and any relevant child (s 38(4)(a));
(2) the respective financial resources of the parties;

(3) the likely effect of any order, or of any decision by the court not to exercise its powers, on the health, safety or well-being of the parties and of any relevant child;[1]

(4) the conduct of the parties in relation to each other and otherwise;

(5) the questions mentioned in s 38(5), which are—

(a) whether the applicant or any relevant child is likely to suffer significant harm attributable to conduct of the respondent if a provision under s 38(3) is not included in the order;[2] and,

(b) whether the harm likely to be suffered by the respondent or child if the provision is included is as great or greater than the harm attributable to conduct of the respondent which is likely to be suffered by the applicant or child if the provision is not included.

As the statute does not provide that any one factor is to be given more weight in the decision making process than another, it is for the judge determining the application to give such weight to each factor as seems appropriate on the facts of each individual case.[3]

1 'Health' includes physical or mental health, see s 63(1).
2 See para 8.23.
3 *Richards v Richards* (see para 1.6).

HARM AND RELATED DEFINITIONS

8.26 The concepts of 'harm' and 'significant harm' were introduced by CA 1989, ss 31(9), (10) and 105(1). The 1996 Act, Part IV develops these concepts in s 63(1). In relation to an adult, 'harm' means 'ill-treatment or the impairment of health'. In relation to a child, 'harm' means 'ill-treatment or the impairment of health or development'. In relation to a child, 'ill-treatment' includes sexual abuse and forms of ill-treatment which are not physical. In relation to an adult, ill-treatment is not defined but it is submitted that it would include violence, threats of violence and forms of ill-treatment which are not physical. It is probably impossible to define 'ill-treatment' but it is relatively simple to say whether specific conduct is or is not 'ill-treatment'.[1] 'Health' includes physical or mental health. 'Development' means physical, intellectual, emotional, social or behavioural development.

1 Similarly 'molestation' is almost impossible to define; see further para 9.1.

Likely to suffer significant harm

8.27 Where the question of whether harm suffered by a child is significant turns on the child's health or development, his health or development should be compared with that which could reasonably be expected of a similar child.[1] Thus the test is objective. The Act uses the words 'is likely to suffer' significant harm, thus decisions on the threshold conditions[2] in care proceedings may assist in interpretation.[3] The word 'likely' has caused some difficulties of interpretation in other contexts.[4] In care proceedings the word 'likely' in CA 1989, s 32(1)(a), is being used in the sense of a real possibility, one that cannot be ignored having regard to the nature and gravity of the feared harm in any particular case.[5] Clearly, the court must evaluate both the chance of harm occurring and the magnitude of the harm if it does in fact occur. It is submitted that Parliament intended these words in the 1996 Act to have the same meaning as in the CA 1989. Thus once a judge has made findings of fact as to the conduct of the parties and the other matters to which the court must have regard, it is then possible to evaluate the future risks to the applicant or child of significant harm attributable to the conduct of the respondent (ss 33(7), 35(8), 36(8), 37(4), 38(5)).

1 See s 63(3), which is in identical terms to CA 1989, s 31(10).
2 See *In re M (a Minor) (Care Orders: Threshold Conditions)* [1994] 2 AC 424, [1994] 3 All ER 298, HL.
3 See *Clarke-Hall and Morrison on Children.*
4 It has been construed as meaning 'a reasonable prospect' of something happening, see *Dunning v United Liverpool Hospitals Board of Governors* [1973] 2 All ER 454 at 460, [1973] 1 WLR 586 at 594 per James LJ; overruled on another point by *McIvor v Southern Health and Social Services Board* [1978] 2 All ER 625, [1978] 1 WLR 757, HL. Equally it has been said that the word 'likely' is imprecise—it is capable of covering a whole range of possibilities from 'it is on the cards' to 'it is more probable than not', see *R v Sheppard* [1981] AC 394, [1980] 3 All ER 899, HL per Lord Diplock.
5 *In re H (minors) (Sexual Abuse: Standard of Proof)* [1996] 1 All ER 1, [1996] 2 WLR 8, HL.

Balancing the risk of significant harm

8.28 On applications by entitled applicants (s 33),[1] or by a non-entitled former spouse (s 35), and in cases where neither spouse or former spouse is entitled (s 37), the court is obliged to make an occupation order in a situation where without such an order the applicant or any relevant child would be likely to suffer significant harm attributable to the conduct of the respondent. However, if it appears that if such an order were made, the respondent or any relevant child would be likely to suffer significant harm *and* that harm is likely to be as great or greater than the harm attributable to the conduct of the respondent which is likely to be suffered by the applicant or child if the order is not made, no order will be made (ss 33(7), 35(8), 37(4), see App 4, Table 3, cols 1–3). It should be noted that in this exercise, the significant harm to the applicant or child likely to be suffered if an order is not made must be attributable to the conduct of the respondent. However, the significant harm likely to be suffered by the respondent or child if an order is made, may arise from any source. Where a respondent establishes a likelihood of equal or greater harm, it is submitted that the court may nonetheless make an occupation order in the exercise of its discretion in accordance with the statutory criteria, where, for example, the harm likely to be suffered by the applicant or child arises from unsatisfactory temporary accommodation.

1 Including spouses with matrimonial home rights.

ORDERS

8.29 Where the court decides to make an occupation order, the type of order may range from regulating the occupation of the dwelling-house to ousting the respondent. In deciding the measure of protection to be afforded to the applicant by an occupation order, the court will apply the statutory criteria to the individual facts of each particular case. It is submitted that an ouster order will continue to be regarded as a drastic measure and only to be made where no lesser measure will adequately protect the applicant or child.[1]

1 *Burke v Burke* [1987] 2 FLR 71, CA; *Bassett v Bassett* [1975] Fam 76, [1975] 1 All ER 513, CA.

Duration of orders

8.30 The maximum duration of occupation orders is specifically addressed in the Act. Previously, courts were required to consider a time limit.[1] Where no other proceedings were instituted to resolve long term housing problems, an order without limitation of time could operate as a summary transfer of property order.[2]

1 *Practice Note* [1978] 2 All ER 1056, sub nom *Practice Direction (Injunction: Domestic Violence)* [1978] 1 WLR 1123, which suggested that in most cases a period of three months would be sufficient.
2 *Hopper v Hopper* [1979] 1 All ER 181, [1978] 1 WLR 1342n, CA.

Orders under s 33

8.31 These orders (s 33(10), see App 4, Table 4, col 1) may be (i) for a specified period, (ii) until the occurrence of a specified event,[1] or (iii) until further order.[2] The court should always specifically consider the appropriate duration of the order. Where an order is limited in time, an application may be made to extend the operation of the order.

1 Such as the hearing of an application for ancillary relief or transfer of tenancy.
2 Where a non-property-owning party has been excluded it may be appropriate for the order to be expressed 'until further order'; *Spencer v Camacho* (1983) 4 FLR 662, 13 Fam Law 114, CA.

Orders under ss 35 and 37

8.32 These orders must be for a specified period not exceeding six months (ss 35(10), 37(5), see App 4, Table 4, cols 2, 4), but may be extended (on one or more occasions) for a further specified period not exceeding six months (ibid). The effect of this is that a respondent excluded under s 35 could be deprived of the enjoyment of property rights indefinitely, by means of repeated extensions of an occupation order. On an application to extend an occupation order under ss 35 or 37 it is submitted that the court should have regard to any changes in circumstances since the order was made and should apply the statutory criteria to those changed circumstances so far as possible, particularly as to the existence or progress of any application for ancillary relief (s 35(6)(g)(i)). It may also be relevant to consider the extent to which the parties have complied with any financial or consequential orders under s 37. Under s 37 where neither spouse has the right to occupy, financial issues are likely to be of some relevance, save that the question of property adjustment in respect of the matrimonial home will probably not arise.

Orders under s 36 and 38

8.33 These orders must be for a specified period not exceeding six months (ss 36(10), 38(6), see App 4, Table 4, cols 3–5), but may be extended on one occasion for a further specified period not exceeding six months (ibid). On an application to extend an order under s 36, the existence of an application for transfer of tenancy or an application under CA 1989, Sch 1 will be relevant. Financial matters will be less relevant on applications under s 38.

Variation and discharge

8.34 An occupation order may be varied or discharged by the court on an application by the respondent (s 49(1)(a)) or by the person on whose application the order was made (s 49(1)(b)). Where a spouse's matrimonial home rights are a charge on the estate or interest of the other spouse or of the trustees for the other spouse[1] an order under s 30 against the other spouse may be varied or discharged by the court on the application of any person deriving title under the other spouse or under the trustees and affected by the charge (s 49(3)). There are no factors prescribed for the court to consider on an application to vary or discharge an occupation order. It is submitted that the court should consider any changes in circumstances since the order was made and apply the statutory criteria to those changed circumstances, so far as possible. It may also be relevant to consider the extent to which the parties have complied with any financial or consequential orders under s 40.

1 See s 31.

FINANCIAL AND CONSEQUENTIAL ORDERS

8.35 Under MHA 1983, s 1(3)(b), the court had power to order a spouse occupying the whole or part of a dwelling-house by virtue of a right of occupation to make periodical payments to the other spouse in respect of that occupation. It could also impose on either spouse obligations as to the repair and maintenance of, or the discharge of liabilities in respect of, the dwelling-house (s 1(3)(c)). Such orders were comparatively rare because, between spouses, such matters were usually dealt with by way of an application for maintenance pending suit or interim periodical payments. Where a party is excluded from a joint home, more immediate matters to consider are what items he can take with him, what will be left behind and how to make sure that nothing is damaged. It is by no means unknown for a party excluded by injunction to remove the entire contents of the home before vacating!

8.36 The 1996 Act, Part IV provides that on making an occupation order under ss 33,[1] 35[2] or 36[3] or at any time thereafter while the occupation order remains in force (s 40(3)) the court may make financial and consequential orders. These orders are those (s 40(1))—

(1) imposing on either party obligations as to the repair and maintenance of the dwelling-house or as to the discharge of rent, mortgage payments[4] or other outgoings affecting the dwelling-house;
(2) ordering a party[5] occupying the dwelling-house or any part of it to make periodical payments to the other party in respect of the accommodation, where the other party would (but for the order) be entitled to occupy the dwelling-house by virtue of a beneficial estate or interest or contract or by virtue of any enactment giving him the right to remain in occupation.
(3) granting either party possession or use of furniture or other contents of the dwelling-house;
(4) ordering either party to take reasonable care of any furniture or other contents of the dwelling-house;
(5) ordering either party to take reasonable steps to keep the dwelling-house and any furniture or other contents secure.

1 Entitled applicants, including those with matrimonial home rights.
2 Non-entitled former spouse.
3 Non-entitled cohabitant or former cohabitant.
4 By s 63(1) 'mortgage payments' includes any payments which the mortgagor is required to make under the mortgage, and so could accordingly include endowment premiums and building insurance depending upon the terms of the deed.
5 Including one who is entitled to occupy by virtue of a beneficial estate or interest or contract or by virtue of any enactment giving him the right to remain in occupation; s 40(1)(b).

8.37 Where a party is excluded the question of consequential orders should always be considered. While 'outgoings' would cover buildings and contents insurance, water rates, council tax, gas, electricity and telephone, it is uncertain whether hire purchase commitments would be included. The Act does not provide any specific provision for enforcement of such orders. Orders in the nature of an injunction would be enforceable by committal, subject to the procedural requirements.[1] Enforcing orders for the payment of money, particularly to third parties is more difficult. Section 40 orders cannot be included in an occupation order under ss 37 or 38.[2] While this is understandable in respect of outgoings and periodical payments, issues as to furniture and contents may nonetheless be important.

1 See the County Court Rules 1981, SI 1981/1687, Ord 29.
2 Ie, cases where neither party is entitled. Section 37 relates to spouses or former spouses and s 38 to cohabitants or former cohabitants.

8.38 In deciding whether and, if so, how to exercise its powers under s 40, the court must have regard to all the circumstances of the case (s 40(2))[1] including—

(1) the financial needs and other resources of the parties, and
(2) the financial obligations which they have or are likely to have in the foreseeable future, including obligations to each other and to any relevant child.[2]

The Act does not contain any specific provision for the variation or discharge of financial and consequential orders, save that such an order ceases to have effect when the occupation order to which it relates ceases to have effect (s 40(3)). It would appear that the provisions of s 46 would not enable the court to vary or discharge an order under s 37 because such an order is not an occupation order.[3]

1 Where the parties have not been married, factors such as the nature and duration of the relationship, and whether or not there are children of the parties should be relevant.
2 This would include an assessment under the CSA 1991. It must be very difficult for a court to take into account such an obligation where the method of calculation is so complex.
3 Section 39(1) defines 'occupation order' as an order under ss 33, 35, 36, 37, or 38. The heading of s 40 refers to additional provisions that may be included in certain occupation orders, but this apparently conflicts with s 40(3) which implies that a s 40 order is not an occupation order.

9 Non-molestation orders

MEANING OF MOLESTATION

9.1 It is, as was recognised by the Law Commission,[1] difficult to define molestation. In *Vaughan v Vaughan*[2] the meaning of 'molestation' was considered and in the absence of any authority,[3] the court considered the definitions in the *Concise Oxford Dictionary*[4] and approved the definition in the *Shorter Oxford Dictionary*[5] which is in the following terms: 'To cause trouble; to vex; to annoy; to put to inconvenience'. Molestation includes acts and threats of violence[6] and 'a multitude of other things'.[7] It could include attempted sexual intercourse without consent[8] and includes vexatious communications by telephone or post[9] especially where they contain threats, although not necessarily threats of violence. Oral harassment, which can not be strictly classed as a threat, is actionable if it causes physical or psychiatric illness to the victim.[10] Where there is a risk that the cumulative effect of such harassment might cause such illness, a *quia timet* injunction may be granted.[11] The jurisdiction of the court is not limited to the restraint of conduct that is in itself tortious or otherwise unlawful.[12]

1 Law Com No 207, para 3.1.
2 [1973] 3 All ER 449, [1973] 1 WLR 1159, CA.
3 Apart from one indirect authority, *Phillips v Phillips* (1905) The Times, 19 December.
4 5th Edn, 'meddle hostilely or injuriously with (person)'.
5 3rd Edn.
6 *Davis v Johnson* [1979] AC 264 at 341A [1978] 1 All ER 1132 at 1150d per Lord Salmon. It is an assault for one person to threaten another with violence if the person making the threat is immediately able to carry out the threat and either intends to do so or the person threatened actually fears violence; see 45 Halsbury's Laws (4th Edn) para 1384 Tort, and *R v Savage* [1992] 1 AC 699, [1991] 4 All ER 698, HL.
7 *Davis v Johnson* (ibid).
8 *Paton v British Pregnancy Advisory Service Trustees* [1979] QB 276 at 280E–F, [1978] 2 All ER 987 at 990h, per Baker J. The so called 'marital exemption' to rape has been abolished, *R v R* [1992] 1 AC 599, [1991] 4 All ER 481, HL.
9 *Horner v Horner* [1982] Fam 90, [1982] 2 All ER 495, CA. See also *R v Ireland* [1996] 23 LS Gaz R 35, CA. See also *Burnett v George* [1992] 1 FLR 525, CA.
10 *Khorasandjian v Bush* [1993] QB 727, [1993] 3 All ER 669, CA.
11 Ibid.
12 *Burris v Azadani* [1995] 4 All ER 802, [1995] 1 WLR 1372, CA.

SCOPE OF POWERS

9.2 A non-molestation order means an order which contains a provision (a) prohibiting the respondent from molesting a person with whom he is associated (s 42(1)(a)),[1] (b) prohibiting the respondent from molesting a relevant child (s 42(1)(b))[2] or (c) both (s 42(1)). The order may be expressed so as to refer to molestation in general, to particular acts of molestation, or both (s 42(6)). Where the applicant and the respondent are associated by virtue of having been engaged (s 62(3)(e)),[3] no application may be made under s 42(2)(a) more than three years after the agreement to marry is terminated (s 42(4)).[4] An application for a non-molestation order may be made in other family proceedings (s 42(2)(a))[5] or in freestanding proceedings under Part IV (s 42(2)(a)). The court may make a non-molestation order of its own motion in any family proceedings to which the respondent is a party, if the court considers that such order should be made for the benefit of any other party or any relevant child (s 42(2)(b)).

1 For the meaning of 'associated persons' see paras 6.8–6.26.
2 For the meaning of 'relevant child' see paras 6.27–6.28.
3 See paras 6.17–6.21.
4 The parties may be associated under some other provision of s 62(3).
5 Family proceedings are defined by s 63(1), (2). Section 42(3) provides that family proceedings include proceedings in which the court has made an emergency protection order under CA 1989, s 44, if an exclusion requirement has been included under ibid, s 44A(3).

CRITERIA FOR MAKING ORDERS

9.3 The jurisdiction to make non-molestation orders may be exercised by the High Court, a county court or a magistrates' court.[1] In deciding whether to make a non-molestation order and, if so, in what manner, the court must have regard to all the circumstances of the case (s 42(5)) including the need to secure the health, safety and well-being of (a) the applicant (s 42(5)(a)), (b) in a case within s 42(2)(b), the person for whose benefit the order would be made (ibid), and (c) any relevant child (s 42(5)(b)). Under the old law, the court would not grant an injunction restraining molestation unless it was proved that the respondent had committed acts of molestation in the past.[2] The purpose of a non-molestation injunction was to protect spouses and children and to ensure that no undue pressure was put on them while proceedings were pending and during the breakup of the marriage.[3] It has been said that as the only remedy for breach of a non-molestation order is an application for committal, an application for such an injunction should not be lightly made,[4] however this should not deter a party from seeking the protection of the court where such protection is necessary. In addition a non-molestation order restraining general acts of molestation[5] does not infringe any rights enjoyed by the respondent.

1 Section 57. Rules of court may specify that certain applications may only be commenced at a particular level and may specify provisions for transfer between levels. See para 14.2.
2 *Spindlow v Spindlow* [1979] Fam 52, [1979] 1 All ER 169, CA.
3 *Paton v British Pregnancy Advisory Service Trustees* [1979] QB 276 at 280E-F, [1979] 2 All ER 987 at 990h, per Baker P.
4 *Freedman v Freedman* [1967] 2 All ER 680n, [1967] 1 WLR 1102.
5 The generally accepted wording of such an order is 'not to use violence against the [applicant or named child] and not to threaten, harass or pester the [applicant or named child]'.

DURATION, VARIATION AND DISCHARGE

9.4 A non-molestation order may be made for a specified period or until further order (s 42(7)). A court granting a non-molestation order should always give consideration as to the length of time for which an order should remain in force. A non-molestation order made in other family proceedings ceases to have effect if those proceedings are withdrawn or dismissed (s 42(8)). A non-molestation order may be varied or discharged by the court on an application by the respondent (s 49(1)(a)) or by the person on whose application the order was made (s 49(1)(b)). Where a non-molestation order has been made by the court of its own motion (s 42(2)(b)) the order may be varied or discharged by the court of its own motion (s 49(2)).[1]

1 The respondent can nonetheless apply under s 49(1)(a) to vary or discharge an order.

10 Powers of arrest and remand

ATTACHMENT OF POWER

10.1 Where the court makes an occupation order or a non-molestation order[1] and it appears to the court that the respondent has used or threatened violence against the applicant it shall attach a power of arrest to one or more provisions of the order unless it is satisfied that in all the circumstances the applicant or child will be adequately protected without a power of arrest (s 47). Previously a power of arrest could only be attached to an injunction where the respondent had caused actual bodily harm[2] to, or physically injured[3] the applicant or child and was considered likely to do so again.[4] A power of arrest was not a routine remedy,[5] and the change in the law made by Part IV of the 1996 Act means that a power of arrest may be attached far more readily than before. However, in considering adequate protection for the applicant and any child, the court should also have regard to any undertakings that may have been offered and the protection thereby offered.[6]

1 An occupation order or a non-molestation order is a 'relevant order' for the purposes of s 47 (s 47(1)).
2 DVMPA 1976, s 2(3). Actual bodily harm included any hurt or injury calculated to interfere with the health or comfort of the victim; see the Offences against the Person Act 1861, s 47; an injury to a person's mind for the time being was within the definition of actual bodily harm, *R v Miller* [1954] 2 QB 282 at 292, [1954] 2 All ER 529 at 534c, per Lynsky J. See also *R v Chan-Fook* [1994] 2 All ER 552, [1994] 1 WLR 689, CA and *R v Ireland* (see para 9.1).
3 DPMCA 1978, s 18(1).
4 DVMPA 1976, s 2(1) and DPMCA 1978, s 18(1).
5 *Lewis v Lewis* [1978] Fam 60 at 63 & 64, [1978] 1 All ER 729 at 731 & 732, CA and *McLean v Nugent* (1980) 1 FLR 26, CA.
6 See paras 14.8, 14.9.

10.2 Where a relevant order is made following an ex parte application,[1] the provisions of s 47(2)[2] do not apply. However, the court may attach a power of arrest to a relevant order where the respondent has used or threatened violence against the applicant or a relevant child (s 47(3)(a)) and there is a risk of significant harm to the applicant or child attributable to the conduct of the respondent if the power of arrest is not attached immediately (s 47(3)(b)). Where a power of arrest is attached to a relevant order on an ex parte application, it may have effect for a shorter period than the ex parte order (s 47(4)) but it may be extended on one or more occasions on any application to vary or discharge the initial order (s 47(5)). In any event, the question of a power of arrest must be reconsidered at the full hearing, when the court will be applying the rather different test under s 44(2) and will be able to make findings of fact having heard evidence from both sides.

1 Ie one under s 45(1). See Ch 11.
2 Automatic attachment where the use or threat of violence is proved.

10.3 Rules of court will be made to prescribe the procedure on grant of a power of arrest and these will probably contain provisions similar to those in the Family Proceedings Rules 1991, SI 1991/1247, rr 3.9(6), (7), 3.10, which provide for the order and also for any order varying or discharging the power of arrest to be sent by the court to the local police station.

ARREST UNDER POWER OF ARREST

10.4 Where a power of arrest has been attached to a relevant order, a constable[1] may arrest without warrant a person whom he has reasonable cause for suspecting to be in breach of the provisions of the order to which a power of arrest has been attached (s 47(6)). This is a significant change from the former law in respect of non-molestation orders; under the former law[2] an arrest could only be made in respect of a violent breach of a non-molestation order. Now it would seem that an arrest could be made for any breach, however trivial or technical. Nevertheless, a constable has discretion whether or not to effect an arrest.

1 'Constable' means any person holding the office of constable (as to which see 36 Halsbury's Laws (4th Edn) paras 201 et seq), not a member of a police force holding the rank of constable. As to the attestation of constables, see the Police Act 1964, s 18, Sch 2, and as to their jurisdiction, see ibid s 19.
2 DVMPA 1976, s 2(3) and DPMCA 1978, s 18(1).

WARRANT FOR ARREST

10.5 Where the court has made a relevant order[1] but has not attached a power of arrest, or has only attached the power to certain provisions, then if the applicant considers that the respondent has failed to comply with the order, he may apply to the relevant judicial authority for a warrant for the arrest of the respondent (s 47(8)). An undertaking[2] is enforceable as if it were an order of the court (s 46(4)).[3] Accordingly it would seem that a warrant for arrest can be issued in respect of an alleged breach of an undertaking. A warrant may only be issued where the application is substantiated on oath (s 47(9)(a)),[4] and the court has reasonable grounds for believing that the respondent has failed to comply with the order (s 47(9)(b)).

1 An occupation order or a non-molestation order (s 47(1), (8)).
2 Given under s 46(1).
3 See further Ch 14.
4 In the High Court and county courts, it is probable that rules of court will provide that an application for a warrant is made ex parte on affidavit; in magistrates' courts such an application will probably be made on the oral evidence of the applicant.

PROCEDURE SUBSEQUENT TO ARREST

10.6 Where a respondent is arrested under a power of arrest for a suspected breach of an order, he must be brought before the relevant judicial authority[1] within 24 hours (s 47(7)(a)).[2] If the matter is not disposed of when the respondent first appears before the relevant judicial authority,[3] he may be remanded (s 47(7)(b)),[4] either in custody[5] or on bail.[6] There may be further periods of remand.[7] A person arrested on a warrant may be remanded by the court (s 47(10)).

1 Relevant judicial authority is defined by s 63(1).
2 No account is taken of Christmas Day, Good Friday or any Sunday (s 47(7)).
3 On such appearance the court should begin to enquire into whether a breach is admitted or proved and if so, decide in what manner to deal with the contempt. See s 58.
4 The power to remand is new. Previously, the court could adjourn the proceedings for evidence to be adduced, *Roberts v Roberts* [1991] 1 FLR 294, CA. There was no power to detain a contemnor between the finding of contempt and passing sentence at a subsequent date; *Delaney v Delaney* [1996] QB 387, [1996] 1 FLR 458, CA.
5 Schedule 5, para 2(1)(a) in the case of the High Court or county courts: the Magistrates' Courts Act 1980, (MCA 1980), s 128 in the case of magistrates' courts.
6 Schedule 5, para 2(1)(b): MCA 1980, s 128.
7 Schedule 5, paras 2(2), 3: MCA 1980, s 129.

10.7 A contemnor may be remanded for the purpose of a medical examination and obtaining a medical report (s 48). A remand for such purpose may be on bail for up to four weeks (s 48(2)) or in custody for up to three weeks (s 48(3)). Where the court[1] has reason to suspect that the contemnor is suffering from mental illness or severe mental impairment, the court has the same power to make an order under the Mental Health Act 1983, s 35 as the Crown Court (s 48(4)). A magistrates' court may make a hospital order or a guardianship order under the Mental Health Act 1983, s 37 or an interim hospital order under s 38 of that Act where the contemnor is suffering from mental illness or severe mental impairment.

1 The relevant judicial authority.

COMMITTAL

10.8 An order for committal is regarded as a last resort.[1] Breach of an order does not automatically lead to committal,[2] and the views of the victim are very relevant.[3] A short term of imprisonment may be appropriate even where there has only been one breach if that is sufficiently serious and flagrant.[4] Blatant and aggravated contempt will justify immediate imprisonment, particularly where the contemnor has been given judicial warnings about his behaviour.[5]

1 *Ansah v Ansah* [1977] Fam 138, [1977] 2 All ER 638, CA.
2 *Smith v Smith* [1988] 1 FLR 179, CA.
3 *Boylan v Boylan* (1980) 11 Fam Law 76, CA.
4 *Pickering v Pickering* [1980] AC Transcript 193, CA.
5 *Jones v Jones* [1993] 2 FCR 82, CA.

Powers of courts

10.9 The High Court and county courts may commit a person to prison for up to two years,[1] and/or impose an unlimited fine.[2] An order for committal may be suspended and consecutive terms may be imposed for different breaches.[3] A magistrates' court may commit a contemnor to prison for up to two months,[4] and may make a suspended order (s 50(1)). A fine may be imposed of £50 for every day of default up to a maximum of £5,000.[5] The relevant judicial authority (as defined by s 63(1), see App 5, Glossary) may exercise these powers in relation to contempt of court arising out of a person's failure to comply with a Part IV order (s 58) either after arrest under a power of arrest, arrest under a warrant or a separate application to commit.

1 Contempt of Court Act 1981, s 14(1), (4A).
2 *Phonographic Performance Ltd v Amusement Caterers (Peckham) Ltd* [1964] 3 Ch 195, [1963] 3 All ER 493.
3 *Lee v Walker* [1985] QB 1191, [1985] 1 All ER 781, CA.
4 MCA 1980, s 63(3)(b).
5 MCA 1980, s 63(3)(a). This is difficult to apply in family cases as the section emphasises the duration not the gravity of the breach.

OTHER POLICE POWERS

10.10 Apart from the powers conferred by statute, the police have common law powers. Where a victim of domestic violence has invited police into premises, the police have an implied licence to enter the home and remain there long enough to take reasonable steps to inquire as to the whereabouts and safety of the complainant and any children, and to be satisfied that there is no reasonable fear of a breach of the peace.[1] The complainant's partner is not able unilaterally to revoke the licence to enter, so as to make the police officers trespassers from the moment that they are told to leave, or as soon thereafter as they could reasonably be expected to leave.[2]

1 *R v Thornley* (1980) 72 Cr App Rep 302.
2 Ibid.

11 Ex parte orders

INTRODUCTION

11.1 Under the former law an ex-parte application could only be made or granted where there was a real immediate danger of serious injury or irreparable damage.[1] On an ex-parte application the court may not be able to reach a rational and balanced decision[2] by virtue of hearing only one side of the facts. The DVMPA 1976 was created and designed to provide an emergency procedure to cope with crisis incidents in domestic life.[3] Accordingly every application will involve a degree of urgency but there must be something out of the ordinary to justify an ex parte application, and such relief will only be granted where it is really necessary to act immediately.[4] An applicant for an order ex parte has a duty to make full and frank disclosure of all relevant facts that *might* affect the exercise of the court's discretion; failure to do so may disentitle the applicant to the relief sought.[5] Therefore, the affidavit or statement of the applicant's evidence must be carefully drafted.

1 *Practice Note (Matrimonial Cause: Injunction)* [1978] 2 All ER 919, [1978] 1 WLR 925. See also *Beese v Woodhouse* [1970] 1 All ER 769, [1970] 1 WLR 586, CA.
2 *Rennick v Rennick* [1978] 1 All ER 817, [1977] 1 WLR 1455, CA.
3 *Mclean v Nugent* (1980) 1 FLR 26, CA.
4 *Ansah v Ansah* (see para 10.8).
5 *R v Kensington Income Tax General Comns ex p Princess de Polignac* [1917] 1 KB 486.

STATUTORY CRITERIA

11.2 In any case where it considers that it is just and convenient to do so, the court may make an occupation order or a non-molestation order even though the respondent has not been given the notice to which he would otherwise be entitled under the rules (s 45(1)). In determining whether or not to make an order ex-parte, the court must have regard to all the circumstances of the case (s 45(2)), including—

(a) any risk of significant harm to the applicant or a relevant child, attributable to the conduct of the respondent, if the order is not made immediately (s 45(2)(a));[1]

(b) whether it is likely that the applicant will be deterred or prevented from pursuing the application if the order is not made immediately (s 45(2)(b));[2] and,

(c) whether there is reason to believe that the respondent is aware of the proceedings but is deliberately evading service and that the applicant or a relevant child will be seriously prejudiced by the delay involved (s 45(2)(c)) in effecting service (s 45(2)(c)(i))[3] or in effecting substituted service (s 45(2)(c)(ii)).[4]

An alternative to granting ex-parte relief is to abridge the time for serving notice on the respondent. This is quite often done where the circumstances are urgent but do not justify the extreme step of granting relief ex-parte.[5] It is submitted that an ex-parte order to exclude a respondent from his or her home will continue to be granted in exceptional cases only.[6]

1 See paras 8.26–8.28.
2 See *Ansah v Ansah* (see para 10.8) where the fear of a violent response to the service of proceedings was held to justify an ex-parte order.
3 Where the court is a magistrates' court.
4 Where the court is the High Court or a county court.
5 *Wookey v Wookey, Re S (A Minor)* [1991] Fam 121, [1991] 3 All ER 365, CA.
6 See *Masich v Masich* (1977) 7 Fam Law 245, CA. See also *G v G (Ouster: ex parte Application)* [1990] 1 FLR 395, CA.

Return date

11.3 Where the court makes an ex-parte order it must afford the respondent an opportunity of making representations relating to the order as soon as it is just and convenient at a full hearing (s 45(4)).[1] An occupation order made ex-parte is referred to as an 'initial order' (s 45(5)). Where at a full hearing the court makes an occupation order[2] then for the purpose of calculating the maximum period for which the full order may be made to have effect, the relevant section[3] applies as if the period for which the full order will have effect began on the date on which the initial order first had effect (s 45(4)(a)). Where the initial order regulates the occupation of the dwelling-house or requires the respondent to leave part of it, but the full order ousts him from the dwelling-house altogether, it is unclear whether the time limit on the full order runs from the date of the initial order because the orders are in different terms. Since the policy of the legislation appears to be to limit the duration of orders it is submitted that the time would run from the date of the initial order. Where at a full hearing the court makes an occupation order, the provisions of ss 36(10) and 38(6) as to the extension of orders apply as if the full order and the initial order were a single order (s 45(4)(b)), thus time runs from the date of the initial order.

1 A full hearing is one in respect of which notice has been given to all parties in accordance with the rules, s 45(5). In *Ansah v Ansah* (see para 10.8) it was said that a return date should take place as soon as possible after the ex-parte hearing.
2 'The full order'.
3 Sections 33(10), 35(10), 36(10), 37(5), or 38(6) (s 45(5)).

11.4 The introduction of a compulsory return date is a new development. Certainly the Court of Appeal has always expressed disapproval of open ended orders,[1] but there are practical reasons for such orders, at least in the case of non-molestation orders. An ex parte non-molestation order does not interfere with the rights of the respondent as he is merely being ordered not to do something, which at common law he should not be doing anyway, namely assaulting, molesting or harassing the applicant. Where the court has not fixed a return date, the respondent should be given leave to apply to vary or discharge the order on, say, 48 hours notice. The avoidance of an automatic return date means that in certain cases potential confrontation can be avoided, not to mention the additional cost of an *inter partes* hearing, particularly to the Legal Aid Fund.

1 *Morgan v Morgan* (1978) 9 Fam Law 87, CA; *Loseby v Newman* [1995] 2 FLR 754, CA.

Power of arrest

11.5 Where an ex parte order[1] is made, the court has a discretion to attach a power of arrest if it appears that the respondent has used or threatened violence to the applicant or a relevant child (s 47(3)(a)), and there is a risk of significant harm to the applicant or child, attributable to the conduct of the respondent, if a power of arrest is not attached immediately (s 47(3)(b)).[2]

1 Under s 45(1).
2 See further para 10.2.

12 Children

INTRODUCTION

12.1 The Cleveland Report[1] expressed concern that children who were alleged to have been sexually abused were removed from the family home, when it might have been in their interests for the alleged abuser to have been required to leave instead. This problem was addressed in CA 1989, which included the power to enable a local authority to provide assistance to the alleged abuser to find alternative accommodation.[2] It was however an imperfect solution because it required the alleged abuser to agree to move from the family home.[3] Subsequent decisions confirmed that the courts were largely powerless to act. A prohibited steps order cannot be used to exclude an alleged abuser, even though children would be at risk of significant harm if he remained.[4] The Court of Appeal decided that CA 1989 did not give the court jurisdiction to exclude a parent from the family home for the protection of a child.[5] Although the inherent jurisdiction of the High Court has been invoked[6] successfully to oust an alleged abuser, there was previously no statutory provision whereby a local authority could do so. The inherent jurisdiction may not always be available.[7]

1 Report of the Enquiry into Child Abuse in Cleveland 1987, (Cm 412) (1988).
2 CA 1989, Sch 2, para 5.
3 CA 1989, Sch 2, para 5(1)(b).
4 *Nottinghamshire County Council v P* [1994] Fam 18, [1993] 2 FLR 134, CA; the inherent jurisdiction was not considered.
5 *Re M (minors) (Disclosure of Evidence)* [1994] 1 FLR 760, CA. The court decided that such an application should be brought under MHA 1983 where the criteria referred to the needs of children without that factor being paramount.
6 *Re S (minors) (Inherent Jurisdiction: Ouster)* [1994] 1 FLR 623.
7 The decision in *Re S (minors) (Inherent Jurisdiction: Ouster)* turned on its own facts, that the local authority wished to leave the children in the family home.

12.2 A prohibited steps order can be used to restrict contact with an alleged abuser who lives away from the family home.[1] The inherent jurisdiction has also been used in such circumstances.[2] However, the absence of a clear statutory power is a limitation on the ability of local authorities who have a statutory duty to safeguard and promote the welfare of children within their area who are in need.[3]

1 *Re H (Prohibited Steps Order)* [1995] 4 All ER 110, [1995] 1 WLR 667, CA.
2 *Devon County Council v S (Inherent Jurisdiction)* [1994] Fam 169, [1995] 1 All ER 243, CA.
3 CA 1989, s 17(1)(a).

12.3 This problem may be eased by s 52, Sch 6 of the 1996 Act, although there are important limitations in the new provisions (see paras 12.15–12.16). At best the amendments to CA 1989 are an improvement, and Parliament has not yet provided sufficient remedies for local authorities.

EMERGENCY PROTECTION ORDERS

12.4 An emergency protection order may be granted in the circumstances set out in CA 1989, s 44.[1] Section 52 of and Sch 6, para 3 to the 1996 Act amend CA 1989 by the insertion of ss 44A and 44B.

1 See *Clark Hall and Morrison on Children*, paras 1 [892]–1 [913].

Exclusion requirement

12.5 Where a court is satisfied as to the requirements for an emergency protection order,[1] and makes such an order, it may include an exclusion requirement in the order if the following conditions are satisfied (CA 1989, s 44A(1))—

(a) there is reasonable cause to believe that if the person[2] is excluded from a dwelling-house[3] in which the child lives, then—
   (i) in the case of an order made on the ground mentioned in CA 1989, s 44(1)(a), the child will not be likely to suffer significant harm,[4] even though the child is not removed, or does not remain in accommodation provided by the applicant; or
   (ii) in the case of an order made on the grounds mentioned in CA 1989, s 44(1)(b) or (c) the enquiries being made with respect to the child will cease to be frustrated; and

(b) another person[5] living in the dwelling-house is able and willing to give to the child the care which it would be reasonable to expect a parent to give him, and consents to the inclusion of the exclusion requirement (CA 1989, s 44A(2)).

1 See CA 1989, s 44(1)(a)–(c) and see *Clark Hall and Morrison on Children*, para 1 [893].
2 'The relevant person', CA 1989, s 44A(2)(a).
3 Defined by CA 1989, s 105(1), as inserted by Sch 6, para 5 in terms identical to s 63(1).
4 See para 8.23, and *In re H (Minors) (Sexual Abuse: Standard of Proof)* [1996] 1 All ER 1 [1996] 2 WLR 8, HL.
5 Whether a parent of the child or some other person (s 44A(2)(b)).

12.6 An exclusion requirement may be one or more of the following provisions—

(a) a provision requiring the relevant person to leave a dwelling-house in which he has been living with a child;

(b) a provision prohibiting the relevant person from entering a dwelling-house in which the child lives;

(c) a provision excluding the relevant person from a defined area in which a dwelling-house in which the child lives is situated (CA 1989, s 44A(3)).

In practice an application for an emergency protection order is made without notice, whereas in order to obtain an exclusion requirement, the person remaining in the dwelling-house will have to be notified to be able to give consent to the exclusion requirement (CA 1989, s 44A(2)(b)(ii)). An exclusion requirement is a draconian provision in relation to the relevant person, even allowing for the fact that an emergency protection order cannot exceed eight days (CA 1989, s 45(1), subject to (2)). Indeed the exclusion requirement may be of a shorter duration than the other provisions of the emergency protection order (CA 1989, s 44A(4)). The period of the exclusion requirement may be extended, on one or more occasions, by the court on an application to vary or discharge the emergency protection order (CA 1989, s 44A(7)).

The exclusion requirement in an emergency protection order ceases to have effect if the applicant removes the child from the dwelling-house from which the relevant person has been excluded to other accommodation for a continuous period of 24 hours (CA 1989, s 44A(10)).

12.7 The court may attach a power of arrest[1] to an exclusion requirement in an emergency protection order (CA 1989, s 44A(5)).[2] The power of arrest may have effect for a shorter duration than the exclusion requirement (CA 1989, s 44A(6)). The period of the power of arrest may be extended, on one or more occasions, by the court on an application to vary or discharge the emergency protection order (CA 1989, s 44A(7)). Where a power of arrest is attached to an exclusion requirement of an emergency protection order, a constable may arrest without warrant any person whom he has reasonable cause to believe to be in breach of the requirement (CA 1989, s 44A(8)).[3] Sections 47(7), (11), (12), 48 and Sch 5 of the 1996 Act have effect in relation to a person arrested under s 44A(8) for breach of an exclusion requirement as they have effect in relation to a person arrested under s 47(6) (CA 1989, s 44A(9)).[4]

1 See Ch 10.
2 The discretion of the court would appear to be unfettered.
3 See also para 10.4.
4 See paras 10.6–10.9.

Undertakings

12.8 Where the court has power to include an exclusion requirement in an emergency protection order, it may accept an undertaking from the relevant person, but cannot attach a power of arrest to the undertaking. Such an undertaking is enforceable as if it were an order of the court. An undertaking ceases to have effect if the applicant removes the child from the dwelling-house from which the relevant person has been excluded to other accommodation for a continuous period of 24 hours (CA 1989, s 44B(1)–(3)).

Variation and discharge

12.9 If the relevant person is not entitled to apply to discharge the emergency protection order[1] he may nonetheless apply to vary or discharge the exclusion requirement (CA 1989, s 45(8A)). The relevant person may apply to vary or discharge any power of arrest, whether or not any application has been made to vary or discharge any other provision of the order (CA 1989, s 45(8B)).

1 See CA 1989, s 44(8).

INTERIM CARE ORDER

12.10 Where a court is satisfied as to the requirements for an interim care order[1] and makes such an order (CA 1989, s 38A(1)(a)), the court may include an exclusion requirement, provided (CA 1989, s 38A(1)(b))—

(a) there is reasonable cause to believe that, if a person[2] is excluded from a dwelling-house in which the child lives, the child will cease to suffer, or cease to be likely to suffer, significant harm (CA 1989, s 38A(2)(a)); and
(b) another person[3] living in the dwelling-house is able and willing to give the child the care which it would be reasonable to expect a parent to give him, and consents to the inclusion of the exclusion requirement (CA 1989, s 38A(2)(b)).

1 See CA 1989, s 38(2); the court must be satisfied that there are reasonable grounds for believing that the circumstances with respect to the child are as mentioned in CA 1989, s 31(2)(a) and (b)(i). See *Clark Hall and Morrison on Children*, paras 1 [701]–1 [723].
2 The relevant person.
3 Whether or not a parent of the child.

12.11 An exclusion requirement may be one or more of the provisions listed in para 12.6. The exclusion requirement may be of a shorter duration than other provisions of the interim care order (CA 1989, s 38A(4)). The period of the exclusion requirement may be extended, on one or more occasions, by the court on an application to vary or discharge the interim care order (CA 1989, s 38A(7)). The exclusion requirement in an emergency protection order ceases to have effect if the applicant removes the child from the dwelling-house, from which the relevant person has been excluded to other accommodation for a continuous period of 24 hours (CA 1989, s 38A(10)).

12.12 The court may attach a power of arrest[1] to an exclusion requirement in an interim care order (CA 1989, s 38A(5)).[2] The power of arrest may have effect for a shorter duration than that of the exclusion requirement (CA 1989, s 38A(6)). The period of the power of arrest may be extended, on one or more occasions, by the court on an application to vary or discharge the interim care order (CA 1989, s 38A(7)). Where a power of arrest is attached to an exclusion requirement of an interim care order, a constable may arrest without warrant any person whom he has reasonable cause to believe to be in breach of the requirement (CA 1989, s 38A(8)).[3] Sections 47(7), (11), (12), 48, and Sch 5 of the 1996 Act have effect in relation to a person arrested under CA 1989, s 38A(8) for breach of an exclusion requirement as they have effect to a person arrested under s 47(6) (CA 1989, s 38A(9)).[4]

1 See Ch 10.
2 The discretion of the court would appear to be unfettered.
3 See also para 10.4.
4 See paras 10.6–10.9.

Undertakings

12.13 Where the court has power to include an exclusion requirement in an interim care order, it may accept an undertaking from the relevant person, but cannot attach a power of arrest to the undertaking. Such an undertaking is enforceable as if it were an order of the court. An undertaking ceases to have effect if the applicant removes the child from the dwelling-house from which the relevant person has been excluded to other accommodation for a continuous period of 24 hours (CA 1989, s 38B(1)–(3)).

Variation and discharge

12.14 If the relevant person is not entitled to apply to discharge the emergency protection order[1] he may nonetheless apply to vary or discharge the exclusion requirement. The relevant person may apply to vary or discharge any power of arrest, whether or not any application has been made to vary or discharge any other provision of the order CA 1989, s 39(3A), (3B)).

[1] See CA 1989, s 39(1).

LIMITATIONS

12.15 The power to impose an exclusion requirement does not extend to a full care order,[1] and accordingly the remedy will only be of a temporary nature. Unlike Part IV of the 1996 Act, the court is not required to consider the entitlement of the relevant person to occupy the dwelling-house. In many cases the mother of children will be placed in the position of having to consent to the inclusion of the exclusion requirement, thus putting her in the position of having to chose between her children and her partner. It is easy to say that she should not hesitate to put her children first, but such a choice may place her in the position of risking domestic violence, particularly if her partner is to have contact with the children.

[1] Under CA 1989, s 31(1)(a).

12.16 Both an emergency protection order and an interim care order provide that the applicant acquires parental responsibility (CA 1989, ss 33(3), 44(4)(c)). If the person who remains in the dwelling-house can adequately care for the child once the alleged abuser has been removed, there should be no need for the local authority to acquire parental responsibility. Indeed, it can be argued that the acquisition of parental responsibility undermines the mother's perception of her parenting ability. Some of these complications could have been avoided if local authorities had the power to make free standing applications to remove alleged abusers from the family home.

13 Transfer of tenancies

INTRODUCTION

13.1 The MHA 1967 enabled courts for the first time to exercise a discretionary jurisdiction to transfer tenancies between former spouses. At that time the courts had no power to make property adjustment orders.[1] The jurisdiction[2] now co-exists with ancillary relief, as a transfer of property order[3] may be made in respect of a local authority tenancy[4] or a contractual tenancy,[5] at least where there is no contractual term prohibiting an assignment. A protected shorthold tenancy can only be assigned by virtue of a property adjustment order.[6] An assured tenancy is subject to limited prohibition on assignment without consent.[7] CA 1989[8] provides that a parent or guardian or a person with a residence order relating to a child may apply for financial provision against a parent of that child, including a transfer of property order to the applicant for the benefit of the child.[9] The term 'parent' as defined[10] does not enable an application to be made against one cohabitant by the other in respect of children of a previous relationship.[11]

1 Introduced by the Matrimonial Proceedings and Property Act 1970, s 4(a) and now contained in MCA 1973, s 24(1)(a).
2 Re-enacted in MHA 1983, Sch 1.
3 Under MCA 1973, s 24(1)(a).
4 *Thompson v Thompson* [1976] Fam 25, [1975] 2 All ER 208, CA; but at that time such tenants had no security of tenure and the courts were reluctant to put pressure on local authorities (see *Regan v Regan* [1977] 1 All ER 428, [1977] 1 WLR 84).
5 *Hale v Hale* [1975] 2 All ER 1090, [1975] 1 WLR 931, CA.
6 HA 1980, s 54(2), (3).
7 HA 1988, s 15. Amendments made by Sch 17, paras 33–34 enabled such tenancies to be transferred under MHA 1983, Sch 1.
8 Section 15 and Sch 1, which primarily re-enacted provisions inserted into the Guardianship of Minors Act 1971 and the Guardianship Act 1973 by FLRA 1987.
9 Schedule 1, para 1(2)(e). 'Property' includes a tenancy; *K v K* [1992] 2 All ER 727, [1992] 1 WLR 530, CA.
10 This term is defined in Sch 1, para 16(2).
11 *J v J (a minor: Property Transfer)* [1993] 2 FLR 56.

13.2 Before the enactment of Part IV of the 1996 Act a childless cohabiting couple had no recourse to the courts to resolve the long term solution to their housing problems if they shared rented accommodation. If the tenancy was in the sole name of one cohabitant, there was no power to transfer the tenancy to the other; an ouster injunction could not operate as a summary transfer of property order.[1] The court would not grant an ouster injunction where the applicant had no intention of returning to the property but merely wanted it to seek an exchange of tenancy.[2] Where a tenancy was in joint names, the long term problem was more acute. If the relationship was terminated the parties could not apply for relief under the DVMPA 1976. Neither party would wish voluntarily to leave as he or she would run the risk of being intentionally homeless for the purposes of HA 1985, Part III.[3] There was no jurisdiction in any court to alter the interests of such parties in respect of a tenancy.[4] The Law Commission considered the problems thereby caused particularly in the context of public sector housing[5] and the decision in *Ainsbury v Millington*.[6]

1 *Hopper v Hopper* (see para 8.30).
2 *Warwick v Warwick* (1981) 3 FLR 393, CA.
3 See however, *Homelessness, Code of Guidance for Local Authorities* (3rd edn revised) 1994, para 7.11(b).
4 The only remedies available would be under LPA 1925, s 30, or under the Married Women's Property Act 1882, s 17; each of these provisions enable the court to declare, but not alter, existing proprietory rights.
5 Law Com No 207, paras 2.18–2.20.
6 [1986] 1 All ER 73, [1986] 1 FLR 331, CA; affd [1987] 1 All ER 929, [1987] 1 WLR 379n, HL.

13.3 One of two (or more) periodic tenants can determine the contractual tenancy by giving notice to quit, which binds all tenants.[1] The other tenants affected have no cause of action for breach of trust against the tenant who determines the tenancy.[2] In the case of a local authority or private sector tenancy, a party who had obtained an ouster injunction against another tenant could seek to come to an arrangement with the landlord whereby he or she would determine the contractual tenancy on condition that he or she would be granted a new sole tenancy of the premises. No consistent approach was adopted by landlords, save that many local authorities were reluctant to come to such an arrangement as the ousted party would usually have a claim to be rehoused by that authority[3] and the authority feared a claim for damages where the right to buy[4] was lost.

1 *Hammersmith & Fulham London Borough Council v Monk* [1992] 1 AC 478, [1992] 1 All ER 1, HL.
2 *Crawley Borough Council v Ure* [1996] QB 13, [1996] 1 All ER 724, CA, even though it would seem they would hold as trustees; LPA 1925, s 36(1).
3 Under HA 1985, Part III.
4 Under HA 1985, Part I.

JURISDICTION

13.4 Section 53 and Sch 7 of the 1996 Act re-enact MHA 1983, s 7, Sch 1[1] which enabled former spouses to apply for a transfer of tenancy and also extend the jurisdiction to cohabitants. The power to order transfer of tenancies may be exercised by the High Court and county courts but not by magistrates' courts (Sch 7, para 1).

1 See App 2 for Derivation and Destination Tables.

13.5 The transfer provisions apply only to 'relevant tenancies'. These are defined (Sch 7, para 1) as—

(a) a protected or statutory tenancy within the meaning of RA 1977,
(b) a statutory tenancy within the meaning of R(A)A 1976,
(c) a secure tenancy within the meaning of HA 1985, s 79, and
(d) an assured tenancy (including an assured shorthold tenancy which is a species of assured tenancy) or assured agricultural occupancy within the meaning of HA 1988, Part I.

'Tenancy' includes sub-tenancy (Sch 7, para 1). A statutory tenancy must be in existence at the date of the application for its transfer.[1] A spouse who remarries after a divorce order or decree annulling the marriage is not entitled to apply by reference to that order or decree for a transfer of tenancy (Sch 7, para 13(1)). In this context, remarriage includes contracting a void or voidable marriage (Sch 7, para 13(2)).

1 *Lewis v Lewis* [1985] AC 828, [1985] 2 All ER 449, HL.

13.6 Where one spouse is entitled[1] to occupy a dwelling-house by virtue of a relevant tenancy, then on pronouncement of a decree in a matrimonial cause[2] or at any time thereafter,[3] the court which granted the decree may make an order under Sch 7, Part II (Sch 7, para 2(2)), provided the dwelling-house is or was a matrimonial home (Sch 7, para 4(a)). A spouse loses the right to apply for an order on remarriage (Sch 7, para 13(1)), including entering into a marriage that is void or voidable (Sch 7, para 13(2)).

1 Either in his own right or jointly with the other spouse. See Sch 7, para 2(1).
2 Ie a decree of divorce, nullity or judicial separation.
3 Whether before or after decree absolute, in the case of divorce or nullity.

13.7 Where one cohabitant is entitled[1] to occupy a dwelling house by virtue of a relevant tenancy and the parties cease to live together as husband and wife,[2] then at any time thereafter the court may make an order under Sch 7, Part II (Sch 7, para 3), provided the dwelling-house is or was a home in which they lived together as husband and wife (Sch 7, para 4(b)). A cohabitant who marries after the termination of the relationship does not lose the right to apply for an order.

1 Either in his own right or jointly with the other cohabitant. See Sch 7, para 3(1).
2 As to what constitutes 'living together as husband and wife', see paras 6.2–6.6.

RANGE OF POWERS

Protected, assured or secure tenancy or assured agricultural occupancy

13.8 Where a spouse or cohabitant is entitled (whether solely or jointly with the other party) to occupy the dwelling-house by virtue of a protected tenancy,[1] a secure tenancy[2] or an assured tenancy or assured agricultural occupancy,[3] the court may by order direct that, as from such date as may be specified in the order,[4] there shall, by virtue of the order and without further assurance, be transferred to and vested in the other spouse or cohabitant the estate or interest which the spouse or cohabitant had in the dwelling house immediately before that date by virtue of the lease or agreement creating the tenancy, including an assignment (Sch 7, para 7(1)(a)). The transfer takes effect with all rights, privileges and appurtenances attaching to the estate or interest but subject to all covenants, obligations, liabilities and incumbrances to which it is subject (ibid). Where the spouse or cohabitant from whom the tenancy is transferred is an assignee of the lease or agreement, the liability of the spouse or cohabitant under any express or implied covenant for indemnity is transferred to and vests in the other spouse or cohabitant (Sch 7, para 7(1)(b)). Liabilities or obligations under any covenant referable to the dwelling-house in the lease or agreement that fall due to be discharged after the date specified in the order are unenforceable against the spouse or cohabitant from whom the tenancy is transferred (Sch 7, para 7(2)). If the spouse so entitled is a successor (within the meaning of HA 1985, Part IV) his former spouse[5] or former cohabitant will be deemed to be a successor (Sch 7, para 7(3)). If the spouse or cohabitant so entitled is a successor (for the purposes of HA 1988, s 17) in relation to the tenancy or occupancy, his former spouse[6] or former cohabitant will be deemed to be a successor in relation to the tenancy or occupancy (Sch 7, para 7(4)). If the transfer under Sch 7, para 7(1) is of an assured agricultural occupancy then[7] the agricultural worker condition is fulfilled with respect to the dwelling-house while the transferee spouse or cohabitant continues to be the occupier under that occupancy (Sch 7, para 7(5)(a)); and the condition is to be treated as so fulfilled[8] as was applicable before the transfer (Sch 7, para 7(5)(b)).

1 Within the meaning of RA 1977.
2 Within the meaning of HA 1985.
3 Within the meaning of the HA 1988, Part I.
4 In the case of divorce or nullity, the order cannot take effect before decree absolute; Sch 7, para 12.
5 Or spouse, if there is in force a separation order or a decree of judicial separation; Sch 7, paras 7(3), (6).
6 Or spouse, if there is in force a separation order or a decree of judicial separation; Sch 7, paras 7(4), (6).
7 For the purposes of HA 1988, Part I, Ch III.
8 Under HA 1988, Sch 3.

Statutory tenancy within RA 1977

13.9 Where a spouse or cohabitant is entitled to occupy a dwelling-house by virtue of a statutory tenancy,[1] the court may by order direct that, as from the date specified in the order, that spouse or cohabitant is to cease to be entitled to occupy the dwelling-house (Sch 7, para 8(2)(a)),[2] and the other spouse or cohabitant is to be deemed to be the tenant, or the sole tenant under the statutory tenancy (Sch 7, para 8(2)(b)). The issue of whether the provisions of RA 1977, Sch 1, paras 1–3 or 5–7[3] are capable of having effect in the event of the death of the person deemed by an order under Sch 7, para 8, to be the tenant or sole tenant under the statutory tenancy depends on whether or not those provisions have or have not already had effect in relation to the statutory tenancy (Sch 7, para 8(3)).

1 Within the meaning of RA 1977.
2 This provision, of itself, does not enable the court to order a party to leave the dwelling-house; see *Maynard v Maynard* [1969] P 88, [1969] 1 All ER 1.
3 Those provisions deal with succession by the surviving spouse of a deceased tenant, or by a member of the deceased tenant's family.

Statutory tenancy within R(A)A 1976

13.10 Where a spouse or cohabitant is entitled to occupy a dwelling house by virtue of a statutory tenancy,[1] the court may by order direct that, as from the date specified in the order, that spouse or cohabitant is to cease to be entitled to occupy the dwelling-house (Sch 7, para 9(2)(a)),[2] and the other spouse or cohabitant is deemed to be the tenant or the sole tenant under the statutory tenancy (Sch 7, para 9(2)(b)). A spouse or cohabitant who is deemed under Sch 7, para 9 to be the statutory tenant[3] is a statutory tenant in his own right, or a statutory tenant by succession, according to whether the other spouse or cohabitant was a statutory tenant in his own right or a statutory tenant by succession (Sch 7, para 9(3)).

1 Within the meaning of R(A)A 1976.
2 This provision, of itself, does not enable the court to order a party to leave the dwelling-house; see *Maynard v Maynard* [1969] P 88, [1969] 1 All ER 1.
3 Within the meaning of R(A)A 1976.

STATUTORY CRITERIA

13.11 In determining whether to exercise its discretionary powers under Sch 7, Part II and if so, in what manner, the court shall have regard to all the circumstances of the case (Sch 7, para 5), including—

(a) the circumstances in which the tenancy was granted to either or both of the spouses or cohabitants or, as the case requires, the circumstances in which either or both of them became tenants under the tenancy;

(b) the matters mentioned in s 33(6)(a)–(c), namely—

  (1) the respective housing needs and housing resources of the parties and any relevant child;

  (2) the financial resources of the parties; and

  (3) the likely effect of any order, or of any decision by the court not to exercise its powers, on the health, safety or well-being of the parties and of any relevant child.

(c) where the parties are cohabitants, and only one of them is entitled to occupy the dwelling-house by virtue of the relevant tenancy, the further matters mentioned in s 36(6)(e)–(h), namely—

  (1) the nature of the parties' relationship;[1]

  (2) the length of time during which they have lived together as husband and wife;

  (3) whether there are or have been children who are children of both parties or for whom both parties have or have had parental responsibility;

  (4) the length of time that has elapsed since the parties ceased to live together;

(d) the suitability of the parties as tenants.[2]

---

1 See s 41, where the court is required to have regard to the fact that the parties have not given each other the commitment involved in marriage.

2 Under rules of court, the landlord will be given the opportunity of being heard before any order is made; see Sch 7, para 14(1). Representations by the landlord may be decisive in deciding which party should have the tenancy.

LIABILITIES

13.12 Where the court makes an order for transfer of tenancy under Sch 7, Part II it may include in the order a direction that both spouses or cohabitants are to be jointly and severally liable to discharge or perform any or all of the liabilities and obligations in respect of the dwelling-house, whether arising under the tenancy or otherwise, which have at the date of the order fallen due to be discharged or performed by only one of them (Sch 7, para 11(1)(a)), or but for the direction, would before the date specified as the date on which the order is to take effect fall to be discharged or performed by only one of them (Sch 7, para 11(1)(b)). Where the court gives such a direction, it may further direct that either spouse or cohabitant is to be liable to indemnify the other in whole or in part against any payment made or expenses incurred by the other in discharging or performing any such liability or obligation (Sch 7, para 1(2)).

COMPENSATION

13.13 Where the court makes an order under Sch 7, Part II transferring a tenancy, it may by that order direct the making of a payment by the spouse or cohabitant to whom the tenancy is transferred[1] to the other spouse or cohabitant.[2] This power to order compensation is new and may well become an important provision. In deciding whether to exercise its powers to order compensation, and if so in what manner, the court shall have regard to all the circumstances (Sch 7, para 10(4)), including—

- (a) the financial loss that would otherwise be suffered by the transferor as a result of the order;[3]
- (b) the financial needs and resources of the parties; and
- (c) the financial obligations which the parties have, or are likely to have in the foreseeable future, including obligations to each other and any relevant child.

1 'The transferee', Sch 7, para 10(1).
2 'The transferor', ibid.
3 Where the transferee has the 'right to buy' under HA 1985, Part V, the discount that would be available on purchase will be one indication of financial loss.

Time for payment

13.14 Where the court orders the payment of compensation, it may direct that payment of the whole or part of the sum be deferred until a specific date, or until the occurrence of a specific event (Sch 7, para 10(2)(a)).[1] In addition the court may direct that payment of the whole or part of the sum is to be made by instalments (Sch 7, para 10(2)(b)). The court may not direct that payment be deferred or made by instalments unless it appears that immediate payment of the sum required by the order would cause the transferee financial hardship which is greater than any financial hardship that would be caused to the transferor if the direction were given (Sch 7, para 10(5)). Balancing the financial hardship may be difficult, particularly where the transferor needs a sum to use as a deposit to secure alternative rented property. Where an order does not provide for deferred payment or payment by instalments, then at any time before full payment is made the court may on the application of the transferee or transferor make a direction for deferred payment or payment by instalments (Sch 7, para 10(3)(a)). Where a direction has been given for deferred payment or payment by instalments, then at any time before full payment is made the court may on the application of the transferee or transferor vary any direction for deferred payment or payment by instalments (Sch 7, para 10(3)(b)).

1 An example of a specific event might be the date on which the transferor vacates the dwelling-house.

14 Jurisdiction and procedure

JURISDICTION

14.1 The jurisdiction to make occupation orders and non-molestation orders may be exercised by the High Court, a county court or a magistrates' court (s 57(1)). However, there are specific restrictions on the jurisdiction of magistrates' courts. A magistrates' court is not competent to entertain any application or make any order involving a disputed question as to a party's entitlement to occupy any property by virtue of any beneficial estate or interest or contract, or by virtue of any enactment giving a party the right to remain in occupation, unless it is unnecessary to determine the question in order to deal with the application or make the order (s 59(1)).[1] A magistrates' court may decline jurisdiction if it considers that the case can more conveniently be dealt with by another court (s 59(2)).

1 Thus the power under s 39(3) (see para 14.6) may be little used in magistrates' courts.

14.2 The Lord Chancellor may by order specify that certain proceedings or proceedings in particular circumstances may only be commenced at a particular level of court or in a certain class of court and that transfer of proceedings is allowed between different levels or classes of court (s 57(3), (4)).[1] Subordinate legislation may also provide that in specified circumstances the whole or any specified part of any specified proceedings may be transferred to a specified level of court, to a court which falls within a specified class of court, or to a particular court determined in accordance with, or specified in, the order (s 57(5)). Subordinate legislation may also specify the circumstances in which appeals may be made against decisions on questions arising in connection with transfer or proposed transfer of proceedings, but except as so provided no appeal will lie against a decision to transfer or not to transfer (s 61(5), (6)). After DPMCA 1978 came into force, the Legal Aid Board tried to direct applications to the magistrates' court, but this attempt was not very successful as any related matrimonial cause had to be brought in a county court.

1 Such an order may be broadly similar to the Children (Allocation of Proceedings) Order 1991, SI 1991/1677.

PROCEDURE

Applications

14.3 An application for an occupation order or non-molestation order may be made in other family proceedings (ss 39(2), 42(2)(a))[1] or in a freestanding application under the 1996 Act, Part IV (ss 39(2), 42(2)(b)).[2] Applications for occupation orders may be brought by entitled applicants and those with matrimonial home rights, by non-entitled former spouses, by non-entitled cohabitants or former cohabitants, and by spouses, former spouses, cohabitants or former cohabitants (neither of whom is entitled) (ss 33, 35–38, see paras 8.2–8.7).

1 Family proceedings are defined by s 63(1), (2). See para 6.25.
2 Rules of court will be made to prescribe that freestanding applications may be made under the Act.

Applications by a representative

14.4 The Law Commission recommended[1] that the police should have power to apply for a civil remedy on behalf of a victim where they had been involved in an incident of molestation or actual or threatened violence or its aftermath. The police would have been obliged to consult the victim, whose views would have been taken into account by the court. However, a 'representative' may act on behalf of another in proceedings under Part IV, and may make an application on behalf of another for an occupation order or a non-molestation order. These provisions will be amplified by extensive rules of court which will prescribe the persons or categories of persons who may be 'representatives',[2] the conditions to be satisfied before a representative brings an application and matters to be considered by the court on such an application (s 60(1)–(3)).

1 Law Com No 207, paras 5.18–5.23 and 7.26–7.27. This was rejected by the Home Affairs Committee and the Government in its Reply to the Third Report from the Home Affairs Committee.
2 Section 60 was introduced as an Opposition amendment at the Report Stage in the House of Commons.

Applications by children

14.5 A child under the age of 16 may not apply for an occupation order or a non-molestation order except with the leave of the court (s 43(1)).[1] The court may grant leave to such a child only if it is satisfied that the child has sufficient understanding to make the proposed application (s 43(2)).[2] This provision raises the question of when a child under the age of 16 might be able to apply for an occupation order;[3] such child would hardly be a spouse,[4] or former spouse,[5] but might be a cohabitant or former cohabitant. Such a child would not be an entitled applicant.[6] In the case of non-molestation orders, a child is associated with a whole range of relatives,[7] against whom the jurisdiction of the court could be invoked. In considering an application for leave the court should have regard to the success of the proposed application.[8]

1 Section 43 was introduced as an Opposition amendment at the Report Stage in the House of Commons.
2 This is broadly similar to CA 1989, s 10(8).
3 See paras 8.2–8.7.
4 Marriage Act 1949, s 2. The exception is in respect of a marriage contracted in a country where the *lex loci celebrationis* permitted marriages below the age of 16.
5 Ibid.
6 See LPA 1925, s 19.
7 See paras 6.14–6.16.
8 *G v Kirklees Metropolitan Borough Council* [1993] 1 FLR 805.

Occupation orders

14.6 Where an application for an occupation order is made under ss 33, 35, 36, 37 or 38 and the court considers that it has no power to make an order under the section concerned but that it has power to make an order under one of the other sections, the court make may an order under that other section (s 39(3)). The fact that a person has applied for an occupation order under ss 35–38, or that an order has been made under one of those sections, does not affect the right of any person to claim a legal or equitable interest in any property in subsequent proceedings, including subsequent proceedings under Part IV of the Act (s 39(4)).

Non-molestation orders

14.7 The court may make a non-molestation order of its own motion in any family proceedings[1] to which the respondent is a party for the benefit of any other party to those proceedings or any relevant child[2] even if no such application has been made (s 42(2)(b)).

1 See para 6.25.
2 See paras 6.27–6.28.

UNDERTAKINGS

14.8 Under the former law, undertakings were frequently offered to narrow the issues in dispute and to save time and money. The offer of an undertaking would not require the person giving the same to make any admission as to past conduct. Under the 1996 Act, where the court has power to make an occupation order or a non-molestation order, it may accept an undertaking from any party to the proceedings (s 46(1)).[1] An undertaking so given to the court is enforceable as if it were an order of the court (s 46(4)).[2] However, a power of arrest cannot be attached to an undertaking (s 46(2)),[3] and the court will not accept an undertaking where a power of arrest would otherwise be attached to the order (s 46(3)).[4]

1 The words 'any party' make it clear that cross-undertakings may be given.
2 This merely confirms the existing law; see eg *Hipgrave v Hipgrave* [1962] P 91, [1962] 1 All ER 75, Scarman J. See also *Hussain v Hussain* [1986] Fam 134, [1986] 1 All ER 961, CA, 'Let it be stated in the clearest possible terms that an undertaking to the court is as solemn, binding and effective as an order of the court in the like terms and that the contrary has never been suggested' per Sir John Donaldson MR.
3 This follows the previous law under DVMPA 1976, s 2 and see *Carpenter v Carpenter* [1988] 1 FLR 121, CA.
4 For the circumstances where a power of arrest is attached to an order, see Ch 10 et seq.

14.9 No doubt undertakings will continue to be offered as a means of trying to resolve applications. It seems that an undertaking will be at least as effective as previously because an undertaking given to the court is enforceable as if it were an order of the court (s 46(4)). For the purposes of arrest for breach of an order under s 47, an occupation order or a non-molestation order is a 'relevant order' (s 47(1)). Where a relevant order has been made without a power of arrest, an applicant, who considers the respondent to be in breach of the order, may apply to the relevant judicial authority[1] for the issue of a warrant for the arrest of the respondent (s 47(8)). Accordingly it seems that the combination of ss 46(4) and 47(8) enable a warrant to be issued for the arrest of a party who has breached an undertaking. Thus the offer of an undertaking will be one of the circumstances to consider under s 47(2) as to whether the applicant will be adequately protected without a power of arrest.[2]

1 See s 63(1).
2 See further Ch 10.

SEPARATE REPRESENTATION OF CHILDREN

14.10 Regulations may provide for the separate representation of children in proceedings relating to a matter in respect of which a question has arisen or may arise under Parts II and IV of the 1996 Act, MCA 1973 or DPMCA 1978 (s 64(1)). The regulations may provide for representation only in specified circumstances (s 64(2)). The existing rules[1] provide for separate representation of children in family proceedings where it appears to the court that any child ought to be separately represented.[2] The court may appoint the Official Solicitor or some other proper person to represent the child. The regulations to be made under s 64 may well be in similar general terms, as it will usually depend on the facts of each individual case whether it is appropriate for children to have separate representation. Where separate representation is ordered, the child should be made a party to the proceedings.[3]

1 Family Proceedings Rules 1991, SI 1991/1247, r 9.5.
2 Ibid, r 9.5(1).
3 *L v L (Minors) (Separate Representation)* [1994] 1 FLR 156, CA.

APPEALS FROM MAGISTRATES' COURT

14.11 Appeals lie to the High Court against the making or refusal of a Part IV order (s 61(1)). No appeal will lie against the decision of a court under s 59(2) to decline jurisdiction (s 61(1)). On appeal, the High Court may make such order as is necessary to give effect to its determination of the appeal (s 61(2)), including such incidental or consequential orders as may be just (s 61(3)). For the purposes of enforcement, variation, revival or discharge, an order of the High Court on appeal is treated as an order of the magistrates' court from which the appeal was brought (s 61(4)). It is important that the correct procedure for appealing is followed as the various methods are not interchangeable.[1]

1 See *Berry v Berry* [1987] Fam 1, [1986] 1 FLR 618, DC; affd 2 All ER 948, CA; and *P v P (Periodical Payments: Appeals)* [1995] 1 FLR 563, DC.

15 Transitional provisions

INTRODUCTION

15.1 The 1996 Act received the Royal Assent on 4 July 1996, and ss 65[1] and 67[2] came into force on that date. The remaining provisions come into force on such day as the Lord Chancellor may appoint, and different days may be appointed for different purposes (s 67(3)).

1 This section deals with rules, regulations and orders. An order under s 5(8) (which varies the specified period, as to which see App 5, Glossary) is subject to an affirmative resolution of each House of Parliament; otherwise all statutory instruments (other than rules of court) under the 1996 Act are subject to a negative resolution (s 65(3)–(5)).

2 This section provides for short title, commencement and extent.

DIVORCE AND SEPARATION PROCEEDINGS

Previous and pending proceedings

15.2 Decrees of divorce and judicial separation already pronounced are not affected by the 1996 Act. Proceedings already begun prior to the coming into force of Part II of the 1996 Act, Part II for divorce and judicial separation are not affected by the 1996 Act, and a decree may be granted in such proceedings (Sch 9, para 5(1)(a)).

Financial relief

15.3 Once Part II of the 1996 Act is brought into force, applications to vary or discharge orders for financial relief made before that date will be determined under MCA 1973, s 31 (Sch 9, para 6(2)).[1] That section relates to orders made under MCA 1973, Part II after the amendments made by the 1996 Act have been brought into force (Sch 9, para 6(1)). Applications for ancillary relief in divorce or judicial separation proceedings begun by petition are not affected by Part II of the 1996 Act (Sch 9, para 5(1)(a)(ii), (b)(i)–(iii)).

1 MCA 1973, s 31 is amended by the 1996 Act, Sch 8, para 1(16); see in particular see s 31(7)–(7F).

The transitional period

15.4 The 'transitional period' is the period of two years beginning with the day that s 3 of the 1996 Act is brought into force (Sch 9, para 1(3)). The Lord Chancellor may by order provide for the application of Part II to marital proceedings which are begun in the transitional period and relate to parties to a marriage who immediately before the beginning of the transitional period were living apart, subject to such modifications (including omissions) as may be prescribed (Sch 9, para 1(1)). The subordinate legislation may make provision for the evidence to be produced to the court in support of a claim that parties to a marriage were living apart at the commencement of the transitional period (Sch 9, para 1(2)). The reason for these provisions would appear to be to ensure that special rules apply for divorces on two years separation and consent and five years separation where that period would end during the transitional period. It would be unfair if parties who were proposing to petition on the basis of separation were to be denied that remedy because Part II of the 1996 Act came into force fully shortly before the period of separation was complete, and therefore they were required to complete the period for reflection and consideration. Until the subordinate legislation is made, one can only speculate as to the provisions, but the cautious practitioner will advise clients to evidence the separation by a deed.

15.5 The Lord Chancellor has very wide powers to make consequential modifications to statute and statutory instruments as appears necessary or expedient in consequence of Part II (Sch 9, para 2).

PART IV PROCEEDINGS

15.6 Once Part IV of the 1996 Act is brought into force,[1] existing orders[2] remain in force (Sch 9, para 10(2)(a)), and may be enforced (Sch 9, para 10(2)(b)). The court may extend, vary or discharge an existing order, but if it thinks it just and convenient to do so it may treat the application as an application for an order under Part IV (Sch 9, para 10(3)). Where a Part IV order is made between parties with respect to whom an existing order is in force, the Part IV order discharges the existing order (Sch 9, para 10(4)). Applications for orders under 'existing enactments' pending immediately before the commencement of Part IV are not affected (Sch 9, para 8(2)).[3] In addition, applications under MHA 1983, Sch 1 pending immediately before the commencement of Part IV are not affected (Sch 9, para 9).

1 On a date to be appointed under s 67(3).
2 That is, orders under 'existing enactments' ie under DVMPA 1976 and under DPMCA 1978, ss 16–18.
3 It is perhaps unfortunate that the court may not treat a pending application as one for an order under Part IV because of the wider powers under Part IV.

Matrimonial home rights

15.7 References in enactments, instruments or documents (whenever made) to rights of occupation within the meaning of MHA 1983 are to be construed as references to matrimonial home rights (Sch 9, para 11(1)).[1] References in enactments, instruments or documents (whenever made) to registration under MHA 1983, s 2(8) are to be construed as references to registration under the 1996 Act (s 31(10), Sch 9, para 12(1)). The effect of previous registrations is preserved (Sch 9, paras 12(2), 14).

1 So far as is required for the continuing effect of the instrument or document.

Appendix 1

Family Law Act 1996

Family Law Act 1996

(1996 c 27)

ARRANGEMENT OF SECTIONS

PART I
PRINCIPLES OF PARTS II AND III

PART II
DIVORCE AND SEPARATION

An Act to make provision with respect to: divorce and separation; legal aid in connection with mediation in disputes relating to family matters; proceedings in cases where marriages have broken down; rights of occupation of certain domestic premises; prevention of molestation; the inclusion in certain orders under the Children Act 1989 of provisions about the occupation of a dwelling-house; the transfer of tenancies between spouses and persons who have lived together as husband and wife; and for connected purposes.

[4 July 1996]

Parliamentary debates

House of Lords:

2nd Reading 30 November 1996: 567 HL Official Report (5th series) cols 700–790.

Committee Stage 11 January 1996: 568 HL Official Report (5th series) cols 277–313, 325–354; 22 January 1996: 568 HL Official Report (5th series) cols 802–852, 861–898; 23 January 1996: 568 HL Official Report (5th series) cols 908–968, 982–1026; 25 January 1996: 568 HL Official Report (5th series) cols 1129–1178, 1188–1224; 30 January 1996: 568 HL Official Report (5th series) cols 1382–1444.

Report 22 February 1996: 569 HL Official Report (5th series) cols 1145–1157, 1173–1202; 29 February 1996: 569 HL Official Report (5th series) cols 1610–1670, 1681–1716; 4 March 1996: 570 HL Official Report (5th series) cols 10–73, 77–146.

3rd Reading 11 March 1996: 570 HL Official Report (5th series) cols 692–730.

Consideration of Commons Amendments 27 June 1996: 573 HL Official Report (5th series) cols 1059–1120.

House of Commons:

2nd Reading 25 March 1996: 274 HC Official Report (6th series) cols 738–806.

Committee Stage 24 April 1996: 276 HC Official Report (6th series) cols 443–543.

Committee Stage 25 April–16 May 1996: HC Official Report, SC E (Family Law Bill).

Remaining stages 17 June 1996: 279 HC Official Report (6th series) cols 536–658.

PART I
PRINCIPLES OF PARTS II AND III

1 The general principles underlying Parts II and III

The court and any person, in exercising functions under or in consequence of Parts II and III, shall have regard to the following general principles—

(a) that the institution of marriage is to be supported;

(b) that the parties to a marriage which may have broken down are to be encouraged to take all practicable steps, whether by marriage counselling or otherwise, to save the marriage;

(c) that a marriage which has irretrievably broken down and is being brought to an end should be brought to an end—

  (i) with minimum distress to the parties and to the children affected;

  (ii) with questions dealt with in a manner designed to promote as good a continuing relationship between the parties and any children affected as is possible in the circumstances; and

  (iii) without costs being unreasonably incurred in connection with the procedures to be followed in bringing the marriage to an end; and

(d) that any risk to one of the parties to a marriage, and to any children, of violence from the other party should, so far as reasonably practicable, be removed or diminished.

Definition For "the court" in Pt II, see s 24(1) post.
References See paras 3.1–3.3.

PART II
DIVORCE AND SEPARATION

Court orders

2 Divorce and separation

(1) The court may—

  (a) by making an order (to be known as a divorce order), dissolve a marriage; or

  (b) by making an order (to be known as a separation order), provide for the separation of the parties to a marriage.

(2) Any such order comes into force on being made.

(3) A separation order remains in force—
- (a) while the marriage continues; or
- (b) until cancelled by the court on the joint application of the parties.

Definitions For "the court", see s 24(1) post.
Reference See para 3.4.

3 Circumstances in which orders are made

(1) If an application for a divorce order or for a separation order is made to the court under this section by one or both of the parties to a marriage, the court shall make the order applied for if (but only if)—
- (a) the marriage has broken down irretrievably;
- (b) the requirements of section 8 about information meetings are satisfied;
- (c) the requirements of section 9 about the parties' arrangements for the future are satisfied; and
- (d) the application has not been withdrawn.

(2) A divorce order may not be made if an order preventing divorce is in force under section 10.

(3) If the court is considering an application for a divorce order and an application for a separation order in respect of the same marriage it shall proceed as if it were considering only the application for a divorce order unless—
- (a) an order preventing divorce is in force with respect to the marriage;
- (b) the court makes an order preventing divorce; or
- (c) section 7(6) or (13) applies.

Definitions For "divorce order", see s 2(1)(a) ante; for "separation order", see s 2(1)(b) ante; for "order preventing divorce", see s 10(1), (2) post; for "the court", see s 24(1) post; as to "the withdrawal of an application", see s 24(2) post.
References See paras 1.3, 3.4, 3.5.

4 Conversion of separation order into divorce order

(1) A separation order which is made before the second anniversary of the marriage may not be converted into a divorce order under this section until after that anniversary.

(2) A separation order may not be converted into a divorce order under this section at any time while—
- (a) an order preventing divorce is in force under section 10; or
- (b) subsection (4) applies.

(3) Otherwise, if a separation order is in force and an application for a divorce order—
- (a) is made under this section by either or both of the parties to the marriage, and
- (b) is not withdrawn,

the court shall grant the application once the requirements of section 11 have been satisfied.

(4) Subject to subsection (5), this subsection applies if—
(a) there is a child of the family who is under the age of sixteen when the application under this section is made; or
(b) the application under this section is made by one party and the other party applies to the court, before the end of such period as may be prescribed by rules of court, for time for further reflection.

(5) Subsection (4)—
(a) does not apply if, at the time when the application under this section is made, there is an occupation order or a non-molestation order in force in favour of the applicant, or of a child of the family, made against the other party;
(b) does not apply if the court is satisfied that delaying the making of a divorce order would be significantly detrimental to the welfare of any child of the family;
(c) ceases to apply—
(i) at the end of the period of six months beginning with the end of the period for reflection and consideration by reference to which the separation order was made; or
(ii) if earlier, on there ceasing to be any children of the family to whom subsection (4)(a) applied.

Definitions For "divorce order", see s 2(1)(a) ante; for "separation order", see s 2(1)(b) ante; for "period for reflection and consideration", see s 7(1), (2) post; for "order preventing divorce", see s 10(1), (2) post; as to "marital proceedings", see s 20 post; for "child of the family", "the court" and "party", see s 24(1) post; as to "the withdrawal of an application", see s 24(2) post.
References See para 3.8.

Marital breakdown

5 Marital breakdown

(1) A marriage is to be taken to have broken down irretrievably if (but only if)—
(a) a statement has been made by one (or both) of the parties that the maker of the statement (or each of them) believes that the marriage has broken down;
(b) the statement complies with the requirements of section 6;
(c) the period for reflection and consideration fixed by section 7 has ended; and
(d) the application under section 3 is accompanied by a declaration by the party making the application that—
(i) having reflected on the breakdown, and
(ii) having considered the requirements of this Part as to the parties' arrangements for the future,
the applicant believes that the marriage cannot be saved.

(2) The statement and the application under section 3 do not have to be made by the same party.

(3) An application may not be made under section 3 by reference to a particular statement if—
(a) the parties have jointly given notice (in accordance with rules of court) withdrawing the statement; or
(b) a period of one year ("the specified period") has passed since the end of the period for reflection and consideration.

(4) Any period during which an order preventing divorce is in force is not to count towards the specified period mentioned in subsection (3)(b).

(5) Subsection (6) applies if, before the end of the specified period, the parties jointly give notice to the court that they are attempting reconciliation but require additional time.

(6) The specified period—
- (a) stops running on the day on which the notice is received by the court; but
- (b) resumes running on the day on which either of the parties gives notice to the court that the attempted reconciliation has been unsuccessful.

(7) If the specified period is interrupted by a continuous period of more than 18 months, any application by either of the parties for a divorce order or for a separation order must be by reference to a new statement received by the court at any time after the end of the 18 months.

(8) The Lord Chancellor may by order amend subsection (3)(b) by varying the specified period.

Definitions For "divorce order", see s 2(1)(a) ante; for "separation order", see s 2(1)(b) ante; for "a statement", see s 6(1) post; for "period for reflection and consideration", see s 7(1), (2) post; for "order preventing divorce", see s 10(1), (2) post; for "the court" and "party", see s 24(1) post.
References See paras 3.9–3.12.

6 Statement of marital breakdown

(1) A statement under section 5(1)(a) is to be known as a statement of marital breakdown; but in this Part it is generally referred to as "a statement".

(2) If a statement is made by one party it must also state that that party—
- (a) is aware of the purpose of the period for reflection and consideration as described in section 7; and
- (b) wishes to make arrangements for the future.

(3) If a statement is made by both parties it must also state that each of them—
- (a) is aware of the purpose of the period for reflection and consideration as described in section 7; and
- (b) wishes to make arrangements for the future.

(4) A statement must be given to the court in accordance with the requirements of rules made under section 12.

(5) A statement must also satisfy any other requirements imposed by rules made under that section.

(6) A statement made at a time when the circumstances of the case include any of those mentioned in subsection (7) is ineffective for the purposes of this Part.

(7) The circumstances are—
- (a) that a statement has previously been made with respect to the marriage and it is, or will become, possible—
  - (i) for an application for a divorce order, or
  - (ii) for an application for a separation order,

  to be made by reference to the previous statement;
- (b) that such an application has been made in relation to the marriage and has not been withdrawn;
- (c) that a separation order is in force.

Definitions For "divorce order", see s 2(1)(a) ante; for "separation order", see s 2(1)(b) ante; for "period for reflection and consideration", see s 7(1), (2) post; for "the court" and "party", see s 24(1) post; as to "the withdrawal of an application", see s 24(2) post.
References See paras 3.13–3.14.

Reflection and consideration

7 Period for reflection and consideration

(1) Where a statement has been made, a period for the parties—

(a) to reflect on whether the marriage can be saved and to have an opportunity to effect a reconciliation, and

(b) to consider what arrangements should be made for the future,

must pass before an application for a divorce order or for a separation order may be made by reference to that statement.

(2) That period is to be known as the period for reflection and consideration.

(3) The period for reflection and consideration is nine months beginning with the fourteenth day after the day on which the statement is received by the court.

(4) Where—

(a) the statement has been made by one party,

(b) rules made under section 12 require the court to serve a copy of the statement on the other party, and

(c) failure to comply with the rules causes inordinate delay in service,

the court may, on the application of that other party, extend the period for reflection and consideration.

(5) An extension under subsection (4) may be for any period not exceeding the time between—

(a) the beginning of the period for reflection and consideration; and

(b) the time when service is effected.

(6) A statement which is made before the first anniversary of the marriage to which it relates is ineffective for the purposes of any application for a divorce order.

(7) Subsection (8) applies if, at any time during the period for reflection and consideration, the parties jointly give notice to the court that they are attempting a reconciliation but require additional time.

(8) The period for reflection and consideration—

(a) stops running on the day on which the notice is received by the court; but

(b) resumes running on the day on which either of the parties gives notice to the court that the attempted reconciliation has been unsuccessful.

(9) If the period for reflection and consideration is interrupted under subsection (8) by a continuous period of more than 18 months, any application by either of the parties for a divorce order or for a separation order must be by reference to a new statement received by the court at any time after the end of the 18 months.

(10) Where an application for a divorce order is made by one party, subsection (13) applies if—

(a) the other party applies to the court, within the prescribed period, for time for further reflection; and

(b) the requirements of section 9 (except any imposed under section 9(3)) are satisfied.

(11) Where any application for a divorce order is made, subsection (13) also applies if there is a child of the family who is under the age of sixteen when the application is made.

(12) Subsection (13) does not apply if—

(a) at the time when the application for a divorce order is made, there is an occupation order or a non-molestation order in force in favour of the applicant, or of a child of the family, made against the other party; or

(b) the court is satisfied that delaying the making of a divorce order would be significantly detrimental to the welfare of any child of the family.

(13) If this subsection applies, the period for reflection and consideration is extended by a period of six months, but—

(a) only in relation to the application for a divorce order in respect of which the application under subsection (10) was made; and

(b) without invalidating that application for a divorce order.

(14) A period for reflection and consideration which is extended under subsection (13), and which has not otherwise come to an end, comes to an end on there ceasing to be any children of the family to whom subsection (11) applied.

Definitions For "divorce order", see s 2(1)(a) ante; for "separation order", see s 2(1)(b) ante; for "a statement", see s 6(1) ante; for "child of the family", "the court" and "party", see s 24(1) post; for "occupation order", see s 39(1) post; for "non-molestation order", see s 42(1) post.
References See paras 2.5, 3.7, 3.18–3.22.

---

8 Attendance at information meetings

(1) The requirements about information meetings are as follows.

(2) A party making a statement must (except in prescribed circumstances) have attended an information meeting not less than three months before making the statement.

(3) Different information meetings must be arranged with respect to different marriages.

(4) In the case of a statement made by both parties, the parties may attend separate meetings or the same meeting.

(5) Where one party has made a statement, the other party must (except in prescribed circumstances) attend an information meeting before—

(a) making any application to the court—

(i) with respect to a child of the family; or

(ii) of a prescribed description relating to property or financial matters; or

(b) contesting any such application.

(6) In this section "information meeting" means a meeting organised, in accordance with prescribed provisions for the purpose—

(a) of providing, in accordance with prescribed provisions, relevant information to the party or parties attending about matters which may arise in connection with the provisions of, or made under, this Part or Part III; and

(b) of giving the party or parties attending the information meeting the opportunity of having a meeting with a marriage counsellor and of encouraging that party or those parties to attend that meeting.

(7) An information meeting must be conducted by a person who—

(a) is qualified and appointed in accordance with prescribed provisions; and

(b) will have no financial or other interest in any marital proceedings between the parties.

(8) Regulations made under this section may, in particular, make provision—

(a) about the places and times at which information meetings are to be held;

(b) for written information to be given to persons attending them;

(c) for the giving of information to parties (otherwise than at information meetings) in cases in which the requirement to attend such meetings does not apply;

(d) for information of a prescribed kind to be given only with the approval of the Lord Chancellor or only by a person or by persons approved by him; and

(e) for information to be given, in prescribed circumstances, only with the approval of the Lord Chancellor or only by a person, or by persons, approved by him.

(9) Regulations made under subsection (6) must, in particular, make provision with respect to the giving of information about—

(a) marriage counselling and other marriage support services;

(b) the importance to be attached to the welfare, wishes and feelings of children;

(c) how the parties may acquire a better understanding of the ways in which children can be helped to cope with the breakdown of a marriage;

(d) the nature of the financial questions that may arise on divorce or separation, and services which are available to help the parties;

(e) protection available against violence, and how to obtain support and assistance;

(f) mediation;

(g) the availability to each of the parties of independent legal advice and representation;

(h) the principles of legal aid and where the parties can get advice about obtaining legal aid;

(i) the divorce and separation process.

(10) Before making any regulations under subsection (6), the Lord Chancellor must consult such persons concerned with the provision of relevant information as he considers appropriate.

(11) A meeting with a marriage counsellor arranged under this section—

(a) must be held in accordance with prescribed provisions; and

(b) must be with a person qualified and appointed in accordance with prescribed provisions.

(12) A person who would not be required to make any contribution towards mediation provided for him under Part IIIA of the Legal Aid Act 1988 shall not be required to make any contribution towards the cost of a meeting with a marriage counsellor arranged for him under this section.

(13) In this section "prescribed" means prescribed by regulations made by the Lord Chancellor.

Definitions For "a statement", see s 6(1) ante; as to "marital proceedings", see s 20 post; for "child of the family", "the court" and "party", see s 24(1) post.
References See paras 2.7, 3.23–3.27.

---

9 Arrangements for the future

(1) The requirements as to the parties' arrangements for the future are as follows.

(2) One of the following must be produced to the court—

(a) a court order (made by consent or otherwise) dealing with their financial arrangements;

(b) a negotiated agreement as to their financial arrangements;
(c) a declaration by both parties that they have made their financial arrangements;
(d) a declaration by one of the parties (to which no objection has been notified to the court by the other party) that—
(i) he has no significant assets and does not intend to make an application for financial provision;
(ii) he believes that the other party has no significant assets and does not intend to make an application for financial provision; and
(iii) there are therefore no financial arrangements to be made.

(3) If the parties—
(a) were married to each other in accordance with usages of a kind mentioned in section 26(1) of the Marriage Act 1949 (marriages which may be solemnized on authority of superintendent registrar's certificate), and
(b) are required to co-operate if the marriage is to be dissolved in accordance with those usages,

the court may, on the application of either party, direct that there must also be produced to the court a declaration by both parties that they have taken such steps as are required to dissolve the marriage in accordance with those usages.

(4) A direction under subsection (3)—
(a) may be given only if the court is satisfied that in all the circumstances of the case it is just and reasonable to give it; and
(b) may be revoked by the court at any time.

(5) The requirements of section 11 must have been satisfied.

(6) Schedule 1 supplements the provisions of this section.

(7) If the court is satisfied, on an application made by one of the parties after the end of the period for reflection and consideration, that the circumstances of the case are—
(a) those set out in paragraph 1 of Schedule 1,
(b) those set out in paragraph 2 of that Schedule,
(c) those set out in paragraph 3 of that Schedule, or
(d) those set out in paragraph 4 of that Schedule,

it may make a divorce order or a separation order even though the requirements of subsection (2) have not been satisfied.

(8) If the parties' arrangements for the future include a division of pension assets or rights under section 25B of the 1973 Act or section 10 of the Family Law (Scotland) Act 1985, any declaration under subsection (2) must be a statutory declaration.

Definitions For "divorce order", see s 2(1)(a) ante; for "separation order", see s 2(1)(b) ante; for "period for reflection and consideration", see s 7(1), (2) ante; for "the 1973 Act", "the court" and "party", see s 24(1) post; for "financial arrangements", see by virtue of Sch 1, para 6 post, the Matrimonial Causes Act 1973, s 34(2); for "negotiated agreement", see Sch 1, para 7 post; as to a "declaration" under this section, see Sch 1, para 8 post.
References See paras 3.28, 4.2–4.9.

Orders preventing divorce

10 Hardship: orders preventing divorce

(1) If an application for a divorce order has been made by one of the parties to a marriage, the court may, on the application of the other party, order that the marriage is not to be dissolved.

(2) Such an order (an "order preventing divorce") may be made only if the court is satisfied—

(a) that dissolution of the marriage would result in substantial financial or other hardship to the other party or to a child of the family; and

(b) that it would be wrong, in all the circumstances (including the conduct of the parties and the interests of any child of the family), for the marriage to be dissolved.

(3) If an application for the cancellation of an order preventing divorce is made by one or both of the parties, the court shall cancel the order unless it is still satisfied—

(a) that dissolution of the marriage would result in substantial financial or other hardship to the party in whose favour the order was made or to a child of the family; and

(b) that it would be wrong, in all the circumstances (including the conduct of the parties and the interests of any child of the family), for the marriage to be dissolved.

(4) If an order preventing a divorce is cancelled, the court may make a divorce order in respect of the marriage only if an application is made under section 3 or 4(3) after the cancellation.

(5) An order preventing divorce may include conditions which must be satisfied before an application for cancellation may be made under subsection (3).

(6) In this section "hardship" includes the loss of a chance to obtain a future benefit (as well as the loss of an existing benefit).

Definitions For "divorce order", see s 2(1)(a) ante; for "child of the family", "the court" and "party", see s 24(1) post.
References See paras 2.4, 4.10–4.20.

Welfare of children

11 Welfare of children

(1) In any proceedings for a divorce order or a separation order, the court shall consider—

(a) whether there are any children of the family to whom this section applies; and

(b) where there are any such children, whether (in the light of the arrangements which have been, or are proposed to be, made for their upbringing and welfare) it should exercise any of its powers under the Children Act 1989 with respect to any of them.

(2) Where, in any case to which this section applies, it appears to the court that—

(a) the circumstances of the case require it, or are likely to require it, to exercise any of its powers under the Children Act 1989 with respect to any such child,

(b) it is not in a position to exercise the power, or (as the case may be) those powers, without giving further consideration to the case, and

(c) there are exceptional circumstances which make it desirable in the interests of the child that the court should give a direction under this section,

it may direct that the divorce order or separation order is not to be made until the court orders otherwise.

(3) In deciding whether the circumstances are as mentioned in subsection (2)(a), the court shall treat the welfare of the child as paramount.

(4) In making that decision, the court shall also have particular regard, on the evidence before it, to—

(a) the wishes and feelings of the child considered in the light of his age and understanding and the circumstances in which those wishes were expressed;

(b) the conduct of the parties in relation to the upbringing of the child;

(c) the general principle that, in the absence of evidence to the contrary, the welfare of the child will be best served by—

(i) his having regular contact with those who have parental responsibility for him and with other members of his family; and

(ii) the maintenance of as good a continuing relationship with his parents as is possible; and

(d) any risk to the child attributable to—

(i) where the person with whom the child will reside is living or proposes to live;

(ii) any person with whom that person is living or with whom he proposes to live; or

(iii) any other arrangements for his care and upbringing.

(5) This section applies to—

(a) any child of the family who has not reached the age of sixteen at the date when the court considers the case in accordance with the requirements of this section; and

(b) any child of the family who has reached that age at that date and in relation to whom the court directs that this section shall apply.

Definitions For "divorce order", see s 2(1)(a) ante; for "separation order", see s 2(1)(b) ante; for "child of the family", "the court" and "party", see s 24(1) post.
References See paras 3.29–3.31.

Supplementary

12 Lord Chancellor's rules

(1) The Lord Chancellor may make rules—

(a) as to the form in which a statement is to be made and what information must accompany it;

(b) requiring the person making the statement to state whether or not, since satisfying the requirements of section 8, he has made any attempt at reconciliation;

(c) as to the way in which a statement is to be given to the court;

(d) requiring a copy of a statement made by one party to be served by the court on the other party;

(e) as to circumstances in which such service may be dispensed with or may be effected otherwise than by delivery to the party;

(f) requiring a party who has made a statement to provide the court with information about the arrangements that need to be made in consequence of the breakdown;

(g) as to the time, manner and (where attendance in person is required) place at which such information is to be given;

(h) where a statement has been made, requiring either or both of the parties—

(i) to prepare and produce such other documents, and

(ii) to attend in person at such places and for such purposes,

as may be specified;

(i) as to the information and assistance which is to be given to the parties and the way in which it is to be given;
(j) requiring the parties to be given, in such manner as may be specified, copies of such statements and other documents as may be specified.

(2) The Lord Chancellor may make rules requiring a person who is the legal representative of a party to a marriage with respect to which a statement has been, or is proposed to be, made—
(a) to inform that party, at such time or times as may be specified—
(i) about the availability to the parties of marriage support services;
(ii) about the availability to them of mediation; and
(iii) where there are children of the family, that in relation to the arrangements to be made for any child the parties should consider the child's welfare, wishes and feelings;
(b) to give that party, at such time or times as may be specified, names and addresses of persons qualified to help—
(i) to effect a reconciliation; or
(ii) in connection with mediation; and
(c) to certify, at such time or times as may be specified—
(i) whether he has complied with the provision made in the rules by virtue of paragraphs (a) and (b);
(ii) whether he has discussed with that party any of the matters mentioned in paragraph (a) or the possibility of reconciliation; and
(iii) which, if any, of those matters they have discussed.

(3) In subsections (1) and (2) "specified" means determined under or described in the rules.

(4) This section does not affect any power to make rules of court for the purposes of this Act.

Definitions For "a statement", see s 6(1) ante; for "child of the family", "the court" and "party", see s 24(1) post.
References See para 3.15–3.17.

Resolution of disputes

13 Directions with respect to mediation

(1) After the court has received a statement, it may give a direction requiring each party to attend a meeting arranged in accordance with the direction for the purpose—
(a) of enabling an explanation to be given of the facilities available to the parties for mediation in relation to disputes between them; and
(b) of providing an opportunity for each party to agree to take advantage of those facilities.

(2) A direction may be given at any time, including in the course of proceedings connected with the breakdown of the marriage (as to which see section 25).

(3) A direction may be given on the application of either of the parties or on the initiative of the court.

(4) The parties are to be required to attend the same meeting unless—
(a) one of them asks, or both of them ask, for separate meetings; or
(b) the court considers separate meetings to be more appropriate.

(5) A direction shall—
(a) specify a person chosen by the court (with that person's agreement) to arrange and conduct the meeting or meetings; and

(b) require such person as may be specified in the direction to produce to the court, at such time as the court may direct, a report stating—
(i) whether the parties have complied with the direction; and
(ii) if they have, whether they have agreed to take part in any mediation.

Definitions For "a statement", see s 6(1) ante; for "the court" and "party", see s 24(1) post; as to "proceedings connected with the breakdown of a marriage", see s 25 post.
References See paras 3.44–3.46.

14 Adjournments

(1) The court's power to adjourn any proceedings connected with the breakdown of a marriage includes power to adjourn—
(a) for the purpose of allowing the parties to comply with a direction under section 13; or
(b) for the purpose of enabling disputes to be resolved amicably.

(2) In determining whether to adjourn for either purpose, the court shall have regard in particular to the need to protect the interests of any child of the family.

(3) If the court adjourns any proceedings connected with the breakdown of a marriage for either purpose, the period of the adjournment must not exceed the maximum period prescribed by rules of court.

(4) Unless the only purpose of the adjournment is to allow the parties to comply with a direction under section 13, the court shall order one or both of them to produce to the court a report as to—
(a) whether they have taken part in mediation during the adjournment;
(b) whether, as a result, any agreement has been reached between them;
(c) the extent to which any dispute between them has been resolved as a result of any such agreement;
(d) the need for further mediation; and
(e) how likely it is that further mediation will be successful.

Definitions For "child of the family" and "the court", see s 24(1) post; as to "proceedings connected with the breakdown of a marriage", see s 25 post.
Reference See para 3.47.

Financial provision

15 Financial arrangements

(1) Schedule 2 amends the 1973 Act.

(2) The main object of Schedule 2 is—
(a) to provide that, in the case of divorce or separation, an order about financial provision may be made under that Act before a divorce order or separation order is made; but
(b) to retain (with minor changes) the position under that Act where marriages are annulled.

(3) Schedule 2 also makes minor and consequential amendments of the 1973 Act connected with the changes mentioned in subsection (1).

Definitions For "divorce order", see s 2(1)(a) ante; for "separation order", see s 2(1)(b) ante; for "the 1973 Act", see s 24(1) post.
References See paras 4.21–4.34.

16 Division of pension rights: England and Wales

(1) The Matrimonial Causes Act 1973 is amended as follows.

(2) In section 25B (benefits under a pension scheme on divorce, etc), in subsection (2), after paragraph (b), insert—

"(c) in particular, where the court determines to make such an order, whether the order should provide for the accrued rights of the party with pension rights ("the pension rights") to be divided between that party and the other party in such a way as to reduce the pension rights of the party with those rights and to create pension rights for the other party.".

(3) After subsection (7) of that section, add—

"(8) If a pensions adjustment order under subsection (2)(c) above is made, the pension rights shall be reduced and pension rights of the other party shall be created in the prescribed manner with benefits payable on prescribed conditions, except that the court shall not have the power—

(a) to require the trustees or managers of the scheme to provide benefits under their own scheme if they are able and willing to create the rights for the other party by making a transfer payment to another scheme and the trustees and managers of that other scheme are able and willing to accept such a payment and to create those rights; or

(b) to require the trustees or managers of the scheme to make a transfer to another scheme—

(i) if the scheme is an unfunded scheme (unless the trustees or managers are able and willing to make such a transfer payment); or

(ii) in prescribed circumstances.

(9) No pensions adjustment order may be made under subsection (2)(c) above—

(a) if the scheme is a scheme of a prescribed type, or

(b) in prescribed circumstances, or

(c) insofar as it would affect benefits of a prescribed type."

(4) In section 25D (pensions: supplementary), insert—

(a) in subsection (2)—

(i) at the end of paragraph (a), the words "or prescribe the rights of the other party under the pension scheme,"; and

(ii) after paragraph (a), the following paragraph—

"(aa) make such consequential modifications of any enactment or subordinate legislation as appear to the Lord Chancellor necessary or expedient to give effect to the provisions of section 25B; and an order under this paragraph may make provision applying generally in relation to enactments and subordinate legislation of a description specified in the order,";

(b) in subsection (4), in the appropriate place in alphabetical order, the following entries—

"'funded scheme' means a scheme under which the benefits are provided for by setting aside resources related to the value of the members' rights as they accrue (and 'unfunded scheme' shall be construed accordingly);

"'subordinate legislation' has the same meaning as in the Interpretation Act 1978;"; and

(c) after subsection (4), the following subsection—

"(4A) Other expressions used in section 25B above shall be construed in accordance with section 124 (interpretation of Part I) of the Pensions Act 1995."

Definitions For the meaning of "the court" in the Matrimonial Causes Act 1973, see s 52(1) of that Act; for "trustees or managers", see s 25D(3) thereof, as inserted by the Pensions Act 1995, s 166; for "the party with pension rights", "the other party", "pension scheme", "prescribed", "subordinate legislation" and "unfunded scheme", see s 25D(4) thereof, as inserted by s 166 of the 1995 Act and amended by sub-(4)(b) above; for "accrued rights", see, by virtue of s 25D(4A) (as inserted by sub-s (4)(c) above), s 124(2) of the 1995 Act.
References See paras 4.35–4.37.

17 Division of pension assets: Scotland

Section 10 of the Family Law (Scotland) Act 1985 (sharing of value of matrimonial property), is amended as follows—

(a) in subsection (5) at the end of paragraph (b), insert

", and

(c) in the assets in respect of which either party has accrued rights to benefits under a pension scheme"; and

(b) after subsection (5) insert—

"(5A) In the case of an unfunded pension scheme, the court may not make an order which would allow assets to be removed from the scheme earlier than would otherwise have been the case.".

Definitions For the meaning of "pension scheme" and "benefits under a pension scheme" in the Family Law (Scotland) Act 1985, see s 10(10) of that Act (as inserted by the Pensions Act 1995, s 167).

18 Grounds for financial provision orders in magistrates' courts

(1) In section 1 of the Domestic Proceedings and Magistrates' Courts Act 1978, omit paragraphs (c) and (d) (which provide for behaviour and desertion to be grounds on which an application for a financial provision order may be made).

(2) In section 7(1) of that Act (powers of magistrates' court where spouses are living apart by agreement), omit "neither party having deserted the other".

Reference See para 4.38.

Jurisdiction and commencement of proceedings

19 Jurisdiction in relation to divorce and separation

(1) In this section "the court's jurisdiction" means—

(a) the jurisdiction of the court under this Part to entertain marital proceedings; and

(b) any other jurisdiction conferred on the court under this Part, or any other enactment, in consequence of the making of a statement.

(2) The court's jurisdiction is exercisable only if—

(a) at least one of the parties was domiciled in England and Wales on the statement date;

(b) at least one of the parties was habitually resident in England and Wales throughout the period of one year ending with the statement date; or

(c) nullity proceedings are pending in relation to the marriage when the marital proceedings commence.

(3) Subsection (4) applies if—

(a) a separation order is in force; or

(b) an order preventing divorce has been cancelled.

(4) The court—

(a) continues to have jurisdiction to entertain an application made by reference to the order referred to in subsection (3); and

(b) may exercise any other jurisdiction which is conferred on it in consequence of such an application.

(5) Schedule 3 amends Schedule 1 to the Domicile and Matrimonial Proceedings Act 1973 (orders to stay proceedings where there are proceedings in other jurisdictions).

(6) The court's jurisdiction is exercisable subject to any order for a stay under Schedule 1 to that Act.

(7) In this section—

"nullity proceedings" means proceedings in respect of which the court has jurisdiction under section 5(3) of the Domicile and Matrimonial Proceedings Act 1973; and

"statement date" means the date on which the relevant statement was received by the court.

Definitions For "separation order", see s 2(1)(b) ante; for "a statement", see s 6(1) ante; for "order preventing divorce", see s 10(1), (2) ante; as to "marital proceedings", see s 20 post; for "the court", see s 24(1) post.

References See paras 3.32–3.34.

20 Time when proceedings for divorce or separation begin

(1) The receipt by the court of a statement is to be treated as the commencement of proceedings.

(2) The proceedings are to be known as marital proceedings.

(3) Marital proceedings are also—

(a) separation proceedings, if an application for a separation order has been made under section 3 by reference to the statement and not withdrawn;

(b) divorce proceedings, if an application for a divorce order has been made under section 3 by reference to the statement and not withdrawn.

(4) Marital proceedings are to be treated as being both divorce proceedings and separation proceedings at any time when no application by reference to the statement, either for a divorce order or for a separation order, is outstanding.

(5) Proceedings which are commenced by the making of an application under section 4(3) are also marital proceedings and divorce proceedings.

(6) Marital proceedings come to an end—

(a) on the making of a separation order;

(b) on the making of a divorce order;

(c) on the withdrawal of the statement by a notice in accordance with section 5(3)(a);

(d) at the end of the specified period mentioned in section 5(3)(b), if no application under section 3 by reference to the statement is outstanding;

(e) on the withdrawal of all such applications which are outstanding at the end of that period;
(f) on the withdrawal of an application under section 4(3).

Definitions For "divorce order", see s 2(1)(a) ante; for "separation order", see s 2(1)(b) ante; for "a statement", see s 6(1) ante; for "the court", see s 24(1) post; as to "the withdrawal of an application", see s 24(2) post.
References See paras 2.2, 2.3, 3.35, 3.36.

Intestacy

21 Intestacy: effect of separation

Where—
(a) a separation order is in force, and
(b) while the parties to the marriage remain separated, one of them dies intestate as respects any real or personal property,

that property devolves as if the other had died before the intestacy occurred.

Definition For "separation order", see see s 2(1)(b) ante.
References See para 3.37.

Marriage support services

22 Funding for marriage support services

(1) The Lord Chancellor may, with the approval of the Treasury, make grants in connection with—
(a) the provision of marriage support services;
(b) research into the causes of marital breakdown;
(c) research into ways of preventing marital breakdown.

(2) Any grant under this section may be made subject to such conditions as the Lord Chancellor considers appropriate.

(3) In exercising his power to make grants in connection with the provision of marriage support services, the Lord Chancellor is to have regard, in particular, to the desirability of services of that kind being available when they are first needed.

References See para 3.38.

23 Provision of marriage counselling

(1) The Lord Chancellor or a person appointed by him may secure the provision, in accordance with regulations made by the Lord Chancellor, of marriage counselling.

(2) Marriage counselling may only be provided under this section at a time when a period for reflection and consideration—
(a) is running in relation to the marriage; or
(b) is interrupted under section 7(8) (but not for a continuous period of more than 18 months).

(3) Marriage counselling may only be provided under this section for persons who would not be required to make any contribution towards the cost of mediation provided for them under Part IIIA of the Legal Aid Act 1988.

(4) Persons for whom marriage counselling is provided under this section are not to be required to make any contribution towards the cost of the counselling.

(5) Marriage counselling is only to be provided under this section if it appears to the marriage counsellor to be suitable in all the circumstances.

(6) Regulations under subsection (1) may—
(a) make provision about the way in which marriage counselling is to be provided; and
(b) prescribe circumstances in which the provision of marriage counselling is to be subject to the approval of the Lord Chancellor.

(7) A contract entered into for the purposes of subsection (1) by a person appointed under that subsection must include such provision as the Lord Chancellor may direct.

(8) If the person appointed under subsection (1) is the Legal Aid Board, the powers conferred on the Board by or under the Legal Aid Act 1988 shall be exercisable for the purposes of this section as they are exercisable for the purposes of that Act.

(9) In section 15 of the Legal Aid Act 1988 (availability of, and payment for, representation under Part IV of the Act), after subsection (3H) insert—

"(3I) A person may be refused representation for the purposes of any proceedings if—
(a) the proceedings are marital proceedings within the meaning of Part II of the Family Law Act 1996; and
(b) he is being provided with marriage counselling under section 23 of that Act in relation to the marriage."

Definitions For "period for reflection and consideration", see s 7(1), (2) ante; as to "marital proceedings", see s 20 ante.
References See paras 3.39–3.41.

Interpretation

24 Interpretation of Part II etc

(1) In this Part—
"the 1973 Act" means the Matrimonial Causes Act 1973;
"child of the family" and "the court" have the same meaning as in the 1973 Act;
"divorce order" has the meaning given in section 2(1)(a);
"divorce proceedings" is to be read with section 20;
"marital proceedings" has the meaning given in section 20;
"non-molestation order" has the meaning given by section 42(1);
"occupation order" has the meaning given by section 39;
"order preventing divorce" has the meaning given in section 10(2);
"party", in relation to a marriage, means one of the parties to the marriage;
"period for reflection and consideration" has the meaning given in section 7;
"separation order" has the meaning given in section 2(1)(b);
"separation proceedings" is to be read with section 20;
"statement" means a statement of marital breakdown;
"statement of marital breakdown" has the meaning given in section 6(1).

(2) For the purposes of this Part, references to the withdrawal of an application are references, in relation to an application made jointly by both parties, to its withdrawal by a notice given, in accordance with rules of court—
(a) jointly by both parties; or
(b) separately by each of them.

(3) Where only one party gives such a notice of withdrawal, in relation to a joint application, the application shall be treated as if it had been made by the other party alone.

Reference See App 5 Glossary.

25 Connected proceedings

(1) For the purposes of this Part, proceedings are connected with the breakdown of a marriage if they fall within subsection (2) and, at the time of the proceedings—

(a) a statement has been received by the court with respect to the marriage and it is or may become possible for an application for a divorce order or separation order to be made by reference to that statement;

(b) such an application in relation to the marriage has been made and not withdrawn; or

(c) a divorce order has been made, or a separation order is in force, in relation to the marriage.

(2) The proceedings are any under Parts I to V of the Children Act 1989 with respect to a child of the family or any proceedings resulting from an application—

(a) for, or for the cancellation of, an order preventing divorce in relation to the marriage;

(b) by either party to the marriage for an order under Part IV;

(c) for the exercise, in relation to a party to the marriage or child of the family, of any of the court's powers under Part II of the 1973 Act;

(d) made otherwise to the court with respect to, or in connection with, any proceedings connected with the breakdown of the marriage.

Definitions For "divorce order", see s 2(1)(a) ante; for "separation order", see s 2(1)(b) ante; for "a statement", see s 6(1) ante; for "order preventing divorce", see s 10(1), (2) ante; for "the 1973 Act", "child of the family" and "the court", see s 24(1) ante; as to "the withdrawal of an application", see s 24(2) ante.

References See paras 3.42, 3.43.

PART III
LEGAL AID FOR MEDIATION IN FAMILY MATTERS

26 Legal aid for mediation in family matters

(1) In the Legal Aid Act 1988 insert, after section 13—

"PART IIIA
MEDIATION

13A Scope of this Part

(1) This Part applies to mediation in disputes relating to family matters.

(2) "Family matters" means matters which are governed by English law and in relation to which any question has arisen, or may arise—

(a) under any provision of—

(i) the 1973 Act;

(ii) the Domestic Proceedings and Magistrates' Courts Act 1978;

(iii) Parts I to V of the Children Act 1989;

(iv) Parts II and IV of the Family Law Act 1996; or

(v) any other enactment prescribed;

(b) under any prescribed jurisdiction of a prescribed court or tribunal; or

(c) under any prescribed rule of law.

(3) Regulations may restrict this Part to mediation in disputes of any prescribed description.

(4) The power to—

(a) make regulations under subsection (2), or

(b) revoke any regulations made under subsection (3),

is exercisable only with the consent of the Treasury.".

(2) In section 2 of the 1988 Act, after subsection (3), insert—

"(3A) "Mediation" means mediation to which Part IIIA of this Act applies; and includes steps taken by a mediator in any case—
- (a) in determining whether to embark on mediation;
- (b) in preparing for mediation; and
- (c) in making any assessment under that Part."

(3) In section 43 of the 1988 Act, after the definition of "legal representative" insert—

""mediator" means a person with whom the Board contracts for the provision of mediation by any person.".

Definitions In the Legal Aid Act 1988, for "mediation", see s 2(3A) thereof, as inserted by sub-s (2) above; for "person", see s 2(10) thereof; for "the Board", see s 3(1) thereof; for "mediator", "prescribed", "regulations" and "tribunal", see s 43 thereof, as amended by sub-s (3) above.
References See para 5.1.

27 Provision and availability of mediation

After section 13A of the 1988 Act, insert—

"13B Provision and availability of mediation

(1) The Board may secure the provision of mediation under this Part.

(2) If mediation is provided under this Part, it is to be available to any person whose financial resources are such as, under regulations, make him eligible for mediation.

(3) A person is not to be granted mediation in relation to any dispute unless mediation appears to the mediator suitable to the dispute and the parties and all the circumstances.

(4) A grant of mediation under this Part may be amended, withdrawn or revoked.

(5) The power conferred by subsection (1) shall be exercised in accordance with any directions given by the Lord Chancellor.

(6) Any contract entered into by the Board for the provision of mediation under this Part must require the mediator to comply with a code of practice.

(7) The code must require the mediator to have arrangements designed to ensure—
- (a) that parties participate in mediation only if willing and not influenced by fear of violence or other harm;
- (b) that cases where either party may be influenced by fear of violence or other harm are identified as soon as possible;
- (c) that the possibility of reconciliation is kept under review throughout mediation; and
- (d) that each party is informed about the availability of independent legal advice.

(8) Where there are one or more children of the family, the code must also require the mediator to have arrangements designed to ensure that the parties are encouraged to consider—
- (a) the welfare, wishes and feelings of each child; and
- (b) whether and to what extent each child should be given the opportunity to express his or her wishes and feelings in the mediation.

(9) A contract entered into by the Board for the provision of mediation under this Part must also include such other provision as the Lord Chancellor may direct the Board to include.

(10) Directions under this section may apply generally to contracts, or to contracts of any description, entered into by the Board, but shall not be made with respect to any particular contract.".

Definitions In the Legal Aid Act 1988, for "mediation", see s 2(3A) thereof, as inserted by s 26(2) ante; for "person", see s 2(10) thereof; for "the Board", see s 3(1) thereof; for "financial resources", "mediator" and "regulations", see s 43 thereof, as amended by s 26(3) ante.
References See paras 5.2, 5.3.

28 Payment for mediation

(1) After section 13B of the 1988 Act, insert—

"13C Payment for mediation under this Part

(1) Except as provided by this section, the legally assisted person is not to be required to pay for mediation provided under this Part.

(2) Subsection (3) applies if the financial resources of a legally assisted person are such as, under regulations, make him liable to make a contribution.

(3) The legally assisted person is to pay to the Board in respect of the costs of providing the mediation, a contribution of such amount as is determined or fixed by or under the regulations.

(4) If the total contribution made by a person in respect of any mediation exceeds the Board's liability on his account, the excess shall be repaid to him.

(5) Regulations may provide that, where—
(a) mediation under this Part is made available to a legally assisted person, and
(b) property is recovered or preserved for the legally assisted person as a result of the mediation,

a sum equal to the Board's liability on the legally assisted person's account is, except so far as the regulations otherwise provide, to be a first charge on the property in favour of the Board.

(6) Regulations under subsection (5) may, in particular, make provision—
(a) as to circumstances in which property is to be taken to have been, or not to have been, recovered or preserved; and
(b) as to circumstances in which the recovery or preservation of property is to be taken to be, or not to be, the result of any mediation.

(7) For the purposes of subsection (5), the nature of the property and where it is situated is immaterial.

(8) The power to make regulations under section 34(2)(f) and (8) is exercisable in relation to any charge created under subsection (5) as it is exercisable in relation to the charge created by section 16.

(9) For the purposes of subsections (4) and (5), the Board's liability on any person's account in relation to any mediation is the aggregate amount of—
(a) the sums paid or payable by the Board on his account for the mediation, determined in accordance with subsection (10);
(b) any sums paid or payable in respect of its net liability on his account, determined in accordance with subsection (11) and the regulations—

(i) in respect of any proceedings, and

(ii) for any advice or assistance under Part III in connection with the proceedings or any matter to which the proceedings relate,

so far as the proceedings relate to any matter to which the mediation relates; and

(c) any sums paid or payable in respect of its net liability on his account, determined in accordance with the regulations, for any other advice or assistance under Part III in connection with the mediation or any matter to which the mediation relates.

(10) For the purposes of subsection (9)(a), the sums paid or payable by the Board on any person's account for any mediation are—

(a) sums determined under the contract between the Board and the mediator as payable by the Board on that person's account for the mediation; or

(b) if the contract does not differentiate between such sums and sums payable on any other person's account or for any other mediation, such part of the remuneration payable under the contract as may be specified in writing by the Board.

(11) For the purposes of subsection (9)(b), the Board's net liability on any person's account in relation to any proceedings is its net liability on his account under section 16(9)(a) and (b) in relation to the proceedings."

(2) In section 16(9), after paragraph (b) insert

"and

(c) if and to the extent that regulations so provide, any sums paid or payable in respect of the Board's liability on the legally assisted persons account in relation to any mediation in connection with any matter to which those proceedings relate.".

(3) At the end of section 16, insert—

"(11) For the purposes of subsection (9)(c) above, the Board's liability on any person's account in relation to any mediation is its liability on his account under section 13C(9)(a) and (c) above in relation to the mediation."

Definitions In the Legal Aid Act 1988, for "mediation", see s 2(3A) thereof, as inserted by s 26(2) ante; for "person", see s 2(10) thereof; for "legally assisted person", see s 2(11) thereof, as amended by s 66(1), Sch 8, para 44(3) post; for "the Board", see s 3(1) thereof; for "financial resources", "mediator" and "regulations", see s 43 thereof, as amended by s 26(3) ante.
References See para 5.4.

29 Mediation and civil legal aid

In section 15 of the 1988 Act, after subsection (3E) insert—

"(3F) A person shall not be granted representation for the purposes of proceedings relating to family matters, unless he has attended a meeting with a mediator—

(a) to determine—

(i) whether mediation appears suitable to the dispute and the parties and all the circumstances, and

(ii) in particular, whether mediation could take place without either party being influenced by fear of violence or other harm; and

(b) if mediation does appear suitable, to help the person applying for representation to decide whether instead to apply for mediation.

(3G) Subsection (3F) does not apply—

(a) in relation to proceedings under—

(i) Part IV of the Family Law Act 1996;

(ii) section 37 of the Matrimonial Causes Act 1973;

(iii) Part IV or V of the Children Act 1989;

(b) in relation to proceedings of any other description that may be prescribed; or

(c) in such circumstances as may be prescribed.

(3H) So far as proceedings relate to family matters, the Board, in determining under subsection (3)(a) whether, in relation to the proceedings, it is reasonable that a person should be granted representation under this Part—

(a) must have regard to whether and to what extent recourse to mediation would be a suitable alternative to taking the proceedings; and

(b) must for that purpose have regard to the outcome of the meeting held under subsection (3F) and to any assessment made for the purposes of section 13B(3)."

Definitions In the Legal Aid Act 1988, for "mediation", see s 2(3A) thereof, as inserted by s 26(2) ante; for "person", see s 2(10) thereof; for "the Board", see s 3(1) thereof; for "family matters", see s 13A(2) thereof, as inserted by s 26(1) ante; for "mediator" and "prescribed", see s 43 thereof, as amended by s 26(3) ante.
References See paras 5.5, 5.6.

PART IV
FAMILY HOMES AND DOMESTIC VIOLENCE

Rights to occupy matrimonial home

30 Rights concerning matrimonial home where one spouse has no estate, etc

(1) This section applies if—

(a) one spouse is entitled to occupy a dwelling-house by virtue of—

(i) a beneficial estate or interest or contract; or

(ii) any enactment giving that spouse the right to remain in occupation; and

(b) the other spouse is not so entitled.

(2) Subject to the provisions of this Part, the spouse not so entitled has the following rights ("matrimonial home rights")—

(a) if in occupation, a right not to be evicted or excluded from the dwelling-house or any part of it by the other spouse except with the leave of the court given by an order under section 33;

(b) if not in occupation, a right with the leave of the court so given to enter into and occupy the dwelling-house.

(3) If a spouse is entitled under this section to occupy a dwelling-house or any part of a dwelling-house, any payment or tender made or other thing done by that spouse in or towards satisfaction of any liability of the other spouse in respect of rent, mortgage payments or other outgoings affecting the dwelling-house is, whether or not it is made or done in pursuance of an order under section 40, as good as if made or done by the other spouse.

(4) A spouse's occupation by virtue of this section—

(a) is to be treated, for the purposes of the Rent (Agriculture) Act 1976 and the Rent Act 1977 (other than Part V and sections 103 to 106 of that Act), as occupation by the other spouse as the other spouse's residence, and

(b) if the spouse occupies the dwelling-house as that spouse's only or principal home, is to be treated, for the purposes of the Housing Act 1985 and Part I of the Housing Act 1988, as occupation by the other spouse as the other spouse's only or principal home.

(5) If a spouse ("the first spouse")—

(a) is entitled under this section to occupy a dwelling-house or any part of a dwelling-house, and

(b) makes any payment in or towards satisfaction of any liability of the other spouse ("the second spouse") in respect of mortgage payments affecting the dwelling-house,

the person to whom the payment is made may treat it as having been made by the second spouse, but the fact that that person has treated any such payment as having been so made does not affect any claim of the first spouse against the second spouse to an interest in the dwelling-house by virtue of the payment.

(6) If a spouse is entitled under this section to occupy a dwelling-house or part of a dwelling-house by reason of an interest of the other spouse under a trust, all the provisions of subsections (3) to (5) apply in relation to the trustees as they apply in relation to the other spouse.

(7) This section does not apply to a dwelling-house which has at no time been, and which was at no time intended by the spouses to be, a matrimonial home of theirs.

(8) A spouse's matrimonial home rights continue—

(a) only so long as the marriage subsists, except to the extent that an order under section 33(5) otherwise provides; and

(b) only so long as the other spouse is entitled as mentioned in subsection (1) to occupy the dwelling-house, except where provision is made by section 31 for those rights to be a charge on an estate or interest in the dwelling-house.

(9) It is hereby declared that a spouse—

(a) who has an equitable interest in a dwelling-house or in its proceeds of sale, but

(b) is not a spouse in whom there is vested (whether solely or as joint tenant) a legal estate in fee simple or a legal term of years absolute in the dwelling-house,

is to be treated, only for the purpose of determining whether he has matrimonial home rights, as not being entitled to occupy the dwelling-house by virtue of that interest.

Definitions For "the court", see s 57(1), (2) post; for "dwelling-house", and "mortgage payments", see s 63(1) post (and note also, in relation to "dwelling-house", s 63(4)).
References See paras 7.1–7.8.

31 Effect of matrimonial home rights as charge on dwelling-house

(1) Subsections (2) and (3) apply if, at any time during a marriage, one spouse is entitled to occupy a dwelling-house by virtue of a beneficial estate or interest.

(2) The other spouse's matrimonial home rights are a charge on the estate or interest.

(3) The charge created by subsection (2) has the same priority as if it were an equitable interest created at whichever is the latest of the following dates—

(a) the date on which the spouse so entitled acquires the estate or interest;

(b) the date of the marriage; and

(c) 1st January 1968 (the commencement date of the Matrimonial Homes Act 1967).

(4) Subsections (5) and (6) apply if, at any time when a spouse's matrimonial home rights are a charge on an interest of the other spouse under a trust, there are, apart from either of the spouses, no persons, living or unborn, who are or could become beneficiaries under the trust.

(5) The rights are a charge also on the estate or interest of the trustees for the other spouse.

(6) The charge created by subsection (5) has the same priority as if it were an equitable interest created (under powers overriding the trusts) on the date when it arises.

(7) In determining for the purposes of subsection (4) whether there are any persons who are not, but could become, beneficiaries under the trust, there is to be disregarded any potential exercise of a general power of appointment exercisable by either or both of the spouses alone (whether or not the exercise of it requires the consent of another person).

(8) Even though a spouse's matrimonial home rights are a charge on an estate or interest in the dwelling-house, those rights are brought to an end by—

- (a) the death of the other spouse, or
- (b) the termination (otherwise than by death) of the marriage,

unless the court directs otherwise by an order made under section 33(5).

(9) If—

- (a) a spouse's matrimonial home rights are a charge on an estate or interest in the dwelling-house, and
- (b) that estate or interest is surrendered to merge in some other estate or interest expectant on it in such circumstances that, but for the merger, the person taking the estate or interest would be bound by the charge,

the surrender has effect subject to the charge and the persons thereafter entitled to the other estate or interest are, for so long as the estate or interest surrendered would have endured if not so surrendered, to be treated for all purposes of this Part as deriving title to the other estate or interest under the other spouse or, as the case may be, under the trustees for the other spouse, by virtue of the surrender.

(10) If the title to the legal estate by virtue of which a spouse is entitled to occupy a dwelling-house (including any legal estate held by trustees for that spouse) is registered under the Land Registration Act 1925 or any enactment replaced by that Act—

- (a) registration of a land charge affecting the dwelling-house by virtue of this Part is to be effected by registering a notice under that Act; and
- (b) a spouse's matrimonial home rights are not an overriding interest within the meaning of that Act affecting the dwelling-house even though the spouse is in actual occupation of the dwelling-house.

(11) A spouse's matrimonial home rights (whether or not constituting a charge) do not entitle that spouse to lodge a caution under section 54 of the Land Registration Act 1925.

(12) If—

- (a) a spouse's matrimonial home rights are a charge on the estate of the other spouse or of trustees of the other spouse, and
- (b) that estate is the subject of a mortgage,

then if, after the date of the creation of the mortgage ("the first mortgage"), the charge is registered under section 2 of the Land Charges Act 1972, the charge is, for the purposes of section 94 of the Law of Property Act 1925 (which regulates the rights of mortgagees to make further advances ranking in priority to subsequent mortgages), to be deemed to be a mortgage subsequent in date to the first mortgage.

(13) It is hereby declared that a charge under subsection (2) or (5) is not registrable under subsection (10) or under section 2 of the Land Charges Act 1972 unless it is a charge on a legal estate.

Definitions For "matrimonial home rights", see s 30(2) ante; for "dwelling-house", "mortgage" and "mortgagees", see s 63(1) post (see also, in relation to "dwelling-house", s 63(4)).
References See paras 7.9–7.11, 7.16.

32 Further provisions relating to matrimonial home rights

Schedule 4 re-enacts with consequential amendments and minor modifications provisions of the Matrimonial Homes Act 1983.

References See paras 7.12–7.15.

Occupation orders

33 Occupation orders where applicant has estate or interest etc or has matrimonial home rights

(1) If—
- (a) a person ("the person entitled")—
  - (i) is entitled to occupy a dwelling-house by virtue of a beneficial estate or interest or contract or by virtue of any enactment giving him the right to remain in occupation, or
  - (ii) has matrimonial home rights in relation to a dwelling-house, and
- (b) the dwelling-house—
  - (i) is or at any time has been the home of the person entitled and of another person with whom he is associated, or
  - (ii) was at any time intended by the person entitled and any such other person to be their home,

the person entitled may apply to the court for an order containing any of the provisions specified in subsections (3), (4) and (5).

(2) If an agreement to marry is terminated, no application under this section may be made by virtue of section 62(3)(e) by reference to that agreement after the end of the period of three years beginning with the day on which it is terminated.

(3) An order under this section may—
- (a) enforce the applicant's entitlement to remain in occupation as against the other person ("the respondent");
- (b) require the respondent to permit the applicant to enter and remain in the dwelling-house or part of the dwelling-house;
- (c) regulate the occupation of the dwelling-house by either or both parties;
- (d) if the respondent is entitled as mentioned in subsection (1)(a)(i), prohibit, suspend or restrict the exercise by him of his right to occupy the dwelling-house;
- (e) if the respondent has matrimonial home rights in relation to the dwelling-house and the applicant is the other spouse, restrict or terminate those rights;
- (f) require the respondent to leave the dwelling-house or part of the dwelling-house; or
- (g) exclude the respondent from a defined area in which the dwelling-house is included.

(4) An order under this section may declare that the applicant is entitled as mentioned in subsection (1)(a)(i) or has matrimonial home rights.

(5) If the applicant has matrimonial home rights and the respondent is the other spouse, an order under this section made during the marriage may provide that those rights are not brought to an end by—

(a) the death of the other spouse; or

(b) the termination (otherwise than by death) of the marriage.

(6) In deciding whether to exercise its powers under subsection (3) and (if so) in what manner, the court shall have regard to all the circumstances including—

(a) the housing needs and housing resources of each of the parties and of any relevant child;

(b) the financial resources of each of the parties;

(c) the likely effect of any order, or of any decision by the court not to exercise its powers under subsection (3), on the health, safety or well-being of the parties and of any relevant child; and

(d) the conduct of the parties in relation to each other and otherwise.

(7) If it appears to the court that the applicant or any relevant child is likely to suffer significant harm attributable to conduct of the respondent if an order under this section containing one or more of the provisions mentioned in subsection (3) is not made, the court shall make the order unless it appears to it that—

(a) the respondent or any relevant child is likely to suffer significant harm if the order is made; and

(b) the harm likely to be suffered by the respondent or child in that event is as great as, or greater than, the harm attributable to conduct of the respondent which is likely to be suffered by the applicant or child if the order is not made.

(8) The court may exercise its powers under subsection (5) in any case where it considers that in all the circumstances it is just and reasonable to do so.

(9) An order under this section—

(a) may not be made after the death of either of the parties mentioned in subsection (1); and

(b) except in the case of an order made by virtue of subsection (5)(a), ceases to have effect on the death of either party.

(10) An order under this section may, in so far as it has continuing effect, be made for a specified period, until the occurrence of a specified event or until further order.

Definitions For "matrimonial home rights", see s 30(2) ante; for "the court"; see s 57(1), (2) post; for "relevant child", see s 62(2) post; for "associated person", see s 62(3)–(6) post; for "child", "dwelling-house", "harm" and "health", see s 63(1) post (and note also, in relation to "dwelling-house", s 63(4)); for "significant harm", see s 63(3) post.

References See paras 8.2, 8.9, 8.19, 8.26–8.29, 8.31.

---

34 Effect of order under s 33 where rights are charge on dwelling-house

(1) If a spouse's matrimonial home rights are a charge on the estate or interest of the other spouse or of trustees for the other spouse—

(a) an order under section 33 against the other spouse has, except so far as a contrary intention appears, the same effect against house. persons deriving title under the other spouse or under the trustees and affected by the charge, and

(b) sections 33(1), (3), (4) and (10) and 30(3) to (6) apply in relation to any person deriving title under the other spouse or under the trustees and affected by the charge as they apply in relation to the other spouse.

(2) The court may make an order under section 33 by virtue of subsection (1)(b) if it considers that in all the circumstances it is just and reasonable to do so.

Definitions For "matrimonial home rights, see s 30(2) ante; for "the court", see s 57(1), (2) post.
References See paras 7.9, 7.10.

35 One former spouse with no existing right to occupy

(1) This section applies if—

(a) one former spouse is entitled to occupy a dwelling-house by virtue of a beneficial estate or interest or contract, or by virtue of any enactment giving him the right to remain in occupation;

(b) the other former spouse is not so entitled; and

(c) the dwelling-house was at any time their matrimonial home or was at any time intended by them to be their matrimonial home.

(2) The former spouse not so entitled may apply to the court for an order under this section against the other former spouse ("the respondent").

(3) If the applicant is in occupation, an order under this section must contain provision—

(a) giving the applicant the right not to be evicted or excluded from the dwelling-house or any part of it by the respondent for the period specified in the order; and

(b) prohibiting the respondent from evicting or excluding the applicant during that period.

(4) If the applicant is not in occupation, an order under this section must contain provision—

(a) giving the applicant the right to enter into and occupy the dwelling-house for the period specified in the order; and

(b) requiring the respondent to permit the exercise of that right.

(5) An order under this section may also—

(a) regulate the occupation of the dwelling-house by either or both of the parties;

(b) prohibit, suspend or restrict the exercise by the respondent of his right to occupy the dwelling-house;

(c) require the respondent to leave the dwelling-house or part of the dwelling-house; or

(d) exclude the respondent from a defined area in which the dwelling-house is included.

(6) In deciding whether to make an order under this section containing provision of the kind mentioned in subsection (3) or (4) and (if so) in what manner, the court shall have regard to all the circumstances including—

(a) the housing needs and housing resources of each of the parties and of any relevant child;

(b) the financial resources of each of the parties;

(c) the likely effect of any order, or of any decision by the court not to exercise its powers under subsection (3) or (4), on the health, safety or well-being of the parties and of any relevant child;

(d) the conduct of the parties in relation to each other and otherwise;

(e) the length of time that has elapsed since the parties ceased to live together;

(f) the length of time that has elapsed since the marriage was dissolved or annulled; and

(g) the existence of any pending proceedings between the parties—

(i) for an order under section 23A or 24 of the Matrimonial Causes Act 1973 (property adjustment orders in connection with divorce proceedings etc);

(ii) for an order under paragraph 1(2)(d) or (e) of Schedule 1 to the Children Act 1989 (orders for financial relief against parents); or

(iii) relating to the legal or beneficial ownership of the dwelling-house.

(7) In deciding whether to exercise its power to include one or more of the provisions referred to in subsection (5) ("a subsection (5) provision") and (if so) in what manner, the court shall have regard to all the circumstances including the matters mentioned in subsection (6)(a) to (e).

(8) If the court decides to make an order under this section and it appears to it that, if the order does not include a subsection (5) provision, the applicant or any relevant child is likely to suffer significant harm attributable to conduct of the respondent, the court shall include the subsection (5) provision in the order unless it appears to the court that—

(a) the respondent or any relevant child is likely to suffer significant harm if the provision is included in the order; and

(b) the harm likely to be suffered by the respondent or child in that event is as great as or greater than the harm attributable to conduct of the respondent which is likely to be suffered by the applicant or child if the provision is not included.

(9) An order under this section—

(a) may not be made after the death of either of the former spouses; and

(b) ceases to have effect on the death of either of them.

(10) An order under this section must be limited so as to have effect for a specified period not exceeding six months, but may be extended on one or more occasions for a further specified period not exceeding six months.

(11) A former spouse who has an equitable interest in the dwelling-house or in the proceeds of sale of the dwelling-house but in whom there is not vested (whether solely or as joint tenant) a legal estate in fee simple or a legal term of years absolute in the dwelling-house is to be treated (but only for the purpose of determining whether he is eligible to apply under this section) as not being entitled to occupy the dwelling-house by virtue of that interest.

(12) Subsection (11) does not prejudice any right of such a former spouse to apply for an order under section 33.

(13) So long as an order under this section remains in force, subsections (3) to (6) of section 30 apply in relation to the applicant—

(a) as if he were the spouse entitled to occupy the dwelling-house by virtue of that section; and

(b) as if the respondent were the other spouse.

Definitions For "the court", see s 57(1), (2) post; for "relevant child", see s 62(2) post; for "child", "dwelling-house" and "health", see s 63(1) post (and note also, in relation to "dwelling-house", s 63(4)); for "significant harm", see s 63(3) post.

References See paras 8.3, 8.10, 8.12, 8.20, 8.21, 8.27–8.29, 8.32.

36 One cohabitant or former cohabitant with no existing right to occupy

(1) This section applies if—

(a) one cohabitant or former cohabitant is entitled to occupy a dwelling-house by virtue of a beneficial estate or interest or contract or by virtue of any enactment giving him the right to remain in occupation;

(b) the other cohabitant or former cohabitant is not so entitled; and

(c) that dwelling-house is the home in which they live together as husband and wife or a home in which they at any time so lived together or intended so to live together.

(2) The cohabitant or former cohabitant not so entitled may apply to the court for an order under this section against the other cohabitant or former cohabitant ("the respondent").

(3) If the applicant is in occupation, an order under this section must contain provision—

(a) giving the applicant the right not to be evicted or excluded from the dwelling-house or any part of it by the respondent for the period specified in the order; and

(b) prohibiting the respondent from evicting or excluding the applicant during that period.

(4) If the applicant is not in occupation, an order under this section must contain provision—

(a) giving the applicant the right to enter into and occupy the dwelling-house for the period specified in the order; and

(b) requiring the respondent to permit the exercise of that right.

(5) An order under this section may also—

(a) regulate the occupation of the dwelling-house by either or both of the parties;

(b) prohibit, suspend or restrict the exercise by the respondent of his right to occupy the dwelling-house;

(c) require the respondent to leave the dwelling-house or part of the dwelling-house; or

(d) exclude the respondent from a defined area in which the dwelling-house is included.

(6) In deciding whether to make an order under this section containing provision of the kind mentioned in subsection (3) or (4) and (if so) in what manner, the court shall have regard to all the circumstances including—

(a) the housing needs and housing-resources of each of the parties and of any relevant child;

(b) the financial resources of each of the parties;

(c) the likely effect of any order, or of any decision by the court not to exercise its powers under subsection (3) or (4), on the health, safety or well-being of the parties and of any relevant child;

(d) the conduct of the parties in relation to each other and otherwise;

(e) the nature of the parties' relationship;

(f) the length of time during which they have lived together as husband and wife;

(g) whether there are or have been any children who are children of both parties or for whom both parties have or have had parental responsibility;

(h) the length of time that has elapsed since the parties ceased to live together; and

(i) the existence of any pending proceedings between the parties—
(i) for an order under paragraph 1 (2)(d) or (e) of Schedule to the Children Act 1989 (orders for financial relief against parents); or
(ii) relating to the legal or beneficial ownership of the dwelling-house.

(7) In deciding whether to exercise its powers to include one or more of the provisions referred to in subsection (5) ("a subsection (5) provision") and (if so) in what manner, the court shall have regard to all the circumstances including—
(a) the matters mentioned in subsection (6)(a) to (d); and
(b) the questions mentioned in subsection (8).

(8) The questions are—
(a) whether the applicant or any relevant child is likely to suffer significant harm attributable to conduct of the respondent if the subsection (5) provision is not included in the order; and
(b) whether the harm likely to be suffered by the respondent or child if the provision is included is as great as or greater than the harm attributable to conduct of the respondent which is likely to be suffered by the applicant or child if the provision is not included.

(9) An order under this section—
(a) may not be made after the death of either of the parties; and
(b) ceases to have effect on the death of either of them.

(10) An order under this section must be limited so as to have effect for a specified period not exceeding six months, but may be extended on one occasion for a further specified period not exceeding six months.

(11) A person who has an equitable interest in the dwelling-house or in the proceeds of sale of the dwelling-house but in whom there is not vested (whether solely or as joint tenant) a legal estate in fee simple or a legal term of years absolute in the dwelling-house is to be treated (but only for the purpose of determining whether he is eligible to apply under this section) as not being entitled to occupy the dwelling-house by virtue of that interest.

(12) Subsection (11) does not prejudice any right of such a person to apply for an order under section 33.

(13) So long as the order remains in force, subsections (3) to (6) of section 30 apply in relation to the applicant—
(a) as if he were a spouse entitled to occupy the dwelling-house by virtue of that section; and
(b) as if the respondent were the other spouse.

Definitions For "the court", see s 57(1), (2) post; for "cohabitants", see s 62(1)(a) post; for "former cohabitants", see s 62(1)(b) post; for "relevant child", see s 62(2) post; for "child", "dwelling-house", "harm", "health" and "parental responsibility", see s 63(1) post (and note also, in relation to "dwelling-house", s 63(4)); for "significant harm", see s 63(3) post.
References See paras 8.4, 8.13–8.15, 8.22, 8.23, 8.27–8.29, 8.33.

37 Neither spouse entitled to occupy

(1) This section applies if—
(a) one spouse or former spouse and the other spouse or former spouse occupy a dwelling-house which is or was the matrimonial home; but
(b) neither of them is entitled to remain in occupation—
(i) by virtue of a beneficial estate or interest or contract; or
(ii) by virtue of any enactment giving him the right to remain in occupation.

(2) Either of the parties may apply to the court for an order against the other under this section.

(3) An order under this section may—
- (a) require the respondent to permit the applicant to enter and remain in the dwelling-house or part of the dwelling-house;
- (b) regulate the occupation of the dwelling-house by either or both of the spouses;
- (c) require the respondent to leave the dwelling-house or part of the dwelling-house; or
- (d) exclude the respondent from a defined area in which the dwelling-house is included.

(4) Subsections (6) and (7) of section 33 apply to the exercise by the court of its powers under this section as they apply to the exercise by the court of its powers under subsection (3) of that section.

(5) An order under this section must be limited so as to have effect for a specified period not exceeding six months, but may be extended on one or more occasions for a further specified period not exceeding six months.

Definitions For "the court", see s 57(1), (2) post; for "dwelling house", see s 63(1) post (and note also s 63(4)).
References See paras 8.6, 8.16, 8.24, 8.27–8.29, 8.32.

38 Neither cohabitant or former cohabitant entitled to occupy

(1) This section applies if—
- (a) one cohabitant or former cohabitant and the other cohabitant or former cohabitant occupy a dwelling-house which is the home in which they live or lived together as husband and wife; but
- (b) neither of them is entitled to remain in occupation—
  - (i) by virtue of a beneficial estate or interest or contract; or
  - (ii) by virtue of any enactment giving him the right to remain in occupation.

(2) Either of the parties may apply to the court for an order against the other under this section.

(3) An order under this section may—
- (a) require the respondent to permit the applicant to enter and remain in the dwelling-house or part of the dwelling-house;
- (b) regulate the occupation of the dwelling-house by either or both of the parties;
- (c) require the respondent to leave the dwelling-house or part of the dwelling-house; or
- (d) exclude the respondent from a defined area in which the dwelling-house is included.

(4) In deciding whether to exercise its powers to include one or more of the provisions referred to in subsection (3) ("a subsection (3) provision") and (if so) in what manner, the court shall have regard to all the circumstances including—
- (a) the housing needs and housing resources of each of the parties and of any relevant child;
- (b) the financial resources of each of the parties;
- (c) the likely effect of any order, or of any decision by the court not to exercise its powers under subsection (3), on the health, safety or well-being of the parties and of any relevant child;
- (d) the conduct of the parties in relation to each other and otherwise; and
- (e) the questions mentioned in subsection (5).

(5) The questions are—

(a) whether the applicant or any relevant child is likely to suffer significant harm attributable to conduct of the respondent if the subsection (3) provision is not included in the order; and

(b) whether the harm likely to be suffered by the respondent or child if the provision is included is as great as or greater than the harm attributable to conduct of the respondent which is likely to be suffered by the applicant or child if the provision is not included.

(6) An order under this section shall be limited so as to have effect for a specified period not exceeding six months, but may be extended on one occasion for a further specified period not exceeding six months.

Definitions For "the court", see s 57(1), (2) post; for "cohabitant", see s 62(1)(a) post; for "former cohabitant", see s 62(1)(b) post; for "relevant child", see s 62(2) post; for "child", "dwelling house", "harm" and "health", see s 63(1) post (and note also, in relation to "dwelling-house", s 63(4)); for "significant harm", see s 63(3) post.
References See paras 8.7, 8.17, 8.25, 8.27–8.29, 8.33.

39 Supplementary provisions

(1) In this Part an "occupation order" means an order under section 33, 35, 36, 37 or 38.

(2) An application for an occupation order may be made in other family proceedings or without any other family proceedings being instituted.

(3) If—

(a) an application for an occupation order is made under section 33, 35, 36, 37 or 38, and

(b) the court considers that it has no power to make the order under the section concerned, but that it has power to make an order under one of the other sections,

the court may make an order under that other section.

(4) The fact that a person has applied for an occupation order under sections 35 to 38, or that an occupation order has been made, does not affect the right of any person to claim a legal or equitable interest in any property in any subsequent proceedings (including subsequent proceedings under this Part).

Definitions For "the court", see s 57(1), (2) post; for "family proceedings", see s 63(1) post.
References See paras 14.3, 14.6.

40 Additional provisions that may be included in certain occupation orders

(1) The court may on, or at any time after, making an occupation order under section 33, 35 or 36—

(a) impose on either party obligations as to—

(i) the repair and maintenance of the dwelling-house; or

(ii) the discharge of rent, mortgage payments or other outgoings affecting the dwelling-house;

(b) order a party occupying the dwelling-house or any part of it (including a party who is entitled to do so by virtue of a beneficial estate or interest or contract or by virtue of any enactment giving him the right to remain in occupation) to make periodical payments to the other party in respect of the accommodation, if the other party would (but for the order) be entitled to occupy the dwelling-house by virtue of a beneficial estate or interest or contract or by virtue of any such enactment;

(c) grant either party possession or use of furniture or other contents of the dwelling-house;

(d) order either party to take reasonable care of any furniture or other contents of the dwelling-house;

(e) order either party to take reasonable steps to keep the dwelling-house and any furniture or other contents secure.

(2) In deciding whether and, if so, how to exercise its powers under this section, the court shall have regard to all the circumstances of the case including—

(a) the financial needs and financial resources of the parties; and

(b) the financial obligations which they have, or are likely to have in the foreseeable future, including financial obligations to each other and to any relevant child.

(3) An order under this section ceases to have effect when the occupation order to which it relates ceases to have effect.

Definitions For "occupation order", see s 39(1) ante; for "the court", see s 57(1), (2) post; for "relevant child", see s 62(2) post; for "child", "dwelling house" and "mortgage payments", see s 63(1) (and note also, in relation to "dwelling-house", s 63(4)).
References See paras 8.36, 8.37.

---

41 Additional considerations if parties are cohabitants or former cohabitants

(1) This section applies if the parties are cohabitants or former cohabitants.

(2) Where the court is required to consider the nature of the parties' relationship, it is to have regard to the fact that they have not given each other the commitment involved in marriage.

Definitions For "the court", see s 57(1), (2) post; for "cohabitants", see s 62(1)(a) post; for "former cohabitants", see s 62(1)(b) post.
Reference See para 8.22.

Non-molestation orders

42 Non-molestation orders

(1) In this Part a "non-molestation order" means an order containing either or both of the following provisions—

(a) provision prohibiting a person ("the respondent") from molesting another person who is associated with the respondent;

(b) provision prohibiting the respondent from molesting a relevant child.

(2) The court may make a non-molestation order—

(a) if an application for the order has been made (whether in other family proceedings or without any other family proceedings being instituted) by a person who is associated with the respondent; or

(b) if in any family proceedings to which the respondent is a party the court considers that the order should be made for the benefit of any other party to the proceedings or any relevant child even though no such application has been made.

(3) In subsection (2) "family proceedings" includes proceedings in which the court has made an emergency protection order under section 44 of the Children Act 1989 which includes an exclusion requirement (as defined in section 44A(3) of that Act).

(4) Where an agreement to marry is terminated, no application under subsection (2)(a) may be made by virtue of section 62(3)(e) by reference to that agreement after the end of the period of three years beginning with the day on which it is terminated.

(5) In deciding whether to exercise its powers under this section and, if so, in what manner, the court shall have regard to all the circumstances including the need to secure the health, safety and well-being—

- (a) of the applicant or, in a case falling within subsection (2)(b), the person for whose benefit the order would be made; and
- (b) of any relevant child.

(6) A non-molestation order may be expressed so as to refer to molestation in general, to particular acts of molestation, or to both.

(7) A non-molestation order may be made for a specified period or until further order.

(8) A non-molestation order which is made in other family proceedings ceases to have effect if those proceedings are withdrawn or dismissed.

Definitions For "the court", see s 57(1), (2) post; for "relevant child", see s 62(2) post; for "associated person", see s 62(3)–(6) post; for "child", "family proceedings" and "health", see s 63(1) post (and see also, in relation to "family proceedings", sub-s (3) above).
References See paras 9.2–9.4.

Further provisions relating to occupation and non-molestation orders

43 Leave of court required for applications by children under sixteen

(1) A child under the age of sixteen may not apply for an occupation order or a non-molestation order except with the leave of the court.

(2) The court may grant leave for the purposes of subsection (1) only if it is satisfied that the child has sufficient understanding to make the proposed application for the occupation order or non-molestation order.

Definitions For "occupation order", see s 39(1) ante; for "non-molestation order", see s 42(1) ante; for "the court", see s 57(1), (2) post.
Reference See para 14.5.

44 Evidence of agreement to marry

(1) Subject to subsection (2), the court shall not make an order under section 33 or 42 by virtue of section 62(3)(e) unless there is produced to it evidence in writing of the existence of the agreement to marry.

(2) Subsection (1) does not apply if the court is satisfied that the agreement to marry was evidenced by—

- (a) the gift of an engagement ring by one party to the agreement to the other in contemplation of their marriage, or
- (b) a ceremony entered into by the parties in the presence of one or more other persons assembled for the purpose of witnessing the ceremony.

Definition For "the court", see s 57(1), (2) post.
References See paras 6.17–6.20.

45 Ex parte orders

(1) The court may, in any case where it considers that it is just and convenient to do so, make an occupation order or a non-molestation order even though the respondent has not been given such notice of the proceedings as would otherwise be required by rules of court.

(2) In determining whether to exercise its powers under subsection (1), the court shall have regard to all the circumstances including—

(a) any risk of significant harm to the applicant or a relevant child, attributable to conduct of the respondent, if the order is not made immediately;

(b) whether it is likely that the applicant will be deterred or prevented from pursuing the application if an order is not made immediately; and

(c) whether there is reason to believe that the respondent is aware of the proceedings but is deliberately evading service and that the applicant or a relevant child will be seriously prejudiced by the delay involved—

(i) where the court is a magistrates' court, in effecting service of proceedings; or

(ii) in any other case, in effecting substituted service.

(3) If the court makes an order by virtue of subsection (1) it must afford the respondent an opportunity to make representations relating to the order as soon as just and convenient at a full hearing.

(4) If, at a full hearing, the court makes an occupation order ("the full order"), then—

(a) for the purposes of calculating the maximum period for which the full order may be made to have effect, the relevant section is to apply as if the period for which the full order will have effect began on the date on which the initial order first had effect; and

(b) the provisions of section 36(10) or 38(6) as to the extension of orders are to apply as if the full order and the initial order were a single order.

(5) In this section—

"full hearing" means a hearing of which notice has been given to all the parties in accordance with rules of court;

"initial order" means an occupation order made by virtue of subsection (1); and

"relevant section" means section 33(10), 35(10), 36(10), 37(5) or 38(6).

Definitions For "occupation order", see s 39(1) ante; for "non-molestation order", see s 42(1) ante; for "the court", see s 57(1), (2) post; for "relevant child", see s 62(2) post; for "child" and "harm", see s 63(1) post; for "significant harm", see s 63(3) post.
References See paras 11.2, 11.3.

---

46 Undertakings

(1) In any case where the court has power to make an occupation order or non-molestation order, the court may accept an undertaking from any party to the proceedings.

(2) No power of arrest may be attached to any undertaking given under subsection (1).

(3) The court shall not accept an undertaking under subsection (1) in any case where apart from this section a power of arrest would be attached to the order.

(4) An undertaking given to a court under subsection (1) is enforceable as if it were an order of the court.

(5) This section has effect without prejudice to the powers of the High Court and the county court apart from this section.

Definitions For "occupation order", see s 39(1) ante; for "non-molestation order", see s 42(1) ante; for "the court", see s 57(1), (2) post.
References See paras 14.8, 14.9.

---

47 Arrest for breach of order

(1) In this section "a relevant order" means an occupation order or a non-molestation order.

(2) If—
- (a) the court makes a relevant order; and
- (b) it appears to the court that the respondent has used or threatened violence against the applicant or a relevant child,

it shall attach a power of arrest to one or more provisions of the order unless satisfied that in all the circumstances of the case the applicant or child will be adequately protected without such a power of arrest.

(3) Subsection (2) does not apply in any case where the relevant order is made by virtue of section 45(1), but in such a case the court may attach a power of arrest to one or more provisions of the order if it appears to it—
- (a) that the respondent has used or threatened violence against the applicant or a relevant child; and
- (b) that there is a risk of significant harm to the applicant or child, attributable to conduct of the respondent, if the power of arrest is not attached to those provisions immediately.

(4) If, by virtue of subsection (3), the court attaches a power of arrest to any provisions of a relevant order, it may provide that the power of arrest is to have effect for a shorter period than the other provisions of the order.

(5) Any period specified for the purposes of subsection (4) may be extended by the court (on one or more occasions) on an application to vary or discharge the relevant order.

(6) If, by virtue of subsection (2) or (3), a power of arrest is attached to certain provisions of an order, a constable may arrest without warrant a person whom he has reasonable cause for suspecting to be in breach of any such provision.

(7) If a power of arrest is attached under subsection (2) or (3) to certain provisions of the order and the respondent is arrested under subsection (6)—
- (a) he must be brought before the relevant judicial authority within the period of 24 hours beginning at the time of his arrest; and
- (b) if the matter is not then disposed of forthwith, the relevant judicial authority before whom he is brought may remand him.

In reckoning for the purposes of this subsection any period of 24 hours, no account is to be taken of Christmas Day, Good Friday or any Sunday.

(8) If the court has made a relevant order but—
- (a) has not attached a power of arrest under subsection (2) or (3) to any provisions of the order, or
- (b) has attached that power only to certain provisions of the order,

then, if at any time the applicant considers that the respondent has failed to comply with the order, he may apply to the relevant judicial authority for the issue of a warrant for the arrest of the respondent.

(9) The relevant judicial authority shall not issue a warrant on an application under subsection (8) unless—

(a) the application is substantiated on oath; and

(b) the relevant judicial authority has reasonable grounds for believing that the respondent has failed to comply with the order.

(10) If a person is brought before a court by virtue of a warrant issued under subsection (9) and the court does not dispose of the matter forthwith, the court may remand him.

(11) Schedule 5 (which makes provision corresponding to that applying in magistrates' courts in civil cases under sections 128 and 129 of the Magistrates' Courts Act 1980) has effect in relation to the powers of the High Court and a county court to remand a person by virtue of this section.

(12) If a person remanded under this section is granted bail (whether in the High Court or a county court under Schedule 5 or in a magistrates' court under section 128 or 129 of the Magistrates' Courts Act 1980), he may be required by the relevant judicial authority to comply, before release on bail or later, with such requirements as appear to that authority to be necessary to secure that he does not interfere with witnesses or otherwise obstruct the course of justice.

Definitions For "occupation order", see s 39(1) ante; for "non-molestation order", see s 42(1) ante; for "the court", see s 57(1), (2) post; for "child", "harm" and "the relevant judicial authority", see s 63(1) post; for "relevant child", see s 62(2) post; for "significant harm", see s 63(3) post.
References See paras 10.1–10.6, 11.5.

48 Remand for medical examination and report

(1) If the relevant judicial authority has reason to consider that a medical report will be required, any power to remand a person under section 47(7)(b) or (10) may be exercised for the purpose of enabling a medical examination and report to be made.

(2) If such a power is so exercised, the adjournment must not be for more than 4 weeks at a time unless the relevant judicial authority remands the accused in custody.

(3) If the relevant judicial authority so remands the accused, the adjournment must not be for more than 3 weeks at a time.

(4) If there is reason to suspect that a person who has been arrested—

(a) under section 47(6), or

(b) under a warrant issued on an application made under section 47(8),

is suffering from mental illness or severe mental impairment, the relevant judicial authority has the same power to make an order under section 35 of the Mental Health Act 1983 (remand for report on accused's mental condition) as the Crown Court has under section 35 of the Act of 1983 in the case of an accused person within the meaning of that section.

Definition For "relevant judicial authority", see s 63(1) post.
Reference See para 10.7.

49 Variation and discharge of orders

(1) An occupation order or non-molestation order may be varied or discharged by the court on an application by—

(a) the respondent, or

(b) the person on whose application the order was made.

(2) In the case of a non-molestation order made by virtue of section 42(2)(b), the order may be varied or discharged by the court even though no such application has been made.

(3) If a spouse's matrimonial home rights are a charge on the estate or interest of the other spouse or of trustees for the other spouse, an order under section 33 against the other spouse may also be varied or discharged by the court on an application by any person deriving title under the other spouse or under the trustees and affected by the charge.

(4) If, by virtue of section 47(3), a power of arrest has been attached to certain provisions of an occupation order or non-molestation order, the court may vary or discharge the order under subsection (1) in so far as it confers a power of arrest (whether or not any application has been made to vary or discharge any other provision of the order).

Definitions For "matrimonial home rights", see s 30(2) ante; for "occupation order", see s 39(1) ante; for "non-molestation order", see s 42(1) ante; for "the court", see s 57(1), (2) post.
References See paras 8.34, 9.4.

Enforcement powers of magistrates' courts

50 Power of magistrates' court to supend execution of committal order

(1) If, under section 63(3) of the Magistrates' Courts Act 1980, a magistrates' court has power to commit a person to custody for breach of a relevant requirement, the court may by order direct that the execution of the order of committal is to be suspended for such period or on such terms and conditions as it may specify.

(2) In subsection (1) "a relevant requirement" means—

- (a) an occupation order or non-molestation order;
- (b) an exclusion requirement included by virtue of section 38A of the Children Act 1989 in an interim care order made under section 38 of that Act; or
- (c) an exclusion requirement included by virtue of section 44A of the Children Act 1989 in an emergency protection order under section 44 of that Act.

Definitions For "occupation order", see s 39(1) ante; for "non-molestation order", see s 42(1) ante.
References See para 10.9, App 5, Glossary.

51 Power of magistrates' court to order hospital admission or guardianship

(1) A magistrates' court has the same power to make a hospital order or guardianship order under section 37 of the Mental Health Act 1983 or an interim hospital order under section 38 of that Act in the case of a person suffering from mental illness or severe mental impairment who could otherwise be committed to custody for breach of a relevant requirement as a magistrates' court has under those sections in the case of a person convicted of an offence punishable on summary conviction with imprisonment.

(2) In subsection (1) "a relevant requirement" has the meaning given by section 50(2).

Reference See para 10.7.

Interim care orders and emergency protection orders

52 Amendment of Children Act 1989

Schedule 6 makes amendments of the provisions of the Children Act 1989 relating to interim care orders and emergency protection orders.

Definition For "cohabitants", see s 62(1)(a) post.
References See paras 12.1–12.16.

Transfer of tenancies

53 Transfer of certain tenancies

Schedule 7 makes provision in relation to the transfer of certain tenancies on divorce etc or on separation of cohabitants.

Definition For "cohabitants", see s 62(1)(a) post.
References See paras 13.1–13.14.

Dwelling-house subject to mortgage

54 Dwelling-house subject to mortgage

(1) In determining for the purposes of this Part whether a person is entitled to occupy a dwelling-house by virtue of an estate or interest, any right to possession of the dwelling-house conferred on a mortgagee of the dwelling-house under or by virtue of his mortgage is to be disregarded.

(2) Subsection (1) applies whether or not the mortgagee is in possession.

(3) Where a person ("A") is entitled to occupy a dwelling-house by virtue of an estate or interest, a connected person does not by virtue of—

(a) any matrimonial home rights conferred by section 30, or

(b) any rights conferred by an order under section 35 or 36,

have any larger right against the mortgagee to occupy the dwelling-house than A has by virtue of his estate or interest and of any contract with the mortgagee.

(4) Subsection (3) does not apply, in the case of matrimonial home rights, if under section 31 those rights are a charge, affecting the mortgagee, on the estate or interest mortgaged.

(5) In this section "connected person", in relation to any person, means that person's spouse, former spouse, cohabitant or former cohabitant.

Definitions For "matrimonial home rights", see s 30(2) ante; for "cohabitants", see s 62(1)(a) post; for "former cohabitants", see s 62(1)(b) post; for "dwelling-house", "mortgage" and "mortgagee", see s 63(1) post (and see also, in relation to "dwelling-house", s 63(4)).
Reference See para 7.17.

55 Actions by mortgagees: joining connected persons as parties

(1) This section applies if a mortgagee of land which consists of or includes a dwelling-house brings an action in any court for the enforcement of his security.

(2) A connected person who is not already a party to the action is entitled to be made a party in the circumstances mentioned in subsection (3).

(3) The circumstances are that—
   (a) the connected person is enabled by section 30(3) or (6) (or by section 30(3) or (6) as applied by section 35(13) or 36(13)), to meet the mortgagor's liabilities under the mortgage;
   (b) he has applied to the court before the action is finally disposed of in that court; and
   (c) the court sees no special reason against his being made a party to the action and is satisfied—
      (i) that he may be expected to make such payments or do such other things in or towards satisfaction of the mortgagor's liabilities or obligations as might affect the outcome of the proceedings; or
      (ii) that the expectation of it should be considered under section 36 of the Administration of Justice Act 1970.

(4) In this section "connected person" has the same meaning as in section 54.

Definitions For "dwelling-house", "mortgage", "mortgagee" and "mortgagor", see s 63(1) post (and note also, in relation to "dwelling-house", s 63(4)).
Reference See para 7.18.

56 Actions by mortgagees: service of notice on certain persons

(1) This section applies if a mortgagee of land which consists, or substantially consists, of a dwelling-house brings an action for the enforcement of his security, and at the relevant time there is—
   (a) in the case of unregistered land, a land charge of Class F registered against the person who is the estate owner at the relevant time or any person who, where the estate owner is a trustee, preceded him as trustee during the subsistence of the mortgage; or
   (b) in the case of registered land, a subsisting registration of—
      (i) a notice under section 31(10);
      (ii) a notice under section 2(8) of the Matrimonial Homes or
      (iii) a notice or caution under section 2(7) of the Matrimonial Homes Act 1967.

(2) If the person on whose behalf—
   (a) the land charge is registered, or
   (b) the notice or caution is entered,

is not a party to the action, the mortgagee must serve notice of the action on him.

(3) If—
   (a) an official search has been made on behalf of the mortgagee which would disclose any land charge of Class F, notice or caution within subsection (1)(a) or (b)
   (b) a certificate of the result of the search has been issued, and
   (c) the action is commenced within the priority period,

the relevant time is the date of the certificate.

(4) In any other case the relevant time is the time when the action is commenced.

(5) The priority period is, for both registered and unregistered land, the period for which, in accordance with section 11(5) and (6) of the Land Charges Act 1972, a certificate on an official search operates in favour of a purchaser.

Definitions For "dwelling-house", "mortgage" and "mortgagee", see s 63(1) post (and note also, in relation to "dwelling-house", s 63(4)).
Reference See para 7.18.

Jurisdiction and procedure etc

57 Jurisdiction of courts

(1) For the purposes of this Part "the court" means the High Court, a county court or a magistrates' court.

(2) Subsection (1) is subject to the provision made by or under the following provisions of this section, to section 59 and to any express provision as to the jurisdiction of any court made by any other provision of this Part.

(3) The Lord Chancellor may by order specify proceedings under this Part which may only be commenced in—

- (a) a specified level of court;
- (b) a court which falls within a specified class of court; or
- (c) a particular court determined in accordance with, or specified in, the order.

(4) The Lord Chancellor may by order specify circumstances in which specified proceedings under this Part may only be commenced in—

- (a) a specified level of court;
- (b) a court which falls within a specified class of court; or
- (c) a particular court determined in accordance with, or specified in, the order.

(5) The Lord Chancellor may by order provide that in specified circumstances the whole, or any specified part of any specified proceedings under this Part is to be transferred to—

- (a) a specified level of court;
- (b) a court which falls within a specified class of court; or
- (c) a particular court determined in accordance with, or specified in, the order.

(6) An order under subsection (5) may provide for the transfer to be made at any stage, or specified stage, of the proceedings and whether or not the proceedings, or any part of them, have already been transferred.

(7) An order under subsection (5) may make such provision as the Lord Chancellor thinks appropriate for excluding specified proceedings from the operation of section 38 or 39 of the Matrimonial and Family Proceedings Act 1984 (transfer of family proceedings) or any other enactment which would otherwise govern the transfer of those proceedings, or any part of them.

(8) For the purposes of subsections (3), (4) and (5), there are three levels of court—

- (a) the High Court;
- (b) any county court; and
- (c) any magistrates' court.

(9) The Lord Chancellor may by order make provision for the principal registry of the Family Division of the High Court to be treated as if it were a county court for specified purposes of this Part, or of any provision made under this Part.

(10) Any order under subsection (9) may make such provision as the Lord Chancellor thinks expedient for the purpose of applying (with or without modifications) provisions which apply in relation to the procedure in county courts to the principal registry when it acts as if it were a county court.

(11) In this section "specified" means specified by an order under this section.

References See paras 14.1, 14.2.

58 Contempt proceedings

The powers of the court in relation to contempt of court arising out of a person's failure to comply with an order under this Part may be exercised by the relevant judicial authority.

Definitions For "the court", see s 57(1), (2) ante; for "the relevant judicial authority", see s 63(1) post.
Reference See para 10.9.

59 Magistrates' courts

(1) A magistrates' court shall not be competent to entertain any application, or make any order, involving any disputed question as to a party's entitlement to occupy any property by virtue of a beneficial estate or interest or contract or by virtue of any enactment giving him the right to remain in occupation, unless it is unnecessary to determine the question in order to deal with the application or make the order.

(2) A magistrates' court may decline jurisdiction in any proceedings under this Part if it considers that the case can more conveniently be dealt with by another court.

(3) The powers of a magistrates' court under section 63(2) of the Magistrates' Courts Act 1980 to suspend or rescind orders shall not apply in relation to any order made under this Part.

Reference See para 14.1.

60 Provision for third parties to act on behalf of victims of domestic violence

(1) Rules of court may provide for a prescribed person, or any person in a prescribed category, ("a representative") to act on behalf of another in relation to proceedings to which this Part applies.

(2) Rules made under this section may, in particular, authorise a representative to apply for an occupation order or for a non-molestation order for which the person on whose behalf the representative is acting could have applied.

(3) Rules made under this section may prescribe—
- (a) conditions to be satisfied before a representative may make an application to the court on behalf of another; and
- (b) considerations to be taken into account by the court in determining whether, and if so how, to exercise any of its powers under this Part when a representative is acting on behalf of another.

(4) Any rules made under this section may be made so as to have effect for a specified period and may make consequential or transitional provision with respect to the expiry of the specified period.

(5) Any such rules may be replaced by further rules made under this section.

Definitions For "occupation order", see s 39(1) ante; for "non-molestation order", see s 42(1) ante; for "the court", see s 57(1), (2) ante.
References See paras 1.10, 14.4.

61 Appeals

(1) An appeal shall lie to the High Court against—

(a) the making by a magistrates' court of any order under this Part, or

(b) any refusal by a magistrates' court to make such an order,

but no appeal shall lie against any exercise by a magistrates' court of the power conferred by section 59(2).

(2) On an appeal under this section, the High Court may make such orders as may be necessary to give effect to its determination of the appeal.

(3) Where an order is made under subsection (2), the High Court may also make such incidental or consequential orders as appear to it to be just.

(4) Any order of the High Court made on an appeal under this section (other than one directing that an application be re-heard by a magistrates' court) shall, for the purposes—

(a) of the enforcement of the order, and

(b) of any power to vary, revive or discharge orders,

be treated as if it were an order of the magistrates' court from which the appeal was brought and not an order of the High Court.

(5) The Lord Chancellor may by order make provision as to the circumstances in which appeals may be made against decisions taken by courts on questions arising in connection with the transfer, or proposed transfer, of proceedings by virtue of any order under section 57(5).

(6) Except to the extent provided for in any order made under subsection (5), no appeal may be made against any decision of a kind mentioned in that subsection.

Reference See para 14.10.

General

62 Meaning of "cohabitants", "relevant child" and "associated persons"

(1) For the purposes of this Part—

(a) "cohabitants" are a man and a woman who, although not married to each other, are living together as husband and wife; and

(b) "former cohabitants" is to be read accordingly, but does not include cohabitants who have subsequently married each other.

(2) In this Part, "relevant child", in relation to any proceedings under this Part, means—

(a) any child who is living with or might reasonably be expected to live with either party to the proceedings;

(b) any child in relation to whom an order under the Adoption Act 1976 or the Children Act 1989 is in question in the proceedings; and

(c) any other child whose interests the court considers relevant.

(3) For the purposes of this Part, a person is associated with another person if—

(a) they are or have been married to each other;

(b) they are cohabitants or former cohabitants;

(c) they live or have lived in the same household, otherwise than merely by reason of one of them being the other's employee, tenant, lodger or boarder;

(d) they are relatives;

(e) they have agreed to marry one another (whether or not that agreement has been terminated);

(f) in relation to any child, they are both persons falling within subsection (4); or

(g) they are parties to the same family proceedings (other than proceedings under this Part).

(4) A person falls within this subsection in relation to a child if—

(a) he is a parent of the child; or

(b) he has or has had parental responsibility for the child.

(5) If a child has been adopted or has been freed for adoption by virtue of any of the enactments mentioned in section 16(1) of the Adoption Act 1976, two persons are also associated with each other for the purposes of this Part if—

(a) one is a natural parent of the child or a parent of such a natural parent; and

(b) the other is the child or any person—

(i) who has become a parent of the child by virtue of an adoption order or has applied for an adoption order, or

(ii) with whom the child has at any time been placed for adoption.

(6) A body corporate and another person are not, by virtue of subsection (3)(f) or (g), to be regarded for the purposes of this Part as associated with each other.

Definitions For "the court", see s 57(1), (2) ante; for "child", "family proceedings", "parental responsibility" and "relative", see s 63(1) post.
References See paras 6.1, 6.26; see also App 5 Glossary.

---

63 Interpretation of Part IV

(1) In this Part—

"adoption order" has the meaning given by section 72(1) of the Adoption Act 1976;

"associated", in relation to a person, is to be read with section 62(3) to (6);

"child" means a person under the age of eighteen years;

"cohabitant" and "former cohabitant" have the meaning given by section 62(1);

"the court" is to be read with section 57;

"development" means physical, intellectual, emotional, social or behavioural development;

"dwelling-house" includes (subject to subsection (4))—

(a) any building or part of a building which is occupied as a dwelling,

(b) any caravan, house-boat or structure which is occupied as a dwelling,

and any yard, garden, garage or outhouse belonging to it and occupied with it;

"family proceedings" means any proceedings—

(a) under the inherent jurisdiction of the High Court in relation to children; or

(b) under the enactments mentioned in subsection (2);

"harm"—

(a) in relation to a person who has reached the age of eighteen years, means ill-treatment or the impairment of health; and

(b) in relation to a child, means ill-treatment or the impairment of health or development;

"health" includes physical or mental health;

"ill-treatment" includes forms of ill-treatment which are not physical and, in relation to a child, includes sexual abuse;

"matrimonial home rights" has the meaning given by section 30;

"mortgage", "mortgagor" and "mortgagee" have the same meaning as in the Law of Property Act 1925;

"mortgage payments" includes any payments which, under the terms of the mortgage, the mortgagor is required to make to any person;

"non-molestation order" has the meaning given by section 42(1);

"occupation order" has the meaning given by section 39;

"parental responsibility" has the same meaning as in the Children Act 1989;

"relative", in relation to a person, means—

(a) the father, mother, stepfather, stepmother, son, daughter, stepson, stepdaughter, grandmother, grandfather, grandson or granddaughter of that person or of that person's spouse or former spouse, or

(b) the brother, sister, uncle, aunt, niece or nephew (whether of the full blood or of the half blood or by affinity) of that person or of that person's spouse or former spouse,

and includes, in relation to a person who is living or has lived with another person as husband and wife, any person who would fall within paragraph (a) or (b) if the parties were married to each other;

"relevant child", in relation to any proceedings under this Part, has the meaning given by section 62(2);

"the relevant judicial authority", in relation to any order under this Part, means—

(a) where the order was made by the High Court, a judge of that court;

(b) where the order was made by a county court, a judge or district judge of that or any other county court; or

(c) where the order was made by a magistrates' court, any magistrates' court.

(2) The enactments referred to in the definition of "family proceedings" are—

(a) Part II;

(b) this Part;

(c) the Matrimonial Causes Act 1973;

(d) the Adoption Act 1976;

(e) the Domestic Proceedings and Magistrates' Courts Act 1978;

(f) Part III of the Matrimonial and Family Proceedings Act 1984;

(g) Parts I, II and IV of the Children Act 1989;

(h) section 30 of the Human Fertilisation and Embryology Act 1990.

(3) Where the question of whether harm suffered by a child is significant turns on the child's health or development, his health or development shall be compared with that which could reasonably be expected of a similar child.

(4) For the purposes of sections 31, 32, 53 and 54 and such other provisions of this Part (if any) as may be prescribed, this Part is to have effect as if paragraph (b) of the definition of "dwelling-house" were omitted.

(5) It is hereby declared that this Part applies as between the parties to a marriage even though either of them is, or has at any time during the marriage been, married to more than one person.

Reference See App 5 Glossary.

PART V
SUPPLEMENTAL

64 Provision for separate representation for children

(1) The Lord Chancellor may by regulations provide for the separate representation of children in proceedings in England and Wales for which relate to any matter in respect of which a question has arisen, or may arise, under—

- (a) Part II;
- (b) Part IV;
- (c) the 1973 Act; or
- (d) the Domestic Proceedings and Magistrates' Courts Act 1978.

(2) The regulations may provide for such representation only in specified circumstances.

Reference See para 14.9.

65 Rules, regulations and orders

(1) Any power to make rules, orders or regulations which is conferred by this Act is exercisable by statutory instrument.

(2) Any statutory instrument made under this Act may—

- (a) contain such incidental, supplemental, consequential and transitional provision as the Lord Chancellor considers appropriate; and
- (b) make different provision for different purposes.

(3) Any statutory instrument containing an order, rules or regulations made under this Act, other than an order made under section 5(8) or 67(3), shall be subject to annulment by a resolution of either House of Parliament.

(4) No order shall be made under section 5(8) unless a draft of the order has been laid before, and approved by a resolution of each House of Parliament.

(5) This section does not apply to rules of court made, or any power to make rules of court, for the purposes of this Act.

Reference See para 15.1.

66 Consequential amendments, transitional provisions and repeals

(1) Schedule 8 makes minor and consequential amendments.

(2) Schedule 9 provides for the making of other modifications consequential on provisions of this Act, makes transitional provisions and provides for savings.

(3) Schedule 10 repeals certain enactments.

67 Short title, commencement and extent

(1) This Act may be cited as the Family Law Act 1996.

(2) Section 65 and this section come into force on the passing of this Act.

(3) The other provisions of this Act come into force on such day as the Lord Chancellor may by order appoint; and different days may be appointed for different purposes.

(4) This Act, other than section 17, extends only to England and Wales, except that—

(a) in Schedule 8—

(i) the amendments of section 38 of the Family Law Act 1986 extend also to Northern Ireland;

(ii) the amendments of the Judicial Proceedings (Regulation of Reports) Act 1926 extend also to Scotland; and

(iii) the amendments of the Maintenance Orders Act 1950, the Civil Jurisdiction and Judgments Act 1982, the Finance Act 1985 and sections 42 and 51 of the Family Law Act 1986 extend also to both Northern Ireland and Scotland; and

(b) in Schedule 10, the repeal of section 2(1)(b) of the Domestic and Appellate Proceedings (Restriction of Publicity) Act 1968 extends also to Scotland.

Reference See para 15.1.

SCHEDULES

SCHEDULE 1

Section 9(6)

ARRANGEMENTS FOR THE FUTURE

The first exemption

1. The circumstances referred to in section 9(7)(a) are that—

(a) the requirements of section 11 have been satisfied;

(b) the applicant has, during the period for reflection and consideration, taken such steps as are reasonably practicable to try to reach agreement about the parties' financial arrangements; and

(c) the applicant has made an application to the court for financial relief and has complied with all requirements of the court in relation to proceedings for financial relief but—

(i) the other party has delayed in complying with requirements of the court or has otherwise been obstructive; or

(ii) for reasons which are beyond the control of the applicant, or of the other party, the court has been prevented from obtaining the information which it requires to determine the financial position of the parties.

The second exemption

2. The circumstances referred to in section 9(7)(b) are that—

(a) the requirements of section 11 have been satisfied;

(b) the applicant has, during the period for reflection and consideration, taken such steps as are reasonably practicable to try to reach agreement about the parties' financial arrangements;

(c) because of

(i) the ill health or disability of the applicant, the other party or a child of the family (whether physical or mental), or

(ii) an injury suffered by the applicant, the other party or a child of the family,

the applicant has not been able to reach agreement with the other party about those arrangements and is unlikely to be able to do so in the foreseeable future; and

(d) a delay in making the order applied for under section 3—

(i) would be significantly detrimental to the welfare of any child of the family; or

(ii) would be seriously prejudicial to the applicant.

The third exemption

3. The circumstances referred to in section 9(7)(c) are that—
  (a) the requirements of section 11 have been satisfied;
  (b) the applicant has found it impossible to contact the other party; and
  (c) as a result, it has been impossible for the applicant to reach agreement with the other party about their financial arrangements.

The fourth exemption

4. The circumstances referred to in section 9(7)(d) are that—
  (a) the requirements of section 11 have been satisfied;
  (b) an occupation order or a non-molestation order is in force in favour of the applicant or a child of the family, made against the other party;
  (c) the applicant has, during the period for reflection and consideration, taken such steps as are reasonably practicable to try to reach agreement about the parties' financial arrangements;
  (d) the applicant has not been able to reach agreement with the other party about those arrangements and is unlikely to be able to do so in the foreseeable future; and
  (e) a delay in making the order applied for under section 3—
    (i) would be significantly detrimental to the welfare of any child of the family; or
    (ii) would be seriously prejudicial to the applicant.

Court orders and agreements

5.—(1) Section 9 is not to be read as requiring any order or agreement to have been carried into effect at the time when the court is considering whether arrangements for the future have been made by the parties.

(2) The fact that an appeal is pending against an order of the kind mentioned in section 9(2)(a) is to be disregarded.

Financial arrangements

6. In section 9 and this Schedule "financial arrangements" has the same meaning as in section 34(2) of the 1973 Act.

Negotiated agreements

7. In section 9(2)(b) "negotiated agreement" means a written agreement between the parties as to future arrangements—
  (a) which has been reached as the result of mediation or any other form of negotiation involving a third party; and
  (b) which satisfies such requirements as may be imposed by rules of court.

Declarations

8.—(1) Any declaration of a kind mentioned in section 9—
  (a) must be in a prescribed form;
  (b) must, in prescribed cases, be accompanied by such documents as may be prescribed; and
  (c) must, in prescribed cases, satisfy such other requirements as may be prescribed.

(2) The validity of a divorce order or separation order made by reference to such a declaration is not to be affected by any inaccuracy in the declaration.

Interpretation

9. In this Schedule—
  "financial relief" has such meaning as may be prescribed; and
  "prescribed" means prescribed by rules of court.

Definitions For "divorce order", see s 2(1)(a) ante; for "separation order", see s 2(1)(b) ante; for "period for reflection and consideration", see s 7(1), (2) ante; for "the 1973 Act", "child of the family", "the court" and "party", see s 24(1) ante; for "occupation order", see s 39(1) ante; for "non-molestation order", see s 42(1) ante.
References See paras 4.5–4.9.

SCHEDULE 2

Section 15

FINANCIAL PROVISION

Introductory

1. Part II of the 1973 Act (financial provision and property adjustment orders) is amended as follows.

The orders

2. For section 21 (definitions) substitute—

"21 Financial provision and property adjustment orders

(1) For the purposes of this Act, a financial provision order is—

(a) an order that a party must make in favour of another person such periodical payments, for such term, as may be specified (a "periodical payments order");

(b) an order that a party must, to the satisfaction of the court, secure in favour of another person such periodical payments, for such term, as may be specified (a "secured periodical payments order");

(c) an order that a party must make a payment in favour of another person of such lump sum or sums as may be specified (an "order for the payment of a lump sum").

(2) For the purposes of this Act, a property adjustment order is—

(a) an order that a party must transfer such of his or her property as may be specified in favour of the other party or a child of the family;

(b) an order that a settlement of such property of a party as may be specified must be made, to the satisfaction of the court, for the benefit of the other party and of the children of the family, or either or any of them;

(c) an order varying, for the benefit of the parties and of the children of the family, or either or any of them, any marriage settlement;

(d) an order extinguishing or reducing the interest of either of the parties under any marriage settlement.

(3) Subject to section 40 below, where an order of the court under this Part of this Act requires a party to make or secure a payment in favour of another person or to transfer property in favour of any person, that payment must be made or secured or that property transferred—

(a) if that other person is the other party to the marriage, to that other party; and

(b) if that other person is a child of the family, according to the terms of the order—

(i) to the child; or

(ii) to such other person as may be specified, for the benefit of that child.

(4) References in this section to the property of a party are references to any property to which that party is entitled either in possession or in reversion.

(5) Any power of the court under this Part of this Act to make such an order as is mentioned in subsection (2)(b) to (d) above is exercisable even though there are no children of the family.

(6) In this section—

"marriage settlement" means an ante-nuptial or post-nuptial settlement made on the parties (including one made by will or codicil);

"party" means a party to a marriage; and

"specified" means specified in the order in question.".

Financial provision: divorce and separation

3. Insert, before section 23—

"22A Financial provision orders: divorce and separation

(1) On an application made under this section, the court may at the appropriate time make one or more financial provision orders in favour of—

(a) a party to the marriage to which the application relates; or
(b) any of the children of the family.

(2) The "appropriate time" is any time—

(a) after a statement of marital breakdown has been received by the court and before any application for a divorce order or for a separation order is made to the court by reference to that statement;
(b) when an application for a divorce order or separation order has been made under section 3 of the 1996 Act and has not been withdrawn;
(c) when an application for a divorce order has been made under section 4 of the 1996 Act and has not been withdrawn;
(d) after a divorce order has been made;
(e) when a separation order is in force.

(3) The court may make—

(a) a combined order against the parties on one occasion,
(b) separate orders on different occasions,
(c) different orders in favour of different children,
(d) different orders from time to time in favour of the same child,

but may not make, in favour of the same party, more than one periodical payments order, or more than one order for payment of a lump sum, in relation to any marital proceedings, whether in the course of the proceedings or by reference to a divorce order or separation order made in the proceedings.

(4) If it would not otherwise be in a position to make a financial provision order in favour of a party or child of the family, the court may make an interim periodical payments order, an interim order for the payment of a lump sum or a series of such orders, in favour of that party or child.

(5) Any order for the payment of a lump sum made under this section may—

(a) provide for the payment of the lump sum by instalments of such amounts as may be specified in the order; and
(b) require the payment of the instalments to be secured to the satisfaction of the court.

(6) Nothing in subsection (5) above affects—

(a) the power of the court under this section to make an order for the payment of a lump sum; or
(b) the provisions of this Part of this Act as to the beginning of the term specified in any periodical payments order or secured periodical payments order.

(7) Subsection (8) below applies where the court—

(a) makes an order under this section ("the main order") for the payment of a lump sum; and
(b) directs—
    (i) that payment of that sum, or any part of it, is to be deferred; or
    (ii) that that sum, or any part of it, is to be paid by instalments.

(8) In such a case, the court may, on or at any time after making the main order, make an order ("the order for interest") for the amount deferred, or the instalments, to carry interest (at such rate as may be specified in the order for interests)—

(a) from such date, not earlier than the date of the main order, as may be so specified;
(b) until the date when the payment is due.

(9) This section is to be read subject to any restrictions imposed by this Act and to section 19 of the 1996 Act.

22B Restrictions affecting section 22A

(1) No financial provision order, other than an interim affecting section order, may be made under section 22A above so as to take effect before the making of a divorce order or separation order in relation to the marriage, unless the court is satisfied—

(a) that the circumstances of the case are exceptional; and

(b) that it would be just and reasonable for the order to be so made.

(2) Except in the case of an interim periodical payments order, the court may not make a financial provision order under section 22A above at any time while the period for reflection and consideration is interrupted under section 7(8) of the 1996 Act.

(3) No financial provision order may be made under section 22A above by reference to the making of a statement of marital breakdown if, by virtue of section 5(3) or 7(9) of the 1996 Act (lapse of divorce or separation process), it has ceased to be possible—

(a) for an application to be made by reference to that statement; or

(b) for an order to be made on such an application.

(4) No financial provision order may be made under section 22A after a divorce order has been made, or while a separation order is in force, except—

(a) in response to an application made before the divorce order or separation order was made; or

(b) on a subsequent application made with the leave of the court.

(5) In this section, "period for reflection and consideration" means the period fixed by section 7 of the 1996 Act.".

Financial provision: nullity of marriage

4. For section 23 substitute—

"23 Financial provision orders: nullity

(1) On or after granting a decree of nullity of marriage (whether before or after the decree is made absolute), the court may, on an application made under this section, make one or more financial provision orders in favour of—

(a) either party to the marriage; or

(b) any child of the family.

(2) Before granting a decree in any proceedings for nullity of marriage, the court may make against either or each of the parties to the marriage—

(a) an interim periodical payments order, an interim order for the payment of a lump sum, or a series of such orders, in favour of the other party;

(b) an interim periodical payments order, an interim order for the payment of a lump sum, a series of such orders or any one or more other financial provision orders in favour of each child of the family.

(3) Where any such proceedings are dismissed, the court may (either immediately or within a reasonable period after the dismissal) make any one or more financial provision orders in favour of each child of the family.

(4) An order under this section that a party to a marriage must pay a lump sum to the other party may be made for the purpose of enabling that other party to meet any liabilities or expenses reasonably incurred by him or her in maintaining himself or herself or any child of the family before making an application for an order under this section in his or her favour.

(5) An order under this section for the payment of a lump sum to or for the benefit of a child of the family may be made for the purpose of enabling any liabilities or expenses reasonably incurred by or for the benefit of that child before the making of an application for an order under this section in his favour to be met.

(6) An order under this section for the payment of a lump sum may
(a) provide for the payment of that sum by instalments of such amount as may be specified in the order; and
(b) require the payment of the instalments to be secured to the satisfaction of the court.

(7) Nothing in subsections (4) to (6) above affects—
(a) the power under subsection (1) above to make an order for the payment of a lump sum; or
(b) the provisions of this Act as to the beginning of the term specified in any periodical payments order or secured periodical payments order.

(8) The powers of the court under this section to make one or more financial provision orders are exercisable against each party to the marriage by the making of—
(a) a combined order on one occasion, or
(b) separate orders on different occasions,
but the court may not make more than one periodical payments order, or more than one order for payment of a lump sum, in favour of the same party.

(9) The powers of the court under this section so far as they consist in power to make one or more orders in favour of the children of the family—
(a) may be exercised differently in favour of different children; and
(b) except in the case of the power conferred by subsection (3) above, may be exercised from time to time in favour of the same child; and
(c) in the case of the power conferred by that subsection, if it is exercised by the making of a financial provision order of any kind in favour of a child, shall include power to make, from time to time, further financial provision orders of that or any other kind in favour of that child.

(10) Where an order is made under subsection (1) above in favour of a party to the marriage on or after the granting of a decree of nullity of marriage, neither the order nor any settlement made in pursuance of the order takes effect unless the decree has been made absolute.

(11) Subsection (10) above does not affect the power to give a direction under section 30 below for the settlement of an instrument by conveyancing counsel.

(12) Where the court—
(a) makes an order under this section ("the main order") for the payment of a lump sum; and
(b) directs—
(i) that payment of that sum or any part of it is to be deferred; or
(ii) that that sum or any part of it is to be paid by instalments,
it may, on or at any time after making the main order, make an order ("the order for interest") for the amount deferred or the instalments to carry interest at such rate as may be specified by the order for interest from such date, not earlier than the date of the main order, as may be so specified, until the date when payment of it is due.

(13) This section is to be read subject to any restrictions imposed by this Act."

Property adjustment orders: divorce and separation

5. Insert, before section 24—

"23A Property adjustment orders: divorce and separation

(1) On an application made under this section, the court may, at any time mentioned in section 22A(2) above, make one or more property adjustment orders.

(2) If the court makes, in favour of the same party to the marriage, more than one property adjustment order in relation to any marital proceedings, whether in the course of the proceedings or by reference to a divorce order or separation order made in the proceedings, each order must fall within a different paragraph of section 21(2) above.

(3) The court shall exercise its powers under this section, so far as is practicable, by making on one occasion all such provision as can be made by way of one or more property adjustment orders in relation to the marriage as it thinks fit.

(4) Subsection (3) above does not affect section 31 or 31A below.

(5) This section is to be read subject to any restrictions imposed by this Act and to section 19 of the 1996 Act.

23B Restrictions affecting section 23A

(1) No property adjustment order may be made under section 23A above so as to take effect before the making of a divorce order or separation order in relation to the marriage unless the court is satisfied—

(a) that the circumstances of the case are exceptional; and

(b) that it would be just and reasonable for the order to be so made.

(2) The court may not make a property adjustment order under section 23A above at any time while the period for reflection and consideration is interrupted under section 7(8) of the 1996 Act.

(3) No property adjustment order may be made under section 23A above by virtue of the making of a statement of marital breakdown if, by virtue of section 5(3) or 7(5) of the 1996 Act (lapse of divorce or separation process), it has ceased to be possible—

(a) for an application to be made by reference to that statement; or

(b) for an order to be made on such an application.

(4) No property adjustment order may be made under section 23A above after a divorce order has been made, or while a separation order is in force, except—

(a) in response to an application made before the divorce order or separation order was made; or

(b) on a subsequent application made with the leave of the court.

(5) In this section, "period for reflection and consideration" means the period fixed by section 7 of the 1996 Act.".

Property adjustment orders: nullity

6. For section 24, substitute—

"24 Property adjustment orders: nullity of marriage

(1) On or after granting a decree of nullity of marriage (whether before or after the decree is made absolute), the court may, on an application made under this section, make one or more property adjustment orders in relation to the marriage.

(2) The court shall exercise its powers under this section, so far as is practicable, by making on one occasion all such provision as can be made by way of one or more property adjustment orders in relation to the marriage as it thinks fit.

(3) Subsection (2) above does not affect section 31 or 31A below.

(4) Where a property adjustment order is made under this section on or after the granting of a decree of nullity of marriage, neither the order nor any settlement made in pursuance of the order is to take effect unless the decree has been made absolute.

(5) That does not affect the power to give a direction under section 30 below for the settlement of an instrument by conveyancing counsel.

(6) This section is to be read subject to any restrictions imposed by this Act."

Period of secured and unsecured payments orders

7.—(1) In section 28(1) (duration of a continuing financial provision order in favour of a party to a marriage), for paragraphs (a) and (b) substitute—

"(a) a term specified in the order which is to begin before the making of the order shall begin no earlier—

(i) where the order is made by virtue of section 22A(2)(a) or (b) above, unless sub-paragraph (ii) below applies, than the beginning of the day on which the statement of marital breakdown in question was received by the court;

(ii) where the order is made by virtue of section 22A(2)(b) above and the application for the divorce order was made following cancellation of an order preventing divorce under section 10 of the 1996 Act, than the date of the making of that application;

(iii) where the order is made by virtue of section 22A(2)(c) above, than the date of the making of the application for the divorce order; or

(iv) in any other case, than the date of the making of the application on which the order is made;

(b) a term specified in a periodical payments order or secured periodical payments order shall be so defined as not to extend beyond—

(i) in the case of a periodical payments order, the death of the party by whom the payments are to be made; or

(ii) in either case, the death of the party in whose favour the order was made or the remarriage of that party following the making of a divorce order or decree of nullity.".

(2) In section 29 (duration of continuing financial provision order in favour of a child of the family) insert after subsection (1)—

"(1A) The term specified in a periodical payments order or secured periodical payments order made in favour of a child shall be such term as the court thinks fit.

(1B) If that term is to begin before the making of the order, it may do so no earlier than—

(a) in the case of an order made by virtue of section 22A(2)(a) or (b) above, except where paragraph (b) below applies, the beginning of the day on which the statement of marital breakdown in question was received by the court;

(b) in the case of an order made by virtue of section 22A(2)(b) above where the application for the divorce order was made following cancellation of an order preventing divorce under section 10 of the 1996 Act, the date of the making of that application;

(c) in the case of an order made by virtue of section 22A(2)(c) above, the date of the making of the application for the divorce order; or

(d) in any other case, the date of the making of the application on which the order is made.".

Variations etc following reconciliations

8. Insert after section 31—

"31A Variation etc following reconciliations

(1) Where, at a time before the making of a divorce order—

(a) an order ("a paragraph (a) order") for the payment of a lump sum has been made under section 22A above in favour of a party,

(b) such an order has been made in favour of a child of the family but the payment has not yet been made, or

(c) a property adjustment order ("a paragraph (c) order") has been made under section 23A above,

the court may, on an application made jointly by the parties to the marriage, vary or discharge the order.

(2) Where the court varies or discharges a paragraph (a) order, it may order the repayment of an amount equal to the whole or any part of the lump sum.

(3) Where the court varies or discharges a paragraph (c) order, it may (if the order has taken effect)—

(a) order any person to whom property was transferred in pursuance of the paragraph (c) order to transfer—

(i) the whole or any part of that property, or

(ii) the whole or any part of any property appearing to the court to represent that property,

in favour of a party to the marriage or a child of the family; or

(b) vary any settlement to which the order relates in favour of any person or extinguish or reduce any person's interest under that settlement.

(4) Where the court acts under subsection (3) it may make such supplemental provision (including a further property adjustment order or an order for the payment of a lump sum) as it thinks appropriate in consequence of any transfer, variation, extinguishment or reduction to be made under paragraph (a) or (b) of that subsection.

(5) Sections 24A and 30 above apply for the purposes of this section as they apply where the court makes a property adjustment order under section 23A or 24 above.

(6) The court shall not make an order under subsection (2), (3) or (4) above unless it appears to it that there has been a reconciliation between the parties to the marriage.

(7) The court shall also not make an order under subsection (3) or (4) above unless it appears to it that the order will not prejudice the interests of—

(a) any child of the family; or

(b) any person who has acquired any right or interest in consequence of the paragraph (c) order and is not a party to the marriage or a child of the family.".

Definitions In the Matrimonial Causes Act 1973, for "child", "child of the family", "statement of marital breakdown", "the court" and "the 1996 Act", see s 52(1) thereof, as amended by s 66(1) ante, Sch 8, para 24 post; as to "financial provision order" and for "periodical payments order", "secured periodical payments order" and "order for the payment of a lump sum", see s 21(1) thereof, as substituted by para 2 above.
References See paras 4.21–4.34.

SCHEDULE 3

Section 19(5)

STAY OF PROCEEDINGS

Introductory

1. Schedule 1 to the Domicile and Matrimonial Proceedings Act 1973 (which relates to the staying of matrimonial proceedings) is amended as follows.

Interpretation

2. In paragraph 1, for "The following five paragraphs" substitute "Paragraphs 2 to 6 below".

3. For paragraph 2 substitute—

"2.—(1) "Matrimonial proceedings" means—

(a) marital proceedings;

(b) proceedings for nullity of marriage;

(c) proceedings for a declaration as to the validity of a marriage of the petitioner; or

(d) proceedings for a declaration as to the subsistence of such a marriage.

(2) "Marital proceedings" has the meaning given by section 20 of the Family Law Act 1996.

(3) "Divorce proceedings" means marital proceedings that are divorce proceedings by virtue of that section."

4. Insert, after paragraph 4—

"4A.—(1)"Statement of marital breakdown" has the same meaning as in the Family Law Act 1996.

(2) "Relevant statement" in relation to any marital proceedings, means—

(a) the statement of marital breakdown with which the proceedings commenced; or

(b) if the proceedings are for the conversion of a separation order into a divorce order under section 4 of the Family Law Act 1996, the statement of marital breakdown by reference to which the separation order was made.".

Duty to furnish particulars of concurrent proceedings

5. For paragraph 7 substitute—

"7.—(1) While marital proceedings are pending in the court with respect to a marriage, this paragraph applies—
- (a) to the party or parties to the marriage who made the relevant statement; and
- (b) in prescribed circumstances where the statement was made by only one party, to the other party.

(2) While matrimonial proceedings of any other kind are pending in the court with respect to a marriage and the trial or first trial in those proceedings has not begun, this paragraph applies—
- (a) to the petitioner; and
- (b) if the respondent has included a prayer for relief in his answer, to the respondent.

(3) A person to whom this paragraph applies must give prescribed information about any proceedings which—
- (a) he knows to be continuing in another jurisdiction; and
- (b) are in respect of the marriage or capable of affecting its validity or subsistence.

(4) The information must be given in such manner, to such persons and on such occasions as may be prescribed.".

Obligatory stays in divorce cases

6.—(1) Paragraph 8 is amended as follows.

(2) For the words before paragraph (a) of sub-paragraph (1) substitute—

"(1) This paragraph applies where divorce proceedings are continuing in the court with respect to a marriage.

(2) Where it appears to the court, on the application of a party to the marriage—".

(3) In sub-paragraph (1), in the words after paragraph (d), for "proceedings" substitute "divorce proceedings".

(4) For sub-paragraph (2) substitute—

"(3) The effect of such an order is that, while it is in force—
- (a) no application for a divorce order in relation to the marriage may be made either by reference to the relevant statement or by reference to any subsequent statement of marital breakdown; and
- (b) if such an application has been made, no divorce order may be made on that application.".

Discretionary stays

7.—(1) Paragraph 9 is amended as follows.

(2) For sub-paragraph (1), substitute—

"(1) Sub-paragraph (1A) below applies where—
- (a) marital proceedings are continuing in the court; or
- (b) matrimonial proceedings of any other kind are continuing in the court, if the trial or first trial in the proceedings has not begun.

(1A) The court may make an order staying the proceedings if it appears to the court—
- (a) that proceedings in respect of the marriage, or capable of affecting its validity or subsistence, are continuing in another jurisdiction; and
- (b) that the balance of fairness (including convenience) as between the parties to the marriage is such that it is appropriate for proceedings in that jurisdiction to be disposed of before further steps are taken in the proceedings to which the order relates.".

(3) For sub-paragraph (3) substitute—

"(3) Where an application for a stay is pending under paragraph 8 above, the court shall not make an order under sub-paragraph (1A) staying marital proceedings in relation to the marriage.".

(4) In sub-paragraph 4, after "pending in the court," insert "other than marital proceedings,".

(5) After sub-paragraph (4), insert—

"(5) The effect of an order under sub-paragraph (1A) for a stay of marital proceedings is that, while it is in force—

(a) no application for a divorce order or separation order in relation to the marriage may be made either by reference to the relevant statement or by reference to any subsequent statement of marital breakdown; and

(b) if such an application has been made, no divorce order or separation order shall be made on that application.".

Discharge of orders

8. In paragraph 10, for sub-paragraph (2), substitute—

"(1A) Where the court discharges an order staying any proceedings, it may direct that the whole or a specified part of any period while the order has been in force—

(a) is not to count towards any period specified in section 5(3) or 7(9) of the Family Law Act 1996; or

(b) is to count towards any such period only for specified purposes.

(2) Where the court discharges an order under paragraph 8 above, it shall not again make such an order in relation to the marriage except in a case where the obligation to do so arises under that paragraph following receipt by the court of a statement of marital breakdown after the discharge of the order.".

Ancillary matters

9.—(1) Paragraph 11 is amended as follows.

(2) For sub-paragraph (1) substitute—

"(1) Sub-paragraphs (2) and (3) below apply where a stay of marital proceedings or proceedings for nullity of marriage—

(a) has been imposed by reference to proceedings in a related jurisdiction for divorce, separation or nullity of marriage, and

(b) is in force.

(1A) In this paragraph—

"lump sum order", in relation to a stay, means an order—

(a) under section 22A or 23, 31 or 31A of the Matrimonial Causes Act 1973 which is an order for the payment of a lump sum for the purposes of Part II of that Act, or

(b) made in any equivalent circumstances under Schedule 1 to the Children Act 1989 and of a kind mentioned in paragraph 1(2)(a) or (b) of that Schedule,

so far as it satisfies the condition mentioned in sub-paragraph (1C) below;

"the other proceedings", in relation to a stay, means the proceedings in another jurisdiction by reference to which the stay was imposed;

"relevant order", in relation to a stay, means—

(a) any financial provision order (including an interim order), other than a lump sum order;

(b) any order made in equivalent circumstances under Schedule 1 to the Children Act 1989 and of a kind mentioned in paragraph 1(2)(a) or (b) of that Schedule;

(c) any section 8 order under the Act of 1989; and

(d) except for the purposes of sub-paragraph (3) below, any order restraining a person from removing a child out of England and Wales or out of the care of another person,

so far as it satisfies the condition mentioned in sub-paragraph (1C) below.

(1C) The condition is that the order is, or (apart from this paragraph) could be, made in connection with the proceedings to which the stay applies.".

(3) In sub-paragraph (2)—
(a) for "any proceedings are stayed" substitute "this paragraph applies in relation to a stay";
(b) in paragraph (a), and in the first place in paragraph (c), omit "in connection with the stayed proceedings"; and
(c) in paragraphs (b) and (c), for "made in connection with the stayed proceedings" substitute "already made".

(4) In sub-paragraph (3)—
(a) for "any proceedings are stayed" substitute "this paragraph applies in relation to a stay";
(b) in paragraph (a), for "made in connection with the stayed proceedings" substitute "already made";
(c) in paragraphs (b) and (c), omit "in connection with the stayed proceedings".

(5) In sub-paragraph (3A), for the words before "any order made" substitute—

"Where a secured periodical payments order within the meaning of the Matrimonial Causes Act 1973—
(a) has been made under section 22A(1)(b) or 23(1)(b) or (2)(b) of that Act, but
(b) ceases to have effect by virtue of sub-paragraph (2) or (3) above,".

(6) For sub-paragraph (4), substitute—

"(4) Nothing in sub-paragraphs (2) and (3) above affects any relevant order or lump sum order or any power to make such an order in so far as—
(a) where the stay applies to matrimonial proceedings other than marital proceedings, the order has been made or the power may be exercised following the receipt by the court of a statement of marital breakdown;
(b) where the stay is of marital proceedings, the order has been made or the power may be exercised in matrimonial proceedings of any other kind; or
(c) where the stay is of divorce proceedings only, the order has been made or the power may be exercised—
(i) in matrimonial proceedings which are not marital proceedings, or
(ii) in marital proceedings in which an application has been made for a separation order.".

(7) In sub-paragraph (5)(c), for the words from "in connection" onwards substitute "where a stay no longer applies".

Definitions In the Domicile and Matrimonial Proceedings Act 1973, Sch 1, for "the court", see s 5(1) of that Act; for "another jurisdiction", see para 3(1) of the said Sch 1; for "trial or first trial", see para 4(1) of that Schedule; as to when proceedings are continuing in the court, see para 4(2) of that Schedule; for "statement of marital breakdown", see, by virtue of para 4A(1) of that Schedule (as inserted by para 4 above), s 6(1) ante; as to when proceedings are continuing in another jurisdiction, see para 5 of that Schedule; for "prescribed", see para 6 of that Schedule.
Reference See para 3.34.

SCHEDULE 4

Section 32

PROVISIONS SUPPLEMENTARY TO SECTIONS 30 AND 31

Interpretation

1.—(1) In this Schedule—
(a) any reference to a solicitor includes a reference to a licensed conveyancer or a recognised body, and
(b) any reference to a person's solicitor includes a reference to a licensed conveyancer or recognised body acting for that person.

(2) In sub-paragraph (1)—

"licensed conveyancer" has the meaning given by section 11(2) of the Administration of Justice Act 1985;

"recognised body" means a body corporate for the time being recognised under section 9 (incorporated practices) or section 32 (provision of conveyancing by recognised bodies) of that Act.

Restriction on registration where spouse entitled to more than one charge

2. Where one spouse is entitled by virtue of section 31 to a registrable charge in respect of each of two or more dwelling-houses, only one of the charges to which that spouse is so entitled shall be registered under section 31(10) or under section 2 of the Land Charges Act 1972 at any one time, and if any of those charges is registered under either of those provisions the Chief Land Registrar, on being satisfied that any other of them is so registered, shall cancel the registration of the charge first registered.

Contract for sale of house affected by registered charge to include term requiring cancellation of registration before completion

3.—(1) Where one spouse is entitled by virtue of section 31 to a charge on an estate in a dwelling-house and the charge is registered under section 31(10) or section 2 of the Land Charges Act 1972, it shall be a term of any contract for the sale of that estate whereby the vendor agrees to give vacant possession of the dwelling-house on completion of the contract that the vendor will before such completion procure the cancellation of the registration of the charge at his expense.

(2) Sub-paragraph (1) shall not apply to any such contract made by a vendor who is entitled to sell the estate in the dwelling-house freed from any such charge.

(3) If, on the completion of such a contract as is referred to in sub-paragraph (1), there is delivered to the purchaser or his solicitor an application by the spouse entitled to the charge for the cancellation of the registration of that charge, the term of the contract for which sub-paragraph (1) provides shall be deemed to have been performed.

(4) This paragraph applies only if and so far as a contrary intention is not expressed in the contract.

(5) This paragraph shall apply to a contract for exchange as it applies to a contract for sale.

(6) This paragraph shall, with the necessary modifications, apply to a contract for the grant of a lease or underlease of a dwelling-house as it applies to a contract for the sale of an estate in a dwelling-house.

Cancellation of registration after termination of marriage, etc

4.—(1) Where a spouse's matrimonial home rights are a charge on an estate in the dwelling-house and the charge is registered under section 31(10) or under section 2 of the Land Charges Act 1972, the Chief Land Registrar shall, subject to sub-paragraph (2), cancel the registration of the charge if he is satisfied—

(a) by the production of a certificate or other sufficient evidence, that either spouse is dead, or

(b) by the production of an official copy of a decree or order of a court, that the marriage in question has been terminated otherwise than by death, or

(c) by the production of an order of the court, that the spouse's matrimonial home rights constituting the charge have been terminated by the order.

(2) Where—

(a) the marriage in question has been terminated by the death of the spouse entitled to an estate in the dwelling-house or otherwise than by death, and

(b) an order affecting the charge of the spouse not so entitled had been made under section 33(5),

then if, after the making of the order, registration of the charge was renewed or the charge registered in pursuance of sub-paragraph (3), the Chief Land Registrar shall not cancel the registration of the charge in accordance with sub-paragraph (1) unless he is also satisfied that the order has ceased to have effect.

(3) Where such an order has been made, then, for the purposes of sub-paragraph (2), the spouse entitled to the charge affected by the order may—

(a) if before the date of the order the charge was registered under section 31(10) or under section 2 of the Land Charges Act 1972, renew the registration of the charge, and

(b) if before the said date the charge was not so registered, register the charge under section 31(10) or under section 2 of the Land Charges Act 1972.

(4) Renewal of the registration of a charge in pursuance of sub-paragraph (3) shall be effected in such manner as may be prescribed, and an application for such renewal or for registration of a charge in pursuance of that sub-paragraph shall contain such particulars of any order affecting the charge made under section 33(5) as may be prescribed.

(5) The renewal in pursuance of sub-paragraph (3) of the registration of a charge shall not affect the priority of the charge.

(6) In this paragraph "prescribed" means prescribed by rules made under section 16 of the Land Charges Act 1972 or section 144 of the Land Registration Act 1925, as the circumstances of the case require.

Release of matrimonial home rights

5.—(1) A spouse entitled to matrimonial home rights may by a release in writing release those rights or release them as respects part only of the dwelling-house affected by them.

(2) Where a contract is made for the sale of an estate or interest in a dwelling-house, or for the grant of a lease or underlease of a dwelling-house, being (in either case) a dwelling-house affected by a charge registered under section 31(10) or under section 2 of the Land Charges Act 1972, then, without prejudice to sub-paragraph (1), the matrimonial home rights constituting the charge shall be deemed to have been released on the happening of whichever of the following events first occurs—

(a) the delivery to the purchaser or lessee, as the case may be, or his solicitor on completion of the contract of an application by the spouse entitled to the charge for the cancellation of the registration of the charge; or

(b) the lodging of such an application at Her Majesty's Land Registry.

Postponement of priority of charge

6. A spouse entitled by virtue of section 31 to a charge on an estate or interest may agree in writing that any other charge on, or interest in, that estate or interest shall rank in priority to the charge to which that spouse is so entitled.

Definitions For "matrimonial home rights", see s 30(2) ante; for "the court", see s 57(1), (2) ante; for "dwelling-house", see s 63(1), (4) ante.
References See paras 7.12–7.16.

SCHEDULE 5

Section 47(11)

POWERS OF HIGH COURT AND COUNTY COURT TO REMAND

Interpretation

1. In this Schedule "the court" means the High Court or a county court and includes—

(a) in relation to the High Court, a judge of that court, and

(b) in relation to a county court, a judge or district judge of that court.

Remand in custody or on bail

2.—(1) Where a court has power to remand a person under section 47, the court may—

(a) remand him in custody, that is to say, commit him to custody to be brought before the court at the end of the period of remand or at such earlier time as the court may require, or

(b) remand him on bail—

(i) by taking from him a recognizance (with or without sureties) conditioned as provided in sub-paragraph (3), or

(ii) by fixing the amount of the recognizances with a view to their being taken subsequently in accordance with paragraph 4 and in the meantime committing the person to custody in accordance with paragraph (a).

(2) Where a person is brought before the court after remand, the court may further remand him.

(3) Where a person is remanded on bail under sub-paragraph (1), the court may direct that his recognizance be conditioned for his appearance—

(a) before that court at the end of the period of remand, or

(b) at every time and place to which during the course of the proceedings the hearing may from time to time be adjourned.

(4) Where a recognizance is conditioned for a person's appearance in accordance with sub-paragraph (1)(b), the fixing of any time for him next to appear shall be deemed to be a remand; but nothing in this sub-paragraph or sub-paragraph (3) shall deprive the court of power at any subsequent hearing to remand him afresh.

(5) Subject to paragraph 3, the court shall not remand a person under this paragraph for a period exceeding 8 clear days, except that—

(a) if the court remands him on bail, it may remand him for a longer period if he and the other party consent, and

(b) if the court adjourns a case under section 48(1), the court may remand him for the period of the adjournment.

(6) Where the court has power under this paragraph to remand a person in custody it may, if the remand is for a period not exceeding 3 clear days, commit him to the custody of a constable.

Further remand

3.—(1) If the court is satisfied that any person who has been remanded under paragraph 2 is unable by reason of illness or accident to appear or be brought before the court at the expiration of the period for which he was remanded, the court may, in his absence, remand him for a further time; and paragraph 2(5) shall not apply.

(2) Notwithstanding anything in paragraph 2(1), the power of the court under sub-paragraph (1) to remand a person on bail for a further time may be exercised by enlarging his recognizance and those of any sureties for him to a later time.

(3) Where a person remanded on bail under paragraph 2 is bound to appear before the court at any time and the court has no power to remand him under sub-paragraph (1), the court may in his absence enlarge his recognizance and those of any sureties for him to a later time; and the enlargement of his recognizance shall be deemed to be a further remand.

Postponement of taking of recognizance

4. Where under paragraph 2(1)(b)(ii) the court fixes the amount in which the principal and his sureties, if any, are to be bound, the recognizance may thereafter be taken by such person as may be prescribed by rules of court, and the same consequences shall follow as if it had been entered into before the court.

Reference See para 10.6.

SCHEDULE 6

Section 52

AMENDMENTS OF CHILDREN ACT 1989

1. After section 38 of the Children Act 1989 insert—

"38A Power to include exclusion requirement in interim care order

(1) Where—

(a) on being satisfied that there are reasonable grounds for believing that the circumstances with respect to a child are as mentioned in section 31(2)(a) and (b)(i), the court makes an interim care order with respect to a child, and

(b) the conditions mentioned in subsection (2) are satisfied,

the court may include an exclusion requirement in the interim care order.

(2) The conditions are—

(a) that there is reasonable cause to believe that, if a person ("the relevant person") is excluded from a dwelling-house in which the child lives, the child will cease to suffer, or cease to be likely to suffer, significant harm, and

(b) that another person living in the dwelling-house (whether a parent of the child or some other person)—

(i) is able and willing to give to the child the care which it would be reasonable to expect a parent to give him, and

(ii) consents to the inclusion of the exclusion requirement.

(3) For the purposes of this section an exclusion requirement is any one or more of the following—

(a) a provision requiring the relevant person to leave a dwelling-house in which he is living with the child,

(b) a provision prohibiting the relevant person from entering a dwelling-house in which the child lives, and

(c) a provision excluding the relevant person from a defined area in which a dwelling-house in which the child lives is situated.

(4) The court may provide that the exclusion requirement is to have effect for a shorter period than the other provisions of the interim care order.

(5) Where the court makes an interim care order containing an exclusion requirement, the court may attach a power of arrest to the exclusion requirement.

(6) Where the court attaches a power of arrest to an exclusion requirement of an interim care order, it may provide that the power of arrest is to have effect for a shorter period than the exclusion requirement.

(7) Any period specified for the purposes of subsection (4) or (6) may be extended by the court (on one or more occasions) on an application to vary or discharge the interim care order.

(8) Where a power of arrest is attached to an exclusion requirement of an interim care order by virtue of subsection (5), a constable may arrest without warrant any person whom he has reasonable cause to believe to be in breach of the requirement.

(9) Sections 47(7), (11) and (12) and 48 of, and Schedule 5 to, the Family Law Act 1996 shall have effect in relation to a person arrested under subsection (8) of this section as they have effect in relation to a person arrested under section 47(6) of that Act.

(10) If, while an interim care order containing an exclusion requirement is in force, the local authority have removed the child from the dwelling-house from which the relevant person is excluded to other accommodation for a continuous period of more than 24 hours, the interim care order shall cease to have effect in so far as it imposes the exclusion requirement.

38B Undertakings relating to interim care orders

(1) In any case where the court has power to include an exclusion requirement in an interim care order, the court may accept an undertaking from the relevant person.

(2) No power of arrest may be attached to any undertaking given under subsection (1).

(3) An undertaking given to a court under subsection (1)—

(a) shall be enforceable as if it were an order of the court, and

(b) shall cease to have effect if, while it is in force, the local authority have removed the child from the dwelling house from which the relevant person is excluded to other accommodation for a continuous period of more than 24 hours.

(4) This section has effect without prejudice to the powers of the High Court and county court apart from this section.

(5) In this section "exclusion requirement" and "relevant person" have the same meaning as in section 38A.".

2. In section 39 of the Children Act 1989 (discharge and variation etc of care orders and supervision orders) after subsection (3) insert—

> "(3A) On the application of a person who is not entitled to apply for the order to be discharged, but who is a person to whom an exclusion requirement contained in the order applies, an interim care order may be varied or discharged by the court in so far as it imposes the exclusion requirement.
>
> (3B) Where a power of arrest has been attached to an exclusion requirement of an interim care order, the court may, on the application of any person entitled to apply for the discharge of the order so far as it imposes the exclusion requirement, vary or discharge the order in so far as it confers a power of arrest (whether or not any application has been made to vary or discharge any other provision of the order)."

3. After section 44 of the Children Act 1989 insert—

"44A Power to include exclusion requirement in emergency protection order

(1) Where—
- (a) on being satisfied as mentioned in section 44(1)(a), (b) emergency or (c), the court makes an emergency protection order protection order with respect to a child, and
- (b) the conditions mentioned in subsection (2) are satisfied,

the court may include an exclusion requirement in the emergency protection order.

(2) The conditions are—
- (a) that there is reasonable cause to believe that, if a person ("the relevant person") is excluded from a dwelling-house in which the child lives, then—
  - (i) in the case of an order made on the ground mentioned in section 44(1)(a), the child will not be likely to suffer significant harm, even though the child is not removed as mentioned in section 44(1)(a)(i) or does not remain as mentioned in section 44(1)(a)(ii), or
  - (ii) in the case of an order made on the ground mentioned in paragraph (b) or (c) of section 44(1), the enquiries referred to in that paragraph will cease to be frustrated, and
- (b) that another person living in the dwelling-house (whether a parent of the child or some other person)—
  - (i) is able and willing to give to the child the care which it would be reasonable to expect a parent to give him, and
  - (ii) consents to the inclusion of the exclusion requirement.

(3) For the purposes of this section an exclusion requirement is any one or more of the following—
- (a) a provision requiring the relevant person to leave a dwelling-house in which he is living with the child,
- (b) a provision prohibiting the relevant person from entering a dwelling-house in which the child lives, and
- (c) a provision excluding the relevant person from a defined area in which a dwelling-house in which the child lives is situated.

(4) The court may provide that the exclusion requirement is to have effect for a shorter period than the other provisions of the order.

(5) Where the court makes an emergency protection order containing an exclusion requirement, the court may attach a power of arrest to the exclusion requirement.

(6) Where the court attaches a power of arrest to an exclusion requirement of an emergency protection order, it may provide that the power of arrest is to have effect for a shorter period than the exclusion requirement.

(7) Any period specified for the purposes of subsection (4) or (6) may be extended by the court (on one or more occasions) on an application to vary or discharge the emergency protection order.

(8) Where a power of arrest is attached to an exclusion requirement of an emergency protection order by virtue of subsection (5), a constable may arrest without

warrant any person whom he has reasonable cause to believe to be in breach of the requirement.

(9) Sections 47(7), (11) and (12) and 48 of, and Schedule 5 to, the Family Law Act 1996 shall have effect in relation to a person arrested under subsection (8) of this section as they have effect in relation to a person arrested under section 47(6) of that Act.

(10) If, while an emergency protection order containing an exclusion requirement is in force, the applicant has removed the child from the dwelling-house from which the relevant person is excluded to other accommodation for a continuous period of more than 24 hours, the order shall cease to have effect in so far as it imposes the exclusion requirement.

44B Undertakings relating to emergency protection orders

(1) In any case where the court has power to include relating to an exclusion requirement in an emergency protection order, the emergency court may accept an undertaking from the relevant person.

(2) No power of arrest may be attached to any undertaking given under subsection (1).

(3) An undertaking given to a court under subsection (1)—

(a) shall be enforceable as if it were an order of the court, and

(b) shall cease to have effect if, while it is in force, the applicant has removed the child from the dwelling-house from which the relevant person is excluded to other accommodation for a continuous period of more than 24 hours.

(4) This section has effect without prejudice to the powers of the High Court and county court apart from this section.

(5) In this section "exclusion requirement" and "relevant person" have the same meaning as in section 44A.".

4. In section 45 of the Children Act 1989 (duration of emergency protection orders and other supplemental provisions), insert after subsection (8)—

"(8A) On the application of a person who is not entitled to apply for the order to be discharged, but who is a person to whom an exclusion requirement contained in the order applies, an emergency protection order may be varied or discharged by the court in so far as it imposes the exclusion requirement.

(8B) Where a power of arrest has been attached to an exclusion requirement of an emergency protection order, the court may, On the application of any person entitled to apply for the discharge of the order so far as it imposes the exclusion requirement, vary or discharge the order in so far as it confers a power of arrest (whether or not any application has been made to vary or discharge any other provision of the order).".

5. In section 105(1) of the Children Act 1989 (interpretation), after the definition of "domestic premises", insert—

"dwelling-house" includes—

(a) any building or part of a building which is occupied as a dwelling;

(b) any caravan, house-boat or structure which is occupied as a dwelling;

and any yard, garden, garage or outhouse belonging to it and occupied with it;".

Definitions In the Children Act 1989, for "harm", see s 31(9) thereof; as to whether harm suffered by a child is significant, see s 31(10) thereof; for "care order", see s 31(11) thereof; for "emergency protection order", see s 44(4) thereof; for "the court", see s 92(7) thereof; for "child", "dwelling-house" and "local authority", see s 105(1) thereof, as amended by para 5 above.
References See paras 12.4–12.14.

SCHEDULE 7

Section 53

TRANSFER OF CERTAIN TENANCIES ON DIVORCE ETC OR ON SEPARATION OF COHABITANTS

PART I

GENERAL

Interpretation

1. In this Schedule—

"cohabitant", except in paragraph 3, includes (where the context requires) former cohabitant;

"the court" does not include a magistrates' court,

"landlord" includes—

(a) any person from time to time deriving title under the original landlord; and

(b) in relation to any dwelling-house, any person other than the tenant who is, or (but for Part VII of the Rent Act 1977 or Part II of the Rent (Agriculture) Act 1976) would be, entitled to possession of the dwelling-house;

"Part II order" means an order under Part II of this Schedule;

"a relevant tenancy" means—

(a) a protected tenancy or statutory tenancy within the meaning of the Rent Act 1977;

(b) a statutory tenancy within the meaning of the Rent (Agriculture) Act 1976;

(c) a secure tenancy within the meaning of section 79 of the Housing Act 1985; or

(d) an assured tenancy or assured agricultural occupancy within the meaning of Part I of the Housing Act 1988;

"spouse", except in paragraph 2, includes (where the context requires) former spouse; and

"tenancy" includes sub-tenancy.

Cases in which the court may make an order

2.—(1) This paragraph applies if one spouse is entitled, either in his own right or jointly with the other spouse, to occupy a dwelling-house by virtue of a relevant tenancy.

(2) At any time when it has power to make a property adjustment order under section 23A (divorce or separation) or 24 (nullity) of the Matrimonial Causes Act 1973 with respect to the marriage, the court may make a Part II order.

3.—(1) This paragraph applies if one cohabitant is entitled, either in his own right or jointly with the other cohabitant, to occupy a dwelling-house by virtue of a relevant tenancy.

(2) If the cohabitants cease to live together as husband and wife, the court may make a Part II order.

4. The court shall not make a Part II order unless the dwelling-house is or was—

(a) in the case of spouses, a matrimonial home; or

(b) in the case of cohabitants, a home in which they lived together as husband and wife.

Matters to which the court must have regard

5. In determining whether to exercise its powers under Part II of this Schedule and, if so, in what manner, the court shall have regard to all the circumstances of the case including—

(a) the circumstances in which the tenancy was granted to either or both of the spouses or cohabitants or, as the case requires, the circumstances in which either or both of them became tenant under the tenancy;

(b) the matters mentioned in section 33(6)(a), (b) and (c) and, where the parties are cohabitants and only one of them is entitled to occupy the dwelling-house by virtue of the relevant tenancy, the further matters mentioned in section 36(6)(e), (f), (g) and (h); and

(c) the suitability of the parties as tenants.

PART II

ORDERS THAT MAY BE MADE

References to entitlement to occupy

6. References in this Part of this Schedule to a spouse or a cohabitant being entitled to occupy a dwelling-house by virtue of a relevant tenancy apply whether that entitlement is in his own right or jointly with the other spouse or cohabitant.

Protected, secure or assured tenancy or assured agricultural occupancy

7.—(1) If a spouse or cohabitant is entitled to occupy the dwelling-house by virtue of a protected tenancy within the meaning of the Rent Act 1977, a secure tenancy within the meaning of the Housing Act 1985 or an assured tenancy or assured agricultural occupancy within the meaning of Part I of the Housing Act 1988, the court may by order direct that, as from such date as may be specified in the order, there shall, by virtue of the order and without further assurance, be transferred to, and vested in, the other spouse or cohabitant—

(a) the estate or interest which the spouse or cohabitant so entitled had in the dwelling-house immediately before that date by virtue of the lease or agreement creating the tenancy and any assignment of that lease or agreement, with all rights, privileges and appurtenances attaching to that estate or interest but subject to all covenants, obligations, liabilities and incumbrances to which it is subject; and

(b) where the spouse or cohabitant so entitled is an assignee of such lease or agreement, the liability of that spouse or cohabitant under any covenant of indemnity by the assignee express or implied in the assignment of the lease or agreement to that spouse or cohabitant.

(2) If an order is made under this paragraph, any liability or obligation to which the spouse or cohabitant so entitled is subject under any covenant having reference to the dwelling-house in the lease or agreement, being a liability or obligation falling due to be discharged or performed on or after the date so specified, shall not be enforceable against that spouse or cohabitant.

(3) If the spouse so entitled is a successor within the meaning of Part IV of the Housing Act 1985, his former spouse or former cohabitant (or, if a separation order is in force, his spouse) shall be deemed also to be a successor within the meaning of that Part.

(4) If the spouse or cohabitant so entitled is for the purpose of section 17 of the Housing Act 1988 a successor in relation to the tenancy or occupancy, his former spouse or former cohabitant (or, if a separation order is in force, his spouse) is to be deemed to be a successor in relation to the tenancy or occupancy for the purposes of that section.

(5) If the transfer under sub-paragraph (1) is of an assured agricultural occupancy, then, for the purposes of Chapter III of Part I of the Housing Act 1988—

(a) the agricultural worker condition is fulfilled with respect to the dwelling-house while the spouse or cohabitant to whom the assured agricultural occupancy is transferred continues to be the occupier under that occupancy, and

(b) that condition is to be treated as so fulfilled by virtue of the same paragraph of Schedule 3 to the Housing Act 1988 as was applicable before the transfer.

(6) In this paragraph, references to a separation order being in force include references to there being a judicial separation in force.

Statutory tenancy within the meaning of the Rent Act 1977

8.—(1) This paragraph applies if the spouse or cohabitant is entitled to occupy the dwelling-house by virtue of a statutory tenancy within the meaning of the Rent Act 1977.

(2) The court may by order direct that, as from the date specified in the order—

(a) that spouse or cohabitant is to cease to be entitled to occupy the dwelling-house; and

(b) the other spouse or cohabitant is to be deemed to be the tenant or, as the case may be, the sole tenant under that statutory tenancy.

(3) The question whether the provisions of paragraphs 1 to 3, or (as the case may be) paragraphs 5 to 7 of Schedule 1 to the Rent Act 1977, as to the succession by the surviving spouse of a deceased tenant, or by a member of the deceased tenant's family, to the right to retain possession are capable of having effect in the event of the death of the person deemed by an order under this paragraph to be the tenant or sole tenant under the statutory tenancy is to be determined according as those provisions have or have not already had effect in relation to the statutory tenancy.

Statutory tenancy within the meaning of the Rent (Agriculture) Act 1976

9.—(1) This paragraph applies if the spouse or cohabitant is entitled to occupy the dwelling-house by virtue of a statutory tenancy within the meaning of the Rent (Agriculture) Act 1976.

(2) The court may by order direct that, as from such date as may be specified in the order—

(a) that spouse or cohabitant is to cease to be entitled to occupy the dwelling-house; and

(b) the other spouse or cohabitant is to be deemed to be the tenant or, as the case may be, the sole tenant under that statutory tenancy.

(3) A spouse or cohabitant who is deemed under this paragraph to be the tenant under a statutory tenancy is (within the meaning of that Act) a statutory tenant in his own right, or a statutory tenant by succession, according as the other spouse or cohabitant was a statutory tenant in his own right or a statutory tenant by succession.

PART III

SUPPLEMENTARY PROVISIONS

Compensation

10.—(1) If the court makes a Part II order, it may by the order direct the making of a payment by the spouse or cohabitant to whom the tenancy is transferred ("the transferee") to the other spouse or cohabitant ("the transferor").

(2) Without prejudice to that, the court may, on making an order by virtue of sub-paragraph (1) for the payment of a sum—

(a) direct that payment of that sum or any part of it is to be deferred until a specified date or until the occurrence of a specified event, or

(b) direct that that sum or any part of it is to be paid by instalments.

(3) Where an order has been made by virtue of sub-paragraph (1), the court may, on the application of the transferee or the transferor—

(a) exercise its powers under sub-paragraph (2), or

(b) vary any direction previously given under that sub-paragraph,

at any time before the sum whose payment is required by the order is paid in full.

(4) In deciding whether to exercise its powers under this paragraph and, if so, in what manner, the court shall have regard to all the circumstances including—

(a) the financial loss that would otherwise be suffered by the transferor as a result of the order;

(b) the financial needs and financial resources of the parties; and

(c) the financial obligations which the parties have, or are likely to have in the foreseeable future, including financial obligations to each other and to any relevant child.

(5) The court shall not give any direction under sub-paragraph (2) unless it appears to it that immediate payment of the sum required by the order would cause the transferee financial hardship which is greater than any financial hardship that would be caused to the transferor if the direction were given.

Liabilities and obligations in respect of the dwelling-house

11.—(1) If the court makes a Part II order, it may by the order direct that both spouses or cohabitants are to be jointly and severally liable to discharge or perform any or all of the liabilities and obligations in respect of the dwelling-house (whether arising under the tenancy or otherwise) which—

(a) have at the date of the order fallen due to be discharged or performed by one only of them; or

(b) but for the direction, would before the date specified as the date on which the order is to take effect fall due to be discharged or performed by one only of them.

(2) If the court gives such a direction, it may further direct that either spouse or cohabitant is to be liable to indemnify the other in whole or in part against any payment made or expenses incurred by the other in discharging or performing any such liability or obligation.

Date when order made between spouses is to take effect

12.—(1) In the case of a decree of nullity of marriage, the date specified in a Part II order as the date on which the order is to take effect must not be earlier than the date on which the decree is made absolute.

(2) In the case of divorce proceedings or separation proceedings, the date specified in a Part II order as the date on which the order is to take effect is to be determined as if the court were making a property adjustment order under section 23A of the Matrimonial Causes Act 1973 (regard being had to the restrictions imposed by section 23B of that Act).

Remarriage of either spouse

13.—(1) If after the making of a divorce order or the grant of a decree annulling a marriage either spouse remarries, that spouse is not entitled to apply, by reference to the making of that order or the grant of that decree, for a Part II order.

(2) For the avoidance of doubt it is hereby declared that the reference in sub-paragraph (1) to remarriage includes a reference to a marriage which is by law void or voidable.

Rules of court

14.—(1) Rules of court shall be made requiring the court, before it makes an order under this Schedule, to give the landlord of the dwelling-house to which the order will relate an opportunity of being heard.

(2) Rules of court may provide that an application for a Part II order by reference to an order or decree may not, without the leave of the court by which that order was made or decree was granted, be made after the expiration of such period from the order or grant as may be prescribed by the rules.

Saving for other provisions of Act

15.—(1) If a spouse is entitled to occupy a dwelling-house by virtue of a tenancy, this Schedule does not affect the operation of sections 30 and 31 in relation to the other spouse's matrimonial home rights.

(2) If a spouse or cohabitant is entitled to occupy a dwelling-house by virtue of a tenancy, the court's powers to make orders under this Schedule are additional to those conferred by sections 33, 35 and 36.

Definitions For "divorce order", see s 2(1)(a) ante; as to "separation proceedings", see s 20(3)(a) ante; as to "divorce proceedings", see s 20(3)(b) ante; for "the court", see s 57(1), (2) ante, and para 1 above; for "cohabitants", see s 62(1)(a) ante, and para 1 above; for "former cohabitants", see s 62(1)(b) ante and para 1 above; for "dwelling-house", see s 63(1), (4) ante.
References See paras 13.4–13.14.

SCHEDULE 8

Section 66(1)

MINOR AND CONSEQUENTIAL AMENDMENTS

PART I

AMENDMENTS CONNECTED WITH PART II

The Wills Act 1837 (c 26)

1. In section 18A(1) of the Wills Act 1837 (effect of dissolution or annulment of marriage on wills), for "a decree" substitute "an order or decree".

The Judicial Proceedings (Regulation of Reports) Act 1926 (c 61)

2. In section 1(1)(b) of the Judicial Proceedings (Regulation of Reports) Act 1926 (restriction on reporting) after "in relation to" insert "any proceedings under Part II of the Family Law Act 1996 or otherwise in relation to".

The Maintenance Orders Act 1950 (c 37)

3. In section 16 of the Maintenance Orders Act 1950 (orders to which Part II of that Act applies)—

(a) in subsection (2)(a)(i), for "23(1), (2) and (4)" substitute "22A, 23"; and

(b) in subsection (2)(c)(v), after "Matrimonial Causes Act 1973" insert "(as that Act had effect immediately before the passing of the Family Law Act 1996)".

The Matrimonial Causes Act 1973 (c 18)

4. The 1973 Act is amended as follows.

5. In section 8 (intervention of Queen's Proctor)—

(a) for "a petition for divorce" substitute "proceedings for a divorce order";

(b) in subsection (1)(b), omit "or before the decree nisi is made absolute"; and

(c) in subsection (2), for "a decree nisi in any proceedings for divorce" substitute "the making of a divorce order".

6. For section 15 (application of provisions relating to divorce to nullity proceedings) substitute—

"15 Decrees of nullity to be decrees nisi

Every decree of nullity of marriage shall in the first instance be a decree nisi and shall not be made absolute before the end of six weeks from its grant unless—

(a) the High Court by general order from time to time fixes a shorter period; or

(b) in any particular case, the court in which the proceedings are for the time being pending from time to time by special order fixes a shorter period than the period otherwise applicable for the time being by virtue of this section.

15A Intervention of Queen's Proctor

(1) In the case of a petition for nullity of marriage—

(a) the court may, if it thinks fit, direct all necessary papers in the matter to be sent to the Queen's Proctor, who shall under the directions of the Attorney-General instruct counsel to argue before the court any question in relation to the matter which the court considers it necessary or expedient to have fully argued;

(b) any person may at any time during the progress of the proceedings or before the decree nisi is made absolute give information to the Queen's Proctor on any matter material to the due decision of the case, and the Queen's Proctor may thereupon take such steps as the Attorney-General considers necessary or expedient.

(2) If the Queen's Proctor intervenes or shows cause against a decree nisi in any proceedings for nullity of marriage, the court may make such order as may be just as to the payment by other parties to the proceedings of the costs incurred by him in so doing or as to the payment by him of any costs incurred by any of those parties by reason of his so doing.

(3) Subsection (3) of section 8 above applies in relation to this section as it applies in relation to that section.

15B Proceedings after decree nisi: general powers of court

(1) Where a decree of nullity of marriage has been decree nisi: granted under this Act but not made absolute, then, without prejudice to section 15A above, any person (excluding a party to the proceedings other than the Queen's Proctor) may show cause why the decree should not be made absolute by reason of material facts not having been brought before the court; and in such a case the court may—

(a) notwithstanding anything in section 15 above (but subject to section 41 below) make the decree absolute; or
(b) rescind the decree; or
(c) require further inquiry; or
(d) otherwise deal with the case as it thinks fit.

(2) Where a decree of nullity of marriage has been granted under this Act and no application for it to be made absolute has been made by the party to whom it was granted, then, at any time after the expiration of three months from the earliest date on which that party could have made such an application, the party against whom it was granted may make an application to the court, and on that application the court may exercise any of the powers mentioned in paragraphs (a) to (d) of subsection (1) above.".

7. In section 19(4) (application of provisions relating to divorce to proceedings under section 19)—

(a) for "1(5), 8 and 9" substitute "15, 15A and 15B"; and
(b) for "divorce" in both places substitute "nullity of marriage".

8. In section 24A(1) (orders for sale of property), for "section 23 or 24 of this Act" substitute "any of sections 22A to 24 above".

9.—(1) Section 25 (matters to which the court is to have regard) is amended as follows.

(2) In subsection (1), for "section 23, 24 or 24A" substitute "any of sections 22A to 24A".

(3) In subsection (2)—

(a) for "section 23(1)(a), (b) or (c)" substitute "section 22A or 23 above to make a financial provision order in favour of a party to a marriage or the exercise of its powers under section 23A,";
(b) in paragraph (g), after "parties" insert ", whatever the nature of the conduct and whether it occurred during the marriage or after the separation of the parties or (as the case may be) dissolution or annulment of the marriage,"; and
(c) in paragraph (h), omit "in the case of proceedings for divorce or nullity of marriage,".

(4) In subsection (3), for "section 23(1)(d), (e) or (f), (2) or (4)" substitute "section 22A or 23 above to make a financial provision order in favour of a child of the family or the exercise of its powers under section 23A,".

(5) In subsection (4), for "section 23(1)(d), (e) or (f), (2) or (4), 24 or 24A" substitute "any of sections 22A to 24A".

(6) After subsection (4) insert—

"(5) In relation to any power of the court to make an interim periodical payments order or an interim order for the payment of a lump sum, the preceding provisions of this section, in imposing any obligation on the court with respect to the matters to which it is to have regard, shall not require the court to do anything which would cause such a delay as would, in the opinion of the court, be inappropriate having regard—

(a) to any immediate need for an interim order;
(b) to the matters in relation to which it is practicable for the court to inquire before making an interim order; and

(c) to the ability of the court to have regard to any matter and to make appropriate adjustments when subsequently making a financial provision order which is not interim.".

10.—(1) Section 25A (requirement to consider need to provide for "a clean break") is amended as follows.

(2) In subsection (1), for the words from the beginning to "the marriage" substitute—

"If the court decides to exercise any of its powers under any of sections 22A to 24A above in favour of a party to a marriage (other than its power to make an interim periodical payments order or an interim order for the payment of a lump sum)".

(3) In subsection (1), for "the decree" substitute "a divorce order or decree of nullity".

(4) For subsection (3) substitute—

"(3) If the court—

(a) would have power under section 22A or 23 above to make a financial provision order in favour of a party to a marriage ("the first party"), but

(b) considers that no continuing obligation should be imposed on the other party to the marriage ("the second party") to make or secure periodical payments in favour of the first party,

it may direct that the first party may not at any time after the direction takes effect, apply to the court for the making against the second party of any periodical payments order or secured periodical payments order and, if the first party has already applied to the court for the making of such an order, it may dismiss the application.

(3A) If the court—

(a) exercises, or has exercised, its power under section 22A at any time before making a divorce order, and

(b) gives a direction under subsection (3) above in respect of a periodical payments order or a secured periodical payments order,

it shall provide for the direction not to take effect until a divorce order is made."

11. In each of sections 25B(2) and (3), 25C(1) and (3) and 25D(1)(a), (2)(a), (c) and (e) (benefits under a pension scheme on divorce, etc) for "section 23" substitute "section 22A or 23".

12. In section 26(1) (commencement of proceedings for ancillary relief), for the words from the beginning to "22 above" substitute—

"(1) If a petition for nullity of marriage has been presented, then, subject to subsection (2) below, proceedings".

13.—(1) Section 27 (financial provision orders etc in case of failure to provide proper maintenance) is amended as follows.

(2) In subsection (5)—

(a) after "an order requiring the respondent" insert

"—

(a)"; and

(b) at the end insert

", or

(b) to pay to the applicant such lump sum or sums as the court thinks reasonable.".

(3) For subsection (6) substitute—

"(6) Subject to the restrictions imposed by the following provisions of this Act, if on an application under this section the applicant satisfies the court of any ground mentioned in subsection (1) above, the court may make one or more financial provision orders against the respondent in favour of the applicant or a child of the family.".

(4) In subsection (7), for "(6)(c) or (f)" substitute "(6)".

14.—(1) Section 28 (duration of continuing financial provision order in favour of a party to a marriage) is amended as follows.

(2) In subsection (1A), for the words from the beginning to "nullity of marriage" substitute—

"(1A) At any time when—

(a) the court exercises, or has exercised, its power under section 22A or 23 above to make a financial provision order in favour of a party to a marriage,

(b) but for having exercised that power, the court would have power under one of those sections to make such an order, and

(c) an application for a divorce order or a petition for a decree of nullity of marriage is outstanding or has been granted in relation to the marriage,".

(3) Insert, after subsection (1A)—

"(1B) If the court—

(a) exercises, or has exercised, its power under section 22A at any time before making a divorce order, and

(b) gives a direction under subsection (1A) above in respect of a periodical payments order or a secured periodical payments order,

it shall provide for the direction not to take effect until a divorce order is made.".

(4) In subsection (2), for the words from "on or after" to "nullity of marriage" substitute "at such a time as is mentioned in subsection (1A)(c) above".

(5) In subsection (3)—

(a) for "a decree" substitute "an order or decree"; and

(b) for "that decree" substitute "that order or decree".

15. In section 29(1) (duration of a continuing financial provision order in favour of a child of the family), for "under section 24(1)(a)" substitute "such as is mentioned in section 21(2)(a)".

16.—(1) Section 31 (variation etc of orders) is amended as follows.

(2) In subsection (2)—

(a) after "following orders" insert "under this Part of this Act";

(b) for paragraph (d) substitute—

"(d) an order for the payment of a lump sum in a case in which the payment is to be by instalments;";

(c) in paragraph (dd), for "23(1)(c)" substitute "21(1)(c)";

(d) after paragraph (dd) insert—

"(de) any other order for the payment of a lump sum, if it is made at a time when no divorce order has been made, and no separation order is in force, in relation to the marriage;";

(e) for paragraph (e) substitute—

"(e) any order under section 23A of a kind referred to in section 21(2)(b),(c) or (d) which is made on or after the making of a separation order;

(ea) any order under section 23A which is made at a time when no divorce order has been made, and no separation order is in force, in relation to the marriage;".

(3) In subsection (4)—

(a) four the words from "for a settlement" to "24(1)(c) or (d)", substitute "referred to in subsection (2)(e)"; and

(b) for paragraphs (a) and (b) substitute "on an application for a divorce order in relation to the marriage".

(4) After subsection (4) insert—

"(4A) In relation to an order which falls within subsection (2)(de) or (ea) above ("the subsection (2) order")—

(a) the powers conferred by this section may be exercised—

(i) only on an application made before the subsection (2) order has or, but for paragraph (b) below, would have taken effect; and

(ii) only if, at the time when the application is made, no divorce order has been made in relation to the marriage and no separation order has been so made since the subsection (2) order was made; and

(b) an application made in accordance with paragraph (a) above prevents the subsection (2) order from taking effect before the application has been dealt with.

(4B) No variation—

(a) of a financial provision order made under section 22A above, other than an interim order, or

(b) of a property adjustment order made under section 23A above,

shall be made so as to take effect before the making of a divorce order or separation order in relation to the marriage, unless the court is satisfied that the circumstances of the case are exceptional, and that it would be just and reasonable for the variation to be so made.".

(5) In subsection (5)—

(a) insert, at the beginning, "Subject to subsections (7A) to (7F) below and without prejudice to any power exercisable by virtue of subsection (2)(d),(dd) or (e) above or otherwise than by virtue of this section,"; and

(b) for "section 23", in each place, substitute "section 22A or 23".

(6) In subsection (7)(a)—

(a) for "on or after" to "consider" substitute "in favour of a party to a marriage, the court shall, if the marriage has been dissolved or annulled, consider"; and

(b) after "sufficient" insert "(in the light of any proposed exercise by the court, where the marriage has been dissolved, of its powers under subsection (7B) below)".

(7) After subsection (7), insert—

"(7A) Subsection (7B) below applies where, after the dissolution of a marriage, the court—

(a) discharges a periodical payments order or secured periodical payments order made in favour of a party to the marriage; or

(b) varies such an order so that payments under the order are required to be made or secured only for such further period as is determined by the court.

(7B) The court has power, in addition to any power it has apart from this subsection, to make supplemental provision consisting of any of—

(a) an order for the payment of a lump sum in favour of a party to the marriage;

(b) one or more property adjustment orders in favour of a party to the marriage;

(c) a direction that the party in whose favour the original order discharged or varied was made is not entitled to make any further application for—

(i) a periodical payments or secured periodical payments order, or

(ii) an extension of the period to which the original order is limited by any variation made by the court.

(7C) An order for the payment of a lump sum made under subsection (7B) above may—

(a) provide for the payment of that sum by instalments of such amount as may be specified in the order; and

(b) require the payment of the instalments to be secured to the satisfaction of the court.

(7D) Subsections (7) and (8) of section 22A above apply where the court makes an order for the payment of a lump sum under subsection (7B) above as they apply where it makes such an order under section 22A above.

(7E) If under subsection (7B) above the court makes more than one property adjustment order in favour of the same party to the marriage, each of those orders must fall within a different paragraph of section 21(2) above.

(7F) Sections 24A and 30 above apply where the court makes a property adjustment order under subsection (7B) above as they apply where it makes such an order under section 23A above.".

17. In section 32(1) (payment of certain arrears to be unenforceable), for the words from "an order" to "financial provision order" substitute "any financial provision order under this Part of this Act or any interim order for maintenance".

18. For section 33(2) (repayment of sums paid under certain orders) substitute—

"(2) This section applies to the following orders under this Part of this Act—
(a) any periodical payments order;
(b) any secured periodical payments order; and
(c) any interim order for maintenance, so far as it requires the making of periodical payments.".

19.—(1) Section 33A (consent orders) is amended as follows.

(2) In subsection (2), after "applies", in the first place, insert "(subject, in the case of the powers of the court under section 31A above, to subsections (6) and (7) of that section)".

(3) In subsection (3), in the definition of "order for financial relief", for "an order under any of sections 23, 24, 24A or 27 above" substitute "any of the following orders under this Part of this Act, that is to say, any financial provision order, any property adjustment order, any order for the sale of property or any interim order for maintenance".

20. In section 35 (alteration of maintenance agreements), after subsection (6), insert—

"(7) Subject to subsection (5) above, references in this Act to any such order as is mentioned in section 21 above shall not include references to any order under this section."

21. In section 37(1) (avoidance of transactions intended to prevent or reduce financial relief), for "22, 23, 24, 27, 31 (except subsection (6))" substitute "22A to 24, 27, 31 (except subsection (6)), 31A".

22. In section 47(2) (relief in cases of polygamous marriages)—
(a) in paragraph (a), after "any" insert the words "divorce order, any separation order under the 1996 Act or any"; and
(b) in paragraph (d), after "this Act" insert "or the 1996 Act" and for "such decree or order" substitute "a statement of marital breakdown or any such order or decree".

23. Omit section 49 (under which a person who is alleged to have committed adultery with a party to a marriage is required to be made a party to certain proceedings).

24.—(1) Section 52(1) (interpretation) is amended as follows.

(2) After "In this Act", insert—

""the 1996 Act" means the Family Law Act 1996;".

(3) After the definition of "maintenance assessment" insert—

""statement of marital breakdown" has the same meaning as in the Family Law Act 1996.".

25. In section 52(2)(a), for "with section 21 above" substitute "(subject to section 35(7) above) with section 21 above and—
(i) in the case of a financial provision order or periodical payments order, as including (except where the context otherwise requires) references to an interim periodical payments order under section 22A or 23 above; and
(ii) in the case of a financial provision order or order for the payment of a lump sum, as including (except where the context otherwise requires) references to an interim order for the payment of a lump sum under section 22A or 23 above;".

The Domicile and Matrimonial Proceedings Act 1973 (c 45)

26. For section 5(5) of the Domicile and Matrimonial Proceedings Act 1973 (jurisdiction in cases of change of domicile or habitual residence) substitute—

"(5) The court shall have jurisdiction to entertain proceedings for nullity of marriage (even though it would not otherwise have jurisdiction) at any time when marital proceedings, as defined by section 20 of the Family Law Act 1996, are pending in relation to the marriage."

The Inheritance (Provision for Family and Dependants) Act 1975 (c 63)

(1) The Inheritance (Provision for Family and Dependants) Act 1975 (meaning of reasonable financial provision) is amended as follows.

(2) In section 1(2)(a), for the words from "the marriage" to "in force" substitute ", at the date of death, a separation order under the Family Law Act 1996 was in force in relation to the marriage".

(3) In section 3(2) (matters to which the court is to have regard)—
- (a) for "decree of judicial separation" substitute "separation order under the Family Law Act 1996"; and
- (b) for "a decree of divorce" substitute "a divorce order".

(4) In section 14 (provision where no financial relief was granted on divorce—
- (a) in subsection (1), for the words from "a decree" to first "granted" substitute "a divorce order or separation order has been made under the Family Law Act 1996 in relation to a marriage or a decree of nullity of marriage has been made absolute";
- (b) in subsection (1)(a), for "section 23" and "section 24" substitute, respectively, "section 22A or 23" and "section 23A or 24";
- (c) after paragraph (b), for the words from "the decree of divorce" to the end substitute ", as the case may be, the divorce order or separation order had not been made or the decree of nullity had not been made absolute"; and
- (d) in subsection (2), for "decree of judicial separation" and "the decree" substitute, respectively, "separation order" and "the order".

(5) In section 15(1) (restriction imposed in divorce proceedings on applications under that Act), for the words from the beginning to "thereafter" substitute—

"At any time when the court—
- (a) has jurisdiction under section 23A or 24 of the Matrimonial Causes Act 1973 to make a property adjustment order in relation to a marriage; or
- (b) would have such jurisdiction if either the jurisdiction had not already been exercised or an application for such an order were made with the leave of the court,".

(6) In section 15, for subsections (2) to (4) substitute—

"(2) An order made under subsection (1) above with respect to any party to a marriage has effect in accordance with subsection (3) below at any time—
- (a) after the marriage has been dissolved;
- (b) after a decree of nullity has been made absolute in relation to the marriage; and
- (c) while a separation order under the Family Law Act 1996 is in force in relation to the marriage and the separation is continuing.

(3) If at any time when an order made under subsection (1) above with respect to any party to a marriage has effect the other party to the marriage dies, the court shall not entertain any application made by the surviving party to the marriage for an order under section 2 of this Act.".

(7) In section 19(2)(b) (effect and duration of certain orders), for the words from "the marriage" to "in force" substitute ", at the date of death, a separation order under the Family Law Act 1996 was in force in relation to the marriage with the deceased".

(8) In section 25 (interpretation), in the definition of "former wife" and "former husband", for "a decree", in the first place, substitute "an order or decree".

The Domestic Proceedings and Magistrates' Courts Act 1978 (c 22)

28.—(1) Section 28(1) of the Domestic Proceedings and Magistrates' Courts Act 1978 (powers of High Court in respect of orders under Part I) is amended as follows.

(2) After "this Act" insert—

"(a) a statement of marital breakdown under section 5 of the Family Law Act 1996 with respect to the marriage has been received by the court but no application has been made under that Act by reference to that statement, or

(b)".

(3) For the words from "then" to "lump sum" substitute "then, except in the case of an order for the payment of a lump sum, any court to which an application may be made under that Act by reference to that statement or, as the case may be,".

The Housing Act 1980 (c 51)

29. In section 54(2) Of the Housing Act 1980 (prohibition of assignment of shorthold tenancy under that section) for "section 24" substitute "sections 23A or 24".

The Supreme Court Act 1981 (c 54)

30. In section 18 of the Supreme Court Act 1981 (restrictions on appeals to Court of Appeal), in paragraph (d) of subsection (1) omit "divorce or" and after that paragraph insert—

"(dd) from a divorce order;".

The Civil Jurisdiction and Judgments Act 1982 (c 27)

31. In section 18(6)(a) of the Civil Jurisdiction and Judgments Act 1982 (decrees of judicial separation), for "a decree" substitute "an order or decree".

The Matrimonial and Family Proceedings Act 1984 (c 42)

32.—(1) The Matrimonial and Family Proceedings Act 1984 is amended as follows.

(2) In section 17(1) (financial relief in the case of overseas divorces etc), for the words from "any" where it first occurs to the end substitute "one or more orders each of which would, within the meaning of Part II of the 1973 Act, be a financial provision order in favour of a party to the marriage or child of the family or a property adjustment order in relation to the marriage."

(3) For section 21(a) (provisions of the 1973 Act applied for the purposes of the powers to give relief in the case of overseas divorces etc) substitute—

"(a) section 22A(5) (provisions about lump sums in relation to divorce or separation);

(aa) section 23(4), (5) and (6) (provisions about lump sums in relation to annulment);".

(4) In section 27 (interpretation), for the definition of "property adjustment order", substitute—

""property adjustment order" and "secured periodical payments order" mean any order which would be a property adjustment order or, as the case may be, secured periodical payments order within the meaning of Part II of the 1973 Act;"

(5) In section 32 (meaning of "family business"), for the definition of "matrimonial cause" substitute—

""matrimonial cause" means an action for nullity of marriage or any marital proceedings under the Family Law Act 1996;".

The Finance Act (c 54)

33. In section 83(1) of the Finance Act 1985 (stamp duty for transfers of property in connection with divorce etc)—

(a) after paragraph (b), insert—

"(bb) is executed in pursuance of an order of a court which is made at any time under section 22A, 23A or 24A of the Matrimonial Causes Act 1973, or"; and

(b) in paragraph (c), for "or their judicial separation" substitute ", their judicial separation or the making of a separation order in respect of them".

The Housing Act 1985 (c 68)

34. In each of sections 39(1)(c), 88(2), 89(3), 90(3)(a), 91(3)(b), 99B(2)(e), 101(3)(c), 160(1)(c), 171B(4)(b)(i) of, and paragraph 1(2)(c) to, Schedule 6A of the Housing Act 1985 (which refers to the 1973 Act), for "section 24" substitute "section 23A or 24".

The Housing Associations Act 1985 (c 69)

35. In paragraph 5(1)(c) of Schedule 2 to the Housing Associations Act 1985 (which refers to the 1973 Act), for "section 24" substitute "section 23A or 24".

The Agricultural Holdings Act 1986 (c 5)

36. In paragraph 1(3) of Schedule 6 to the Agricultural Holdings Act 1986 (spouse of close relative not to be treated as such when marriage subject to decree nisi etc), for the words from "when" to the end substitute "when a separation order or a divorce order under the Family Law Act 1996 is in force in relation to the relative's marriage or that marriage is the subject of a decree nisi of nullity."

The Family Law Act 1986 (c 55)

37.—(1) The Family Law Act 1986 is amended as follows.

(2) For section 2(1) and (2) (jurisdiction to make orders under section 1) substitute—

"(1) A court in England and Wales shall not have jurisdiction to make a section 1(1)(a) order with respect to a child unless—
(a) the case falls within section 2A below; or
(b) in any other case, the condition in section 3 below is satisfied.".

(3) For section 2A(1) (jurisdiction in or in connection with matrimonial proceedings), substitute—

"(1) Subject to subsections (2) to (4) below, a case falls within this section for the purposes of the making of a section 1(1)(a) order if that order is made—
(a) at a time when—
(i) a statement of marital breakdown under section 5 of the Family Law Act 1996 with respect to the marriage of the parents of the child concerned has been received by the court; and
(ii) it is or may become possible for an application for a divorce order or for a separation order to be made by reference to that statement; or
(b) at a time when an application in relation to that marriage for a divorce order, or for a separation order under the Act of 1996, has been made and not withdrawn.

(1A) A case also falls within this section for the purposes of the making of a section 1(1)(a) order if that order is made in or in connection with any proceedings for the nullity of the marriage of the parents of the child concerned and—
(a) those proceedings are continuing; or
(b) the order is made—
(i) immediately on the dismissal, after the beginning of the trial, of the proceedings; and
(ii) on an application made before the dismissal.".

(4) In section 2A(2), for the words from the beginning to "judicial separation" substitute "A case does not fall within this section if a separation order under the Family Law Act 1996 is in force in relation to the marriage of the parents of the child concerned if,".

(5) In section 2A(3), for "in which the other proceedings there referred to" substitute "in Scotland, Northern Ireland or a specified dependent territory in which the proceedings for divorce or nullity".

(6) In section 2A(4)—
(a) for "in or in connection with matrimonial proceedings" substitute "by virtue of the case falling within this section"; and
(b) for "in or in connection with those proceedings" substitute "by virtue of section 2(1)(a) of this Act".

(7) In section 3 (child habitually resident or present in England and Wales), for "section 2(2)" substitute "section 2(1)(b)".

(8) In section 6 (duration and variation of Part I orders), for subsections (3A) and (3B) substitute—

"(3A) Subsection (3) above does not apply if the Part I order was made in a case falling within section 2A of this Act.".

(9) In section 38 (restriction on removal of wards of court from the jurisdiction), insert after subsection (3)—

"(4) The reference in subsection (2) above to a time when proceedings for divorce or judicial separation are continuing in respect of a marriage in another part of the United Kingdom includes, in relation to any case in which England and Wales would be another part of the United Kingdom, any time when—

(a) a statement of marital breakdown under section 5 of the Family Law Act 1996 with respect to that marriage has been received by the court and it is or may become possible for an application for a divorce order or for a separation order to be made by reference to that statement; or

(b) an application in relation to that marriage for a divorce order, or for a separation order under the Act of 1996, has been made and not withdrawn.".

(10) In section 42(2) (times when divorce etc proceedings are to be treated as continuing for the purposes of certain restrictions on the removal of children from the jurisdiction), for the words from "unless" to the end substitute "be treated as continuing (irrespective of whether a divorce order, separation order or decree of nullity has been made)—

(a) from the time when a statement of marital breakdown under section 5 of the Family Law Act 1996 with respect to the marriage is received by the court in England and Wales until such time as the court may designate or, if earlier, until the time when—

(i) the child concerned attains the age of eighteen; or

(ii) it ceases, by virtue of section 5(3) or 7(9) of that Act (lapse of divorce or separation process) to be possible for an application for a divorce order, or for a separation order, to be made by reference to that statement; and

(b) from the time when a petition for nullity is presented in relation to the marriage in England and Wales or a petition for divorce, judicial separation or nullity is presented in relation to the marriage in Northern Ireland or a specified dependent territory, until the time when—

(i) the child concerned attains the age of eighteen; or

(ii) if earlier, proceedings on the petition are dismissed."

(11) In section 51(4) (definitions), after the definition of "the relevant date" insert—

"'judicial separation' includes a separation order under the Family Law Act 1996;".

The Landlord and Tenant Act 1987 (c 31)

38. In section 4(2)(c) of the Landlord and Tenant Act 1987 (which refers to the 1973 Act), for "section 24" substitute "section 23A, 24".

The Legal Aid Act 1988 (c 34)

39. In paragraph 5A of Part II of Schedule 2 to the Legal Aid Act 1988 (excepted proceedings)—

(a) for "decree of divorce or judicial separation" substitute "a divorce order or a separation order"; and

(b) in sub-paragraph (b) of that paragraph, for "petition" substitute "application.

The Housing Act 1988 (c 50)

40. In paragraph 4(1)(c) of Schedule 11 (which refers to the 1973 Act), for "section 24" substitute "section 23A or 24".

The Children Act 1989 (c 41)

41.—(1) The Children Act 1989 is amended as follows.

(2) In section 6(3A) (revocation or appointment of guardian) for paragraph (a) substitute—

"(a) a court of civil jurisdiction in England and Wales by order dissolves, or by decree annuls, a marriage, or".

(3) In section 8(3) after "means" insert "(subject to subsection (5))".

(4) In section 8, insert after subsection (4)—

"(5) For the purposes of any reference in this Act to family proceedings powers which under this Act are exercisable in family proceedings shall also be exercisable in relation to a child, without any such proceedings having been commenced or any application having been made to the court under this Act, if—

(a) a statement of marital breakdown under section 5 of the Family Law Act 1996 with respect to the marriage in relation to which that child is a child of the family has been received by the court; and

(b) it may, in due course, become possible for an application for a divorce order or for a separation order to be made by reference to that statement."

The Local Government and Housing Act 1989 (c 42)

42. In section 124(3)(c) of the Local Government and Housing Act 1989 (which refers to the 1973 Act), for "section 24" substitute "section 23A or 24".

Pensions Act 1995 (c 26)

43. In section 166(4) of the Pensions Act 1995 (jurisdiction of the court under the Matrimonial Causes Act 1973 in respect of pensions to which that section applies) for "section 23" substitute section 22A or 23".

Definitions In the Matrimonial Causes Act 1973, for "financial provision order", "periodical payments order", "secured periodical payments order" and "order for the payment of a lump sum", see s 21(1) thereof, as substituted by s 15, Sch 2, para 2 ante (and note also s 52(2)(a) thereof, as amended by para 25 above); as to "orders for the sale of property", see s 24A thereof, as amended by para 8 above and s 66(3) ante, Sch 10 post; as to "interim order for maintenance", see s 27(5) thereof; for "child", "child of the family" and "the court", see s 52(1) thereof. In the Domicile and Matrimonial Proceedings Act 1973, for "the court", see s 5(1) thereof. In the Inheritance (Provision for Family and Dependants) Act 1975, for "the court", see s 25(1) thereof. In the Matrimonial and Family Proceedings Act 1984, for "child of the family", see s 27 thereof. In the Finance Act 1985, for "executed", see, by virtue of s 98(4) thereof, the Stamp Act 1891, s 122(1). In the Family Law Act 1986, for "Part I order", see ss 1(1), 42(5), thereof; for "child" and "section 1(1)(a) order", see s 7 thereof; for "specified dependant territory", see s 42(1) thereof; for "proceedings for divorce or judicial separation are continuing", see s 42(2) thereof, as amended by para 37(10) above; for "dependant territory", see s 43(2) thereof; for "judicial separation", see s 51(4) thereof, as amended by para 37(11) above. In the Children Act 1989, for "family proceedings", see s 8(3), (5) thereof, as amended (in the case of sub-s (3)) by para 41(3) above and inserted (in the case of sub-s (5)) by para 41(4) above; for "the court", see s 92(7) thereof; for "child" and "child of the family", see s 105(1) thereof.

PART II

AMENDMENTS CONNECTED WITH PART III

The Legal Aid Act 1988 (c 34)

44.—(1) The 1988 Act is amended as follows.

(2) In section 1, after "III" insert "IIIA".

(3) In sections 1, 2(11), 3(2), 4(1), (2) and (4), 5(1) and (6), 6(2)(a) and (3)(a), 34(2)(c) and (d) and (11), 38(1) and (6) and 39(1) and (4)(a), after "assistance", in each place, insert ", mediation".

(4) In section 3(9), after paragraph (a) insert—

"(aa) the provision of mediation;".

(5) In section 6, after subsection (3)(c) insert—

"(ca) any sum which is to be paid out of property on which it is charged under regulations under section 13C(5) below".

(6) In section 15—

(a) in subsection (1), after "(3D)" insert "and (3F)"; and

(b) in subsection (3D), after "(3)" insert "and (3F)".

(7) In section 16(9), leave out "and" at the end of paragraph (a).

(8) In section 38—

(a) in subsection (1)(f), after "legal representatives" insert "or mediators"; and

(b) in subsection (6), after "legal representative" insert "or mediator".

(9) In section 43—

(a) after "“assistance insert", "mediation"";

(b) after "(3)" insert", (3A)"; and

(c) after the definition of "financial resources" insert—

"“family matters" has the meaning assigned by section 13A(2);".

Definitions In the Legal Aid Act 1988, for "mediation", see s 2(3A) thereof, as inserted by s 26(2) ante; for "legal representative" and "mediator", see s 43 thereof, as amended by s 26(3) ante.

PART III

AMENDMENTS CONNECTED WITH PART IV

The Land Registration Act 1925 (c 21)

45. In section 64 of the Land Registration Act 1925 (certificates to be produced and noted on dealings) in subsection (5) for "section 2(8) of the Matrimonial Homes Act 1983" substitute "section 31(10) of the Family Law Act 1996 and for "rights of occupation" substitute "matrimonial home rights"".

The Land Charges Act 1972 (c 61)

46. In section 1(6A) of the Land Charges Act 1972 (cases where county court has jurisdiction to vacate registration) in paragraph (d)—

(a) after "section 1 of the Matrimonial Homes Act 1983" insert "or section 33 of the Family Law Act 1996"; and

(b) for "that section" substitute "either of those sections".

47. In section 2(7) of that Act (Class F land charge) for "Matrimonial Homes Act 1983" substitute "Part IV of the Family Law Act 1996".

The Land Compensation Act 1973 (c 26)

48.—(1) Section 29A of the Land Compensation Act 1973 (spouses having statutory rights of occupation) is amended as follows.

(2) In subsection (1), for "rights of occupation (within the meaning of the Matrimonial Homes Act 1983)" substitute "matrimonial home rights (within the meaning of Part IV of the Family Law Act 1996)".

(3) In subsection (2)(a), for "rights of occupation" substitute "matrimonial home rights".

The Magistrates' Court Act 1980 (c 43)

49. In section 65(1) of the Magistrates' Courts Act 1980 (meaning of family proceedings) after paragraph (o) insert—

"(p) Part IV of the Family Law Act 1996;".

The Contempt of Court Act 1981 (c 49)

50. In Schedule 3 to the Contempt of Court Act 1981 (application of Magistrates' Courts Act 1980 to civil contempt proceedings), in paragraph 3 for the words from "“or, having been arrested" onwards substitute—

"“or, having been arrested under section 47 of the Family Law Act 1996 in connection with the matter of the complaint, is at large after being remanded under subsection (7)(b) or (10) of that section."".

The Supreme Court Act 1981 (c 54)

51. In Schedule 1 to the Supreme Court Act 1981 (distribution of business in High Court), in paragraph 3 (Family Division)—

(a) in paragraph (d), after "matrimonial proceedings " insert "or proceedings under Part IV of the Family Law Act 1996", and

(b) in paragraph (f)(i), for "Domestic Violence and Matrimonial Proceedings Act 1976" substitute "Part IV of the Family Law Act 1996".

The Matrimonial and Family Proceedings Act 1984 (c 42)

52. For section 22 of the Matrimonial and Family Proceedings Act 1984 substitute—

"22 Powers of court in relation to certain tenancies of dwelling-houses

(1) This section applies if—

(a) an application is made by a party to a marriage for an order for financial relief; and

(b) one of the parties is entitled, either in his own right or jointly with the other party, to occupy a dwelling-house situated in England or Wales by virtue of a tenancy which is a relevant tenancy within the meaning of Schedule 7 to the Family Law Act 1996 (certain statutory tenancies).

(2) The court may make in relation to that dwelling-house any order which it could make under Part II of that Schedule if—

(a) a divorce order,

(b) a separation order, or

(c) a decree of nullity of marriage,

had been made or granted in England and Wales in respect of the marriage.

(3) The provisions of paragraphs 10, 11 and 14(1) in Part III of that Schedule apply in relation to any order under this section as they apply to any order under Part II of that Schedule.".

The Housing Act 1985 (c 68)

53.—(1) Section 85 of the Housing Act 1985 (extended discretion of court in certain proceedings for possession) is amended as follows.

(2) In subsection (5)—

(a) in paragraph (a), for "rights of occupation under the Matrimonial Homes Act 1983" substitute "matrimonial home rights under Part IV of the Family Law Act 1996"; and

(b) for "those rights of occupation" substitute "those matrimonial home rights".

(3) After subsection (5) insert—

"(5A) If proceedings are brought for possession of a dwelling-house which is let under a secure tenancy and—

(a) an order is in force under section 35 of the Family Law Act 1996 conferring rights on the former spouse of the tenant or an order is in force under section 36 of that Act conferring rights on a cohabitant or former cohabitant (within the meaning of that Act) of the tenant,

(b) the former spouse, cohabitant or former cohabitant is then in occupation of the dwelling-house, and

(c) the tenancy is terminated as a result of those proceedings,

the former spouse, cohabitant or former cohabitant shall, so long as he or she remains in occupation, have the same rights in relation to, or in connection with, any adjournment, stay, suspension or postponement in pursuance of this section as he or she would have if the rights conferred by the order referred to in paragraph (a) were not affected by the termination of the tenancy.".

54. In section 99B of that Act (persons qualifying for compensation for improvements) in subsection (2) for paragraph (f) substitute—

"(f) a spouse, former spouse, cohabitant or former cohabitant of the improving tenant to whom the tenancy has been transferred by an order made under Schedule 1 to the Matrimonial Homes Act 1983 or Schedule 7 to the Family Law Act 1996."

55. In section 101 of that Act (rent not to be increased on account of tenant's improvements) in subsection (3) for paragraph (d) substitute—

"(d) a spouse, former spouse, cohabitant or former cohabitant of the tenant to whom the tenancy has been transferred by an order made under Schedule 1 to the Matrimonial Homes Act 1983 or Schedule 7 to the Family Law Act 1996."

56. In section 171B of that Act (extent of preserved right to buy: qualifying persons and dwelling-houses) in subsection (4)(b)(ii) after "Schedule 1 to the Matrimonial Homes Act 1983" insert "or Schedule 7 to the Family Law Act 1996".

The Insolvency Act 1986 (c 45)

57.—(1) Section 336 of the Insolvency Act 1986 (rights of occupation etc of bankrupt's spouse) is amended as follows.

(2) In subsection (1), for "rights of occupation under the Matrimonial Homes Act 1983" substitute "matrimonial home rights under Part IV of the Family Law Act 1996".

(3) In subsection (2)—

(a) for "rights of occupation under the Act of 1983" substitute "matrimonial home rights under the Act of 1996", and

(b) in paragraph (b), for "under section 1 of that Act" substitute "under section 33 of that Act".

(4) In subsection (4), for "section 1 of the Act of 1983" substitute "section 33 of the Act of 1996".

58.—(1) Section 337 of that Act is amended as follows.

(2) In subsection (2), for "rights of occupation under the Matrimonial Homes Act 1983" substitute "matrimonial home rights under Part IV of the Family Law Act 1996".

(3) For subsection (3) substitute—

"(3) The Act of 1996 has effect, with the necessary modifications, as if—

(a) the rights conferred by paragraph (a) of subsection (2) were matrimonial home rights under that Act,

(b) any application for such leave as is mentioned in that paragraph were an application for an order under section 33 of that Act, and

(c) any charge under paragraph (b) of that subsection on the estate or interest of the trustee were a charge under that Act on the estate or interest of a spouse."

(4) In subsections (4) and (5) for "section 1 of the Act of 1983" substitute "section 33 of the Act of 1996".

The Housing Act 1988 (c 50)

59.—(1) Section 9 of the Housing Act 1988 (extended discretion of court in possession claims) is amended as follows.

(2) In subsection (5)—

(a) in paragraph (a), for "rights of occupation under the Matrimonial Homes Act 1983" substitute "matrimonial home rights under Part IV of the Family Law Act 1996", and

(b) for "those rights of occupation" substitute "those matrimonial home rights".

(3) After subsection (5) insert—

"(5A) In any case where—

(a) at a time when proceedings are brought for possession of a dwelling-house let on an assured tenancy—

(i) an order is in force under section 35 of the Family Law Act 1996 conferring rights on the former spouse of the tenant, or

(ii) an order is in force under section 36 of that Act conferring rights on a cohabitant or former cohabitant (within the meaning of that Act) of the tenant,

(b) that cohabitant, former cohabitant or former spouse is then in occupation of the dwelling-house, and

(c) the assured tenancy is terminated as a result of those proceedings,

the cohabitant, former cohabitant or former spouse shall have the same rights in relation to, or in connection with, any such adjournment as is referred to in subsection (1) above or any such stay, suspension or postponement as is referred to in subsection (2) above as he or she would have if the rights conferred by the order referred to in paragraph (a) above were not affected by the termination of the tenancy.".

The Children Act 1989 (c 41)

60.—(1) In section 8(4) of the Children Act 1989 (meaning of "family proceedings" for purposes of that Act), omit paragraphs (c) and (f) and after paragraph (g) insert—

"(h) the Family Law Act 1996."

(2) In Schedule 11 to that Act, in paragraph 6(a) (amendment of the Domestic Proceedings and Magistrates' Courts Act 1978), for "sections 16(5)(c) and" substitute "section".

The Courts and Legal Services Act 1990 (c 41)

61. In section 58 of the Courts and Legal Services Act 1990 (conditional fee agreements) in subsection (10), omit paragraphs (b) and (e) and immediately before the "or" following paragraph (g) insert—

"(gg) Part IV of the Family Law Act 1996".

Definitions In the Matrimonial and Family Proceedings Act 1984, for "order for financial relief", see s 12(4); for "the court" and "dwelling-house", see s 27 thereof. In the Housing Act 1985, for "secure tenancy", see s 79 thereof; for "improving tenant", see s 99B(5) thereof, as inserted by the Leasehold Reform, Housing and Urban Development Act 1993, s 124; for "dwelling-house", see s 112 of the 1985 Act; for "tenancy" and "tenant", see s 621 of that Act. In the Insolvency Act 1986, for "estate" and "the trustee", see s 385(1) thereof. In the Housing Act 1988, for "assured tenancy", see s 1 thereof; for "dwelling-house" and "tenant", see s 45(1) thereof.

SCHEDULE 9

Section 66(2)

MODIFICATIONS, SAVING AND TRANSITIONAL

Transitional arrangements for those who have been living apart

1.—(1) The Lord Chancellor may by order provide for the application of Part II to marital proceedings which—

(a) are begun during the transitional period, and
(b) relate to parties to a marriage who immediately before the beginning of that period were living apart,

subject to such modifications (which may include omissions) as may be prescribed.

(2) An order made under this paragraph may, in particular, make provision as to the evidence which a party who claims to have been living apart from the other party immediately before the beginning of the transitional period must produce to the court.

(3) In this paragraph—

"marital proceedings" has the same meaning as in section 24;
"prescribed" means prescribed by the order; and
"transitional period" means the period of two years beginning with the day on which section 3 is brought into force."

Modifications of enactments etc

2.—(1) The Lord Chancellor may by order make such consequential modifications of any enactment or subordinate legislation as appear to him necessary or expedient in consequence of Part II in respect of any reference (in whatever terms) to—

(a) a petition;
(b) the presentation of a petition;
(c) the petitioner or respondent in proceedings on a petition;
(d) proceedings on a petition;
(e) proceedings in connection with any proceedings on a petition;
(f) any other matrimonial proceedings;
(g) a decree; or
(h) findings of adultery in any proceedings.

(2) An order under sub-paragraph (1) may, in particular—

(a) make provision applying generally in relation to enactments and subordinate legislation of a description specified in the order;

(b) modify the effect of sub-paragraph (3) in relation to documents and agreements of a description so specified.

(3) Otherwise a reference (in whatever terms) in any instrument or agreement to the presentation of a petition or to a decree has effect, in relation to any time after the coming into force of this paragraph—

(a) in the case of a reference to the presentation of a petition, as if it included a reference to the making of a statement; and

(b) in the case of a reference to a decree, as if it included a reference to a divorce order or (as the case may be) a separation order.

3. If an Act or subordinate legislation—

(a) refers to an enactment repealed or amended by or under this Act, and

(b) was passed or made before the repeal or amendment came into force,

the Lord Chancellor may by order make such consequential modifications of any provision contained in the Act or subordinate legislation as appears to him necessary or expedient in respect of the reference.

Expressions used in paragraphs 2 and 3

4. In paragraphs 2 and 3—

"decree" means a decree of divorce (whether a decree nisi or a decree which has been made absolute) or a decree of judicial separation;

"instrument" includes any deed, will or other instrument or document

"petition" means a petition for a decree of divorce or a petition for a decree of judicial separation; and

"subordinate legislation" has the same meaning as in the Interpretation Act 1978.

Proceedings under way

5.—(1) Except for paragraph 6 of this Schedule, nothing in any provision of Part II, Part I of Schedule 8 or Schedule 10—

(a) applies to, or affects—

(i) any decree granted before the coming into force of the provision;

(ii) any proceedings begun, by petition or otherwise, before that time; or

(iii) any decree granted in any such proceedings;

(b) affects the operation of—

(i) the 1973 Act,

(ii) any other enactment, or

(iii) any subordinate legislation,

in relation to any such proceedings or decree or to any proceedings in connection with any such proceedings or decree; or

(c) without prejudice to paragraph (b), affects any transitional provision having effect under Schedule 1 to the 1973 Act.

(2) In this paragraph, "subordinate legislation" has the same meaning as in the Interpretation Act 1978.

6.—(1) Section 31 of the 1973 Act has effect as amended by this Act in relation to any order under Part II of the 1973 Act made after the coming into force of the amendments.

(2) Subsections (7) to (7F) of that section also have effect as amended by this Act in relation to any order made before the coming into force of the amendments.

Interpretation

7. In paragraphs 8 to 15 "the 1983 Act" means the Matrimonial Homes Act 1983.

Pending applications for orders relating to occupation and molestation

8.—(1) In this paragraph and paragraph 10 "the existing enactments" means—

(a) the Domestic Violence and Matrimonial Proceedings Act 1976;

(b) sections 16 to 18 of the Domestic Proceedings and Magistrates' Courts Act 1978; and

(c) sections 1 and 9 of the 1983 Act.

(2) Nothing in Part IV, Part III of Schedule 8 or Schedule 10 affects any application for an order or injunction under any of the existing enactments which is pending immediately before the commencement of the repeal of that enactment.

Pending applications under Schedule 1 to the Matrimonial Homes Act 1983

9. Nothing in Part IV, Part III of Schedule 8 or Schedule 10 affects any application for an order under Schedule 1 to the 1983 Act which is pending immediately before the commencement of the repeal of that Schedule.

Existing orders relating to occupation and molestation

10.—(1) In this paragraph "an existing order" means any order or injunction under any of the existing enactments which—

(a) is in force immediately before the commencement of the repeal of that enactment; or

(b) was made or granted after that commencement in proceedings brought before that commencement.

(2) Subject to sub-paragraphs (3) and (4), nothing in Part IV, Part III of Schedule 8 or Schedule 10—

(a) prevents an existing order from remaining in force; or

(b) affects the enforcement of an existing order.

(3) Nothing in Part IV, Part III of Schedule 8 or Schedule 10 affects any application to extend, vary or discharge an existing order, but the court may, if it thinks it just and reasonable to do so, treat the application as an application for an order under Part IV.

(4) The making of an order under Part IV between parties with respect to whom an existing order is in force discharges the existing order.

Matrimonial home rights

11.—(1) Any reference (however expressed) in any enactment, instrument or document (whether passed or made before or after the passing of this Act) to rights of occupation under, or within the meaning of, the 1983 Act shall be construed, so far as is required for continuing the effect of the instrument or document, as being or as the case requires including a reference to matrimonial home rights under, or within the meaning of, Part IV.

(2) Any reference (however expressed) in this Act or in any other enactment, instrument or document (including any enactment amended by Schedule 8) to matrimonial home rights under, or within the meaning of, Part IV shall be construed as including, in relation to times, circumstances and purposes before the commencement of sections 30 to 32, a reference to rights of occupation under, or within the meaning of, the 1983 Act.

12.—(1) Any reference (however expressed) in any enactment, instrument or document (whether passed or made before or after the passing of this Act) to registration under section 2(8) of the 1983 Act shall, in relation to any time after the commencement of sections 30 to 32, be construed as being or as the case requires including a reference to registration under section 31(10).

(2) Any reference (however expressed) in this Act or in any other enactment, instrument or document (including any enactment amended by Schedule 8) to registration under section 31(10) shall be construed as including a reference to—

(a) registration under section 2(7) of the Matrimonial Homes Act 1967 or section 2(8) of the 1983 Act, and

(b) registration by caution duly lodged under Section 2(7) of the Matrimonial Homes Act 1967 before 14th February 1983 (the date of the commencement of section 4(2) of the Matrimonial Homes and Property Act 1981.

13. In sections 30 and 31 and Schedule 4—

(a) any reference to an order made under section 33 shall be construed as including a reference to an order made under section 1 of the 1983 Act, and

(b) any reference to an order made under section 33(5) shall be construed as including a reference to an order made under section 1 of the 1983 Act by virtue of section 2(4) of that Act.

14. Neither section 31(11) nor the repeal by the Matrimonial Homes and Property Act 1981 of the words "or caution" in section 2(7) of the Matrimonial Homes Act 1967, affects any caution duly lodged as respects any estate or interest before 14th February 1983.

15. Nothing in this Schedule is to be taken to prejudice the operation of sections 16 and 17 of the Interpretation Act 1978 (which relate to the effect of repeals).

Definitions For "divorce order", see s 2(1)(a) ante; for "separation order", see s 2(1)(b) ante; for "a statement", see s 6(1) ante; for "matrimonial home rights", see s 30(2) ante.
References See para 15.2–15.7.

SCHEDULE 10

Section 66(3)

REPEALS

Chapter	Short Title	Extent of Repeal
1968 c 63	The Domestic and Appellate Proceedings (Restriction of Publicity) Act 1968	Section 2(1)(b)
1973 c 18	The Matrimonial Causes Act 1973	Sections 1 to 7
		In section 8(1)(b), the words "or before the decree nisi is made absolute"
		Sections 9 and 10
		Sections 17 and 18
		Section 20
		Section 22
		In section 24A(3), the words "divorce or"
		In section 25(2)(h), the words "in the case of proceedings for divorce or nullity of marriage,"
		In section 28(1), the words from "in", in the first place where it occurs, to "nullity of marriage" in the first place where those words occur
		In section 29(2), the words from "may begin" to "but"
		In section 30, the words "divorce" and "or judicial separation"
		In section 31, in subsection (2)(a), the words "order for maintenance pending suit and any"
		In section 41, in subsection (1) the words "divorce or" and "or a decree of judicial separation" and in subsection (2) the words "divorce or" and "or that the decree of judicial separation is not to be granted"
		Section 49
		In section 52(2)(b), the words "to orders for maintenance pending suit and", "respectively" and "section 22 and"
		In Schedule 1, paragraph 8

Chapter	Short Title	Extent of Repeal
1973 c 45	The Domicile and Matrimonial Proceedings Act 1973	In section 5, in subsection (1), the words "subject to section 6(3) and (4) of this Act" and, in paragraph (a), "divorce, judicial separation or" and subsection (2)
		Section 6(3) and (4)
		In Schedule 1, in paragraph 11, in sub-paragraph (2)(a), in sub-paragraph (2)(c), in the first place where they occur and in sub-paragraph (3)(b) and (c), the words "in connection with the stayed proceedings"
1976 c 50	The Domestic Violence and Matrimonial Proceedings Act 1976	The whole Act
1978 c 22	The Domestic Proceedings and Magistrates' Courts Act 1978	In section 1, paragraphs (c) and (d) and the word "or" preceding paragraph (c)
		In section 7(1), the words "neither party having deserted the other"
		Sections 16 to 18
		Section 28(2)
		Section 63(3)
		In Schedule 2, paragraphs 38 and 53
1980 c 43	The Magistrates' Courts Act 1980	In Schedule 7, paragraph 159
1981 c 54	The Supreme Court Act 1981	In section 18(1)(d), the words "divorce or"
1982 c 53	The Administration of Justice Act 1982	Section 16
1983 c 19	The Matrimonial Homes Act 1983	The whole Act
1984 c 42	The Matrimonial and Family Proceedings Act 1984	Section 1
		In section 21(f) the words "except subsection (2)(e) and subsection (4)"
		In section 27, the definition of "secured periodical payments order"
		In Schedule 1, paragraph 10
1985 c 61	The Administration of Justice Act 1985	In section 34(2), paragraph (f) and the word "and" immediately preceding it
		In Schedule 2, in paragraph 37, paragraph (e) and the word "and" immediately preceding it

Chapter	Short Title	Extent of Repeal
1985 c 71	The Housing (Consequential Provisions) Act 1985	In Schedule 2, paragraph 56
1986 c 53	The Building Societies Act 1986	In Schedule 21, paragraph 9(f)
1985 c 55	The Family Law Act 1986	In Schedule 1, paragraph 27
1988 c 34	The Legal Aid Act 1988	In section 16(9), the word "and" at the end of paragraph (a)
1988 c 50	The Housing Act 1988	In Schedule 17, paragraphs 33 and 34
1989 c 41	The Children Act 1989	Section 8(4)(c) and (f) In Schedule 11, paragraph 6(b) In Schedule 13, paragraphs 33(1) and 65(1)
1990 c 41	The Courts and Legal Services Act 1990	Section 58(10)(b) and (e) In Schedule 18, paragraph 21
1995 c 42	The Private International Law (Miscellaneous Provisions) Act 1995	In the Schedule, paragraph 3

Appendix 2

Tables of derivations and destinations

Table 1	Family Law Act 1996—Derivation Table
Table 2	Matrimonial Homes Act 1983—Destination Table
Table 3	Matrimonial Homes Act 1983—Enactments repealed by MHA 1983

The Family Law Act 1996, Pt IV has its origins in the Domestic Violence and Matrimonial Proceedings Act 1976, the Domestic Proceedings and Magistrates' Courts Act 1978 and the Matrimonial Homes Act 1983 (MHA). Because of the extension of jurisdiction in Pt IV of the 1996 Act some provisions have been substantially altered although retaining the character of the previous enactment. In other cases the new provision may have been altered only by a drafting change. In addition, an attempt has been made to draft the 1996 Act in plainer English. When using the Tables, practitioners are strongly advised to check the extent of the changes by referring to the legislation itself in all cases.

Table 3, in conjunction with Tables 1 and 2, enables certain provisions of Pt IV of the 1996 Act to be traced back to their statutory origins.

Table 1

Family Law Act 1996—Derivation Table

This Table shows in column (1) the enactments of the 1996 Act which are derived from the repealed enactments of the MHA 1983 listed in column (2).

(1) Family Law Act 1996 Pt VI (c 27)	(2) Matrimonial Homes Act 1983 (c 19)	(1) Family Law Act 1996 Pt VI (c 27)	(2) Matrimonial Homes Act 1983 (c 19)
s 30(1), (2)	s 1(1)	s 55	s 8(2)
s 30(3)	s 1(5)	s 56(1), (2)	s 8(3)
s 30(4)	s 1(6)	s 56(3), (4)	s 8(4)
s 30(5)	s 1(7)	s 56(5)	s 8(5)
s 30(6)	s 1(8)	s 63(5)	s 10(2)
s 30(7)	s 1(10)	Sch 4, para 2	s 3
s 30(9)	s 1(11)	para 3	s 4
s 31(1)–(3)	s 2(1)	para 4	s 5
s 31(4)–(6)	s 2(2)	para 5(1)	s 6(1)
s 31(7)	s 2(3)	para 5(2)	s 6(2)
s 31(8)	s 2(4)	para 6	s 6(3)
s 31(9)	s 2(6)	Sch 7, para 1	Sch 1, para 10(1)
s 31(10)	s 2(8)	para 2	para 1(1)
s 31(11)	s 2(9)	para 7	para 2
s 31(12)	s 2(10)	para 8	para 3
s 31(13)	s 2(11)	para 9	para 4
s 33(3)(a), (e), (4)	s 1(2)(a)	para 11	para 5
s 33(3)(b)	s 1(2)(c)	para 12	para 6
s 33(3)(d)	s 1(2)(b)	para 13(1)	para 7
s 34	s 2(5)	para 13(2)	para 10(2)
s 40(1)(a)	s 1(3)(c)	para 14(1)	para 8(1)
s 40(1)(b)	s 1(3)(b)	para 14(2)	para 8(2)
s 53	s 7	para 15	para 9
s 54(1), (2)	s 9(4)	Sch 9, para 14	ss 10(3), 11
s 54(1)–(5)	s 8(1)		

Table 2

Matrimonial Homes Act 1983—Destination Table

This Table shows in column (1) the enactments of the MHA 1983 which have been repealed by the 1996 Act and in column (2) the provisions of that Act corresponding to the repealed provisions.

(1)	(2)	(1)	(2)
Matrimonial Homes Act 1983 (c 19)	Family Law Act 1996 Pt IV (c 27)	Matrimonial Homes Act 1983 (c 19)	Family Law Act 1996 Pt IV (c 27)
s 1(1)	s 30(1), (2)	s 5	Sch 4, para 4
s 1(2)(a)	s 33(3)(a), (e), (4)	s 6(1)	para 5(1)
s 1(2)(b)	s 33(3)(d)	s 6(2)	para 5(2)
s 1(2)(c)	s 33(3)(b)	s 6(3)	para 6
s 1(3)(b)	s 40(1)(b)	s 7	s 53
s 1(3)(c)	s 40(1)(a)	s 8(1)	s 54(1)–(4)
s 1(5)	s 30(3)	s 8(2)	s 55
s 1(6)	s 30(4)	s 8(3)	s 56(1), (2)
s 1(7)	s 30(5)	s 8(4)	s 56(3), (4)
s 1(8)	s 30(6)	s 8(5)	s 56(5)
s 1(10)	s 30(7)	s 9(4)	s 54(1), (2)
s 1(11)	s 30(9)	s 11	Sch 9, para 14
s 2(1)	s 31(1)–(3)	Sch 1, para 1(1)	Sch 7, para 2
s 2(2)	s 31(4)–(6)	para 2	para 7
s 2(3)	s 31(7)	para 3	para 8
s 2(4)	s 31(8)	para 4	para 9
s 2(5)	s 34	para 5	para 11
s 2(6)	s 31(9)	para 6	para 12
s 2(7)*	—	para 7	para 13(1)
s 2(8)	s 31(10)	para 8(1)	para 14(1)
s 2(9)	s 31(11)	para 8(2)	para 14(2)
s 2(10)	s 31(12)	para 9	para 15(1)
s 2(11)	s 31(13)	para 10(1)	para 1
s 3	Sch 4, para 2	para 10(2)	para 13(2)
s 4	para 3		

*See the Insolvency Act 1986, s 336(2).

Table 3

Matrimonial Homes Act 1983

This Table shows in column (1) the enactments repealed by the Matrimonial Homes Act 1983, and in column (2) the provisions of that Act corresponding to the repealed provisions.

(1)	(2)
Matrimonial Homes Act 1967 (c 75)	Matrimonial Homes Act 1983 (c 19)
s 1(1)–(4)	s 1(1)–(4)
s 1(5)	s 1(5)–(7)
s 1(5A)	s 1(8)
s 1(6)	s 1(9)
s 1(7)	s 10(1)
s 1(8), (9)	s 1(10), (11)
s 2(1)	s 2(1)
s 2(1A)	s 2(2), (3)
s 2(2)–(5)	s 2(4)–(7)
s 2(6)*	—
s 2(7)	s 2(8)
s 2(7A)	s 2(9)
s 2(8), (9)	s 2(10), (11)
s 3	s 3
s 4(1)	s 4(1), (2)
s 4(2)–(5)	s 4(3)–(6)
s 5	s 5
s 6	s 6
s 7	s 7
s 7A(1)–(3)(a)	s 8(1)–(3)
s 7A(3)(b)	s 8(4), (5)
s 7A(4)	s 10(1)
s 8(1)	—
s 8(2)	s 13(3)
s 8(3)	—
Sch 1, para 1	Rep 1969, c 59, s 17, Sch 2, Pt II
para 2	Rep 1972, c 61, s 18(3), Sch 5
Sch 2	Sch 1

(1)	(2)
Matrimonial Proceedings and Property Act 1970 (c 24)	Matrimonial Homes Act 1983 (c 19)
s 38	s 1(11)

(1)	(2)
Land Charges Act 1972 (c 61)	Matrimonial Homes Act 1983 (c 19)
Sch 3, para 8(1)	s 2(7)
para 8(2)	s 2(10)
para 9	s 3
para 10	s 4(1)
para 11	s 5(1), (3), (6)
Sch 3, para 12	s 6(2)

(1)	(2)
Domestic Violence and Matrimonial Proceedings Act 1976 (c 50)	Matrimonial Homes Act 1983 (c 19)
s 3	s 1(2)
s 4(1)–(3)	s 1(1)–(3)
s 4(4)	ss 9(4), 10(1)

(1)	(2)
Rent Act 1977 (c 42)	Matrimonial Homes Act 1983 (c 19)
Sch 23, para 40	s 1(6)

(1)	(2)
Housing Act 1980 (c 51)	Matrimonial Homes Act 1983 (c 19)
Sch 25, para 14	s 1(6)

(1)	(2)
Matrimonial Homes and Property Act 1981 (c 24)	Matrimonial Homes Act 1983 (c 19)
s 1(1)	ss 1(1), 2(1)
s 1(2)	s 1(8)
s 1(3)	s 2(5)
s 1(4)	s 2(2), (3)
s 1(5)	ss 2, 3, 5, 6
s 2	ss 8, 10(1)
s 3	s 10(2)
s 4(2)	s 2(9), (11)
s 4(3)	s 2(11)
s 5(1)	s 1(6)
s 5(2)	s 2(10)
s 5(3)	ss 9(4), 10(1)
s 6(1)	—
s 6(2)	s 7
s 6(3)	Sch 1
s 6(4)	—
Sch 1, para 1	s 2(5)–(8), (10)(a)
para 2	s 3
para 3	s 5(1)
para 4	s 6(3)
Sch 2	Sch 1

*Repealed in part

Appendix 3

Timetable for marital proceedings

Timetable for marital proceedings

1	Attend information meeting	S 8	Regulations under s 8 will prescribe details about such a meeting.
2	File statement of marital breakdown	S 8(2)	.Must be more than three months after attending information meeting.
		S 7(6)	A statement made before first anniversary of marriage is ineffective for the purposes of an application for a divorce order.
		S 5(3)(a)	A statement may be withdrawn.
3	Serve statement	S 12(1)(d)	Statement will be served by the court on the other party in accordance with rules under s 12; where a joint statement is made, service is unlikely to be required.
4	Start of period for reflection and consideration (PRC)	S 7(3)	On the fourteenth day after the day on which statement is received by the court.
5	PRC is nine months	S 7(3)	Unless s 7(13) applies in which case PRC is extended by six months to 15 months.
6	Delay in service	S 7(4)	Where a statement made by one party is required to be served by the court and failure to comply with the rules causes inordinate delay in service the other party may apply to the court for an extension of PRC.
7	Extension of PRC (delay)	S 7(5)	The court may extend PRC for any period between the beginning of PRC and the actual date of service.
8	Suspension of PRC (joint notice)	S 7(7)	Parties may give joint notice to the court that they are attempting a reconciliation but require additional time.
		S 7(8)(a)	PRC stops running on the day on which joint notice is received from the court.
		S 7(8)(b)	PRC resumes running on the day on which either of the parties gives notice that attempted reconciliation has been unsuccessful.
		S 7(9)	If PRC is interrupted under s 7(8) by a continuous period of more than 18 months any application for a divorce or separation order must be by reference to a new statement received by the court at any time after the period of 18 months.
9	PRC ends	S 7(3)	PRC ends nine months after the start, plus any extension under s 7(5), plus any suspension under s 7(8).

Timetable for marital proceedings—*contd*

10	Application for divorce order	S 3	Application for a divorce order triggers a prescribed period (whose length is yet unknown) for certain applications. Must be accompanied by a declaration specified in s 5(1)(d).
		S 5(2)	The application under s 3 and the statement do not have to be made by the same party.
11	Further reflection	S 7(10)	Where an application for a divorce order is made by either party under s 3, then if the other party applies to the court within the prescribed period for time for further reflection and requirements of s 9 (arrangements for the future) are satisfied (other than under s 9(3)) the PRC is extended by six months subject to the exceptions in 13 below, but only in relation to the application for a divorce order in respect of which application under s 7(10) was made and without invalidating the application for the divorce order.
12	Children under sixteen	S 7(11)	Where an application for a divorce order is made under s 3, then if at that time there is a child of the family under the age of sixteen the PRC is extended by six months subject to the exceptions in 13 below, but only in relation to the application for the divorce order in respect of which application under s 7(10) was made and without invalidating the application for the divorce order. A PRC so extended comes to an end on there ceasing to be a child of the family under the age of sixteen.
13	Exceptions	S 7(12)	(a) at the time when the application for the divorce order is made under s 3 there is an occupation order or a non-molestation order in force in favour of the applicant or a child of the family, made against the other party; or (b) the court is satisfied that delaying making the divorce order would be significantly detrimental to the welfare of any child of the family.
14	Order preventing divorce	S 10(1), (2)	If an application for a divorce order has been made, the court may on the application of the other party order that the marriage is not to be dissolved only if— (a) the dissolution of the marriage would result in substantial financial or other hardship to the other party or to a child of the family; and (b) it would be wrong in all the circumstances (including the conduct of the parties and the interests of any child of the family) for the marriage to be dissolved.
15	Cancellation of order preventing divorce	S 10(3)	If an application for the cancellation of an order preventing divorce is made by one or both of the parties, the court shall cancel the order unless it is still satisfied that— (a) dissolution of the marriage would result in substantial financial or other hardship to the other party or to a child of the family; and (b) it would be wrong, in all the circumstances (including the conduct of the parties and the interests of any child of the family), for the marriage to be dissolved

16	Marital breakdown	S 5	(a) A statement has been made that the maker believes that the marriage has broken down. (b) The statement complies with s 6. (c) The PRC under s 7 has ended. (d) The application under s 3 is accompanied by a declaration by the applicant that having reflected on the breakdown and having considered the requirements as to the arrangements for the future, believes that the marriage cannot be saved.
17	Arrangements for the future	S 9(2)	One of the following must be produced— (a) A court order dealing with financial arrangements. (b) A negotiated agreement as to financial arrangements. (c) A declaration by both parties that they have made financial arrangements. (d) A declaration by one (to which objection is not made) that— (i) he has no significant assets and does not intend to apply for financial provision, (ii) he believes that the other party has no significant assets and does not intend to apply for financial provision, and (iii) there are no financial arrangements to be made.
18	Specified period	S 5(3)(b)	A period of one year since the end of PRC.
19	Suspension of specified period (joint notice)	S 5(5)	Parties may give joint notice to the court that they are attempting a reconciliation but require additional time.
		S 5(6)(a)	Specified period stops running on the day on which joint notice is received by the court.
		S 5(6)(b)	Specified period resumes running on date on which either of the parties gives notice that attempted reconciliation has been unsuccessful.
		S 5(7)	If PRC is interrupted under s 5(6) by a continuous period of more than 18 months any application for a divorce or separation order must be by reference to a new statement received by the court at any time after the period of 18 months.
20	Application under s 3 not allowed	S 5(3)	An application under s 3 may not be made if the parties have jointly given notice withdrawing the statement (s 5(3)(a)). An application under s 3 may not be made if one year (the specified period) has passed since the end of PRC (s 5(3)(b)).

Appendix 4

Occupation orders

Table1—Entitlement to apply

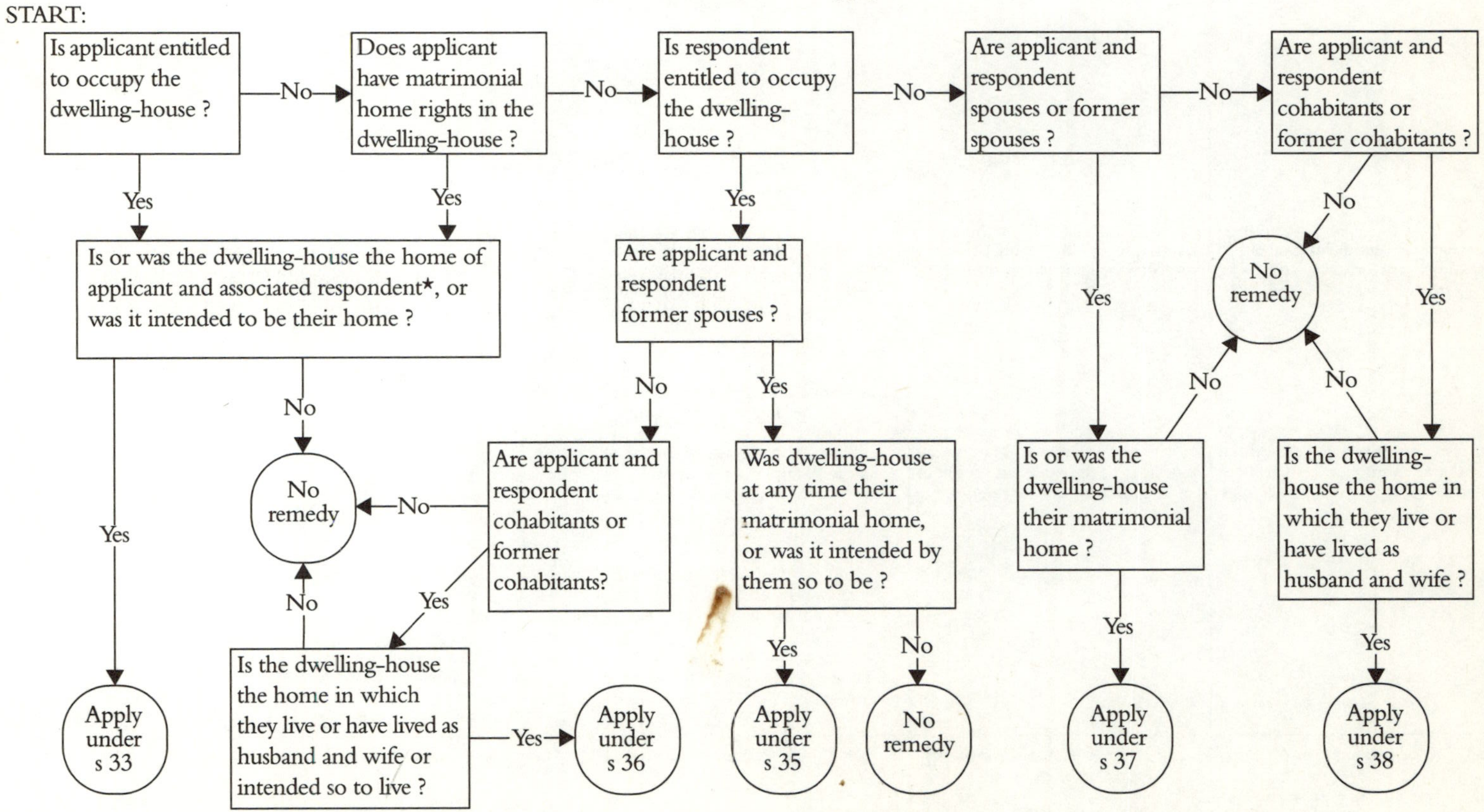

* Where the applicant and respondent are associated persons only by virtue of having agreed to marry one another (s 62(3)(e)), no application for an occupation order may be made more than three years after the date on which the agreement to marry was terminated (s 33(2))

Table 2—Range of orders available

Section 33 applicants Entitled applicants and those with matrimonial home rights Discretionary orders: S 33(3)	*Section 35 applicants* Non-entitled former spouse Mandatory orders: S 35(3), (4)	*Section 36 applicants* Non-entitled cohabitant or former cohabitant Mandatory orders: S 36(3), (4)	*Section 37 applicants* Neither spouse nor former spouse entitled Discretionary orders: S 37(3)	*Section 38 applicants* Neither cohabitant nor former cohabitant entitled Discretionary orders: s 38(3)
S 33(3)(a): Enforce the applicant's right to remain in occupation.	If applicant in occupation: S 35(3)(a): The right not to be evicted or excluded from the dwelling-house or part of it and S 35(3)(b): Prohibiting the respondent from excluding or evicting the applicant, or	If applicant in occupation: S 36(3)(a): The right not to be evicted or excluded from the dwelling-house or part of it and S 36(3)(b): Prohibiting the respondent from excluding or evicting the applicant, or		
S 33(3)(b): Require the respondent to permit the applicant to enter and remain in the dwelling-house or part of it.	If applicant not in occupation: S 35(4)(a): The right to enter into and occupy the dwelling-house, and S 35(4)(b): Requiring the respondent to permit the exercise of that right. Discretionary orders: S 35(5)	If applicant not in occupation: S 36(4)(a): The right to enter into and occupy the dwelling-house, and S 36(4)(b): Requiring the respondent to permit the exercise of that right. Discretionary orders: S 36(5)	S 37(3)(a): Require the respondent to permit the applicant to enter and remain in the dwelling-house or part of it.	S 38(3)(a): Require the respondent to permit the applicant to enter and remain in the dwelling-house or part of it.
S 33(3)(c): Regulate the occupation of the dwelling-house by either or both parties.	S 35(5)(a): Regulate the occupation of the dwelling-house by either or both parties.	S 36(5)(a): Regulate the occupation of the dwelling-house by either or both parties.	S 37(3)(b): Regulate the occupation of the dwelling-house by either or both parties.	S 38(3)(b): Regulate the occupation of the dwelling-house by either or both parties.
S 33(3)(d): If the respondent is entitled under s 33(1)(a)(i), prohibit, suspend or restrict the exercise of his right to occupy the dwelling-house.	S 35(5)(b): Prohibit, suspend or restrict the exercise by the respondent of his right to occupy the dwelling-house.	S 36(5)(b): Prohibit, suspend or restrict the exercise by the respondent of his right to occupy the dwelling-house.		

S 33(3)(e): If the respondent has matrimonial home rights and the applicant is the other spouse, terminate those rights.				
S 33(3)(f): Require the respondent to leave the dwelling-house or part of it.	S 35(5)(e): Require the respondent to leave the dwelling-house or part of it.	S 36(5)(c): Require the respondent to leave the dwelling-house or part of it.	S 37(3)(c): Require the respondent to leave the dwelling-house or part of it.	S 38(3)(c): Require the respondent to leave the dwelling-house or part of it.
S 33(3)(g): Exclude the respondent from a defined area in which the dwelling-house is included.	S 35(5)(d): Exclude the respondent from a defined area in which the dwelling-house is included.	S 36(5)(d): Exclude the respondent from a defined area in which the dwelling-house is included.	S 37(3)(d): Exclude the respondent from a defined area in which the dwelling-house is included.	S 38(3)(d): Exclude the respondent from a defined area in which the dwelling-house is included.
S 33(4): Declare the applicant is entitled under s 33(1)(a)(i), or has matrimonial rights.				
S 33(5): During the subsistence of the marriage: If the applicant has matrimonial home rights and the respondent is the other spouse, order that the rights shall not be brought to an end by (a) the death of the other spouse, or (b) the termination (otherwise than by death) of the marriage.				

Table 3—Criteria for exercise of powers

Section 33 applicants Entitled applicants and those with matrimonial home rights	*Section 35 applicants* Non-entitled former spouse	*Section 36 applicants* Non-entitled cohabitant or former cohabitant	*Section 37 applicants* Neither spouse nor former spouse entitled	*Section 38 applicants* Neither cohabitant nor former cohabitant entitled
In deciding whether, and (if so) in what manner, to exercise its powers under sub-s (3) the court SHALL have regard to— S 33(6) All the circumstances including— (a) the respective housing needs and housing resources of the parties and any relevant child; (b) the respective financial resources of the parties; (c) the likely effect of any order or decision not to exercise its powers under sub-s (3) on the health, safety or well-being of the parties and any relevant child; (d) the conduct of the parties in relation to each other and otherwise;	In deciding whether, and (if so) in what manner, to make an order of the kind mentioned in sub-ss (3) or (4) the court SHALL have regard to— S 35(6) All the circumstances including— (a) the respective housing needs and housing resources of the parties and any relevant child; (b) the respective financial resources of the parties; (c) the likely effect of any order or decision not to exercise its powers under sub-s (3) on the health, safety or well-being of the parties and any relevant child; (d) the conduct of the parties in relation to each other and otherwise; (e) the length of time that has elapsed since the parties ceased to live together; (f) the length of time that has elapsed since the marriage was dissolved or annulled; (g) the existence of any pending proceedings between them— (i) for an order under MCA 1973, ss 23A or 24, or (ii) for an order under CA 1989, Sch 1, para 1(2)(d) or (e), (iii) relating to the legal or beneficial ownership of the dwelling-house.	In deciding whether, and (if so) in what manner, to make an order of the kind mentioned in sub-ss (3) or (4) the court SHALL have regard to— S 36(6) All the circumstances including— (a) the respective housing needs and housing resources of the parties and any relevant child; (b) the respective financial resources of the parties; (c) the likely effect of any order or decision not to exercise its powers under sub-s (3) on the health, safety or well-being of the parties and any relevant child; (d) the conduct of the parties in relation to each other and otherwise; (e) the nature of the parties' relationship; (f) the length of time during which they have lived together as husband and wife; (g) whether there are or have been any children who are children of both parties or for whom the parties have or have had parental responsibility; (h) the length of time that has elapsed since the parties ceased to live together; (j) the existence of any pending proceedings between them— (i) for an order under CA 1989, Sch 1, para 1(2)(d) or (e), or (ii) relating to the legal or beneficial ownership of the dwelling-house.	In deciding whether, and (if so) in what manner, to exercise its powers under sub-s (3) the court SHALL have regard to— S 33(6) All the circumstances including— (a) the respective housing needs and housing resources of the parties and any relevant child; (b) the respective financial resources of the parties; (c) the likely effect of any order or decision not to exercise its powers under sub-s (3) on the health, safety or well-being of the parties and any relevant child; (d) the conduct of the parties in relation to each other and otherwise.	In deciding whether, and (if so) in what manner, to exercise its powers under sub-s (3) the court SHALL have regard to— S 38(4) All the circumstances including— (a) the respective housing needs and housing resources of the parties and any relevant child; (b) the respective financial resources of the parties; (c) the likely effect of any order or decision not to exercise its powers under sub-s (3) on the health, safety or well-being of the parties and any relevant child; (d) the conduct of the parties in relation to each other and otherwise; and (e) the questions mentioned in sub-s (5) (see below).

	S 35(7) In deciding whether and (if so) in what manner to exercise its power to include a sub-s (5) provision, the court SHALL have regard to all the circumstances including the matters in sub-s (6)(a) to (e).	S 36(7) In deciding whether and (if so) in what manner to exercise its power to include a sub-s (5) provision, the court SHALL have regard to all the circumstances including— (a) the matters in sub-s (6)(a) to (d), and (b) the questions mentioned in sub-s (8).		
S 33(7) If it appears that the applicant or any relevant child is likely to suffer significant harm attributable to conduct of the respondent if an order is not made, the court SHALL make an order containing a sub-s (3) provision unless it appears that— (a) the respondent or any relevant child is likely to suffer significant harm if the order is made, and (b) the harm likely to be suffered by the respondent or child in that event is as great as, or greater than, the harm attributable to conduct of the respondent which is likely to be suffered by the applicant or child if the order is not made.	S 35(8) If the court decides to make an order and it appears that, if the order does not include a sub-s (5) provision, the applicant or any relevant child is likely to suffer significant harm attributable to conduct of the respondent, the court SHALL include a sub-s (5) provision unless it appears that— (a) the respondent or any relevant child is likely to suffer significant harm if the provision is included, and (b) the harm likely to be suffered by the respondent or child in that event is as great as or greater than the harm attributable to conduct of the respondent which is likely to be suffered by the applicant or child if the provision is not included.	S 36(8) The questions are— (a) whether the applicant or any relevant child is likely to suffer significant harm attributable to conduct of the respondent if a sub-s (5) provision is not included; and (b) whether the harm likely to be suffered by the respondent or child is as great as or greater than the harm attributable to conduct of the respondent which is likely to be suffered by the applicant or child if the provision is not included.	S 33(7) If it appears that the applicant or any relevant child is likely to suffer significant harm attributable to conduct of the respondent, if an order is not made, the court SHALL make an order containing a sub-s (3) provision unless it appears that— (a) the respondent or any relevant child is likely to suffer significant harm if the order is made, and (b) the harm likely to be suffered by the respondent or child in that event is as great as, or greater than, the harm attributable to conduct of the respondent which is likely to be suffered by the applicant or child if the order is not made.	S 38(5) The questions are— (a) whether the applicant or any relevant child is likely to suffer significant harm attributable to conduct of the respondent if a sub-s sub-s (5) provision is not included; and (b) whether the harm likely to be suffered by the respondent or child in that event is as great as or greater than the harm attributable to conduct of the respondent which is likely to be suffered by the applicant or child if the provision is not included.
		S 41(1), (2) Where the parties are cohabitants or former cohabitants, and the court is required to consider the nature of the parties' relationship, it is to have regard to the fact that the parties have not given each other the commitment involved in marriage.		

Table 4—Duration

Section 33 orders Entitled applicants and those with matrimonial home rights	*Section 35 irders* Non-entitled former spouse	*Section 36 orders* Non-entitled cohabitant or former cohabitant	*Section 37 orders* Neither spouse nor former spouse entitled	*Section 38 orders* Neither cohabitant nor former cohabitant entitled
S 33 (10)— MAY be— (a) for a specified period, (b) until the occurrence of a specified event or (c) until further order.	S 35(10)— MUST be limited for a specified period not exceeding six months, MAY be extended (on one or more occasions) for a further specified period exceeding six months.	S 36(10)— MUST be limited for a specified period not exceeding six months, MAY be extended on one occasion for a further specified period not exceeding six months.	S 37(5)— MUST be limited for a specified period not exceeding six months, MAY be extended (on one or more occasions) for a further specified period not exceeding six months.	S 38(6)— MUST be limited for a specified period not exceeding six months, MAY be extended on one occasion for a further specified period not exceeding six months.
S 33(9)(b)— Unless order under s 33(5)(a), orders cease to have effect on the death of either party.	S 35(9)(b)— Orders cease to have effect on the death of either party.	S 36(9)(b)— Orders cease to have effect on the death of either party.		
S 49(1): An occupation order MAY be varied or discharged by the court on the application of (a) the respondent or (b) the person on whose application the order was made.				
S 49(3): If a spouse's matrimonial home rights are a charge on the estate or interest of the other spouse or the trustees for the other spouse, an order under s 33 against the other spouse MAY also be varied or discharged by the court on application by any person deriving title under the other spouse or under the trustees and affected by the charge.				

Appendix 5

Glossary of terms

Glossary of terms

The Family Law Act 1996 introduces a variety of new terms. This Glossary lists those terms that are defined by the Act or included in the interpretation sections with details of the provision where the term is used or defined, followed by the meaning of the term or a cross reference to another statute or paragraph in the narrative where the meaning is discussed. It should be noted that some terms have different meanings in different Parts of the Act and some definitions only apply to particular sections or schedules.

Term	Provision in FLA 1996	Meaning
Adoption order	S 63(1)	See Adoption Act 1976, s 72(1)
Arrangements for the future	S 9	See para 3.28.
Associated persons	S 62(3)–(6)	Spouses and former spouses; cohabitants and former cohabitants; common householders; relatives; engaged or formerly engaged couple; parents of a child or those with parental responsibility for that child; parties to the same family proceedings. See paras 6.8–6.26.
Child	S 63(1)	Person under the age of 18. See para 6.27.
Child of the family	S 24(1)	See Matrimonial Causes Act 1973, s 52(1). In relation to the parties to a marriage, (a) a child of both those parties; and (b) any other child, not being a child who is placed with those parties by a local authority or another organisation, who has been treated by both of those parties as a child of their family.
Cohabitants	S 62(1)(a)	A man and woman who, although not married to each other, live together as husband and wife. See paras 6.2–6.6.
Connected persons	Ss 54(5), 55(4)	In relation to any person, that person's spouse, former spouse, cohabitant or former cohabitant. See para 7.17.
Connected proceedings	S 25	Proceedings are connected with the breakdown of a marriage if marital proceedings are pending at the time of proceedings— (a) under Children Act 1989, Parts I to V with respect to a child of the family; (i) for, or for the cancellation of, an order preventing divorce in relation to the marriage; (ii) by either party to the marriage under Family Law Act 1996, Part IV; (iii) for the exercise, in relation to a party to the marriage or a child of the family, of any of the court's powers under Matrimonial Causes Act 1973, Part II; (iv) made otherwise to the court with respect to, or in connection with, any proceedings connected with the breakdown of the marriage. See para 3.42–3.43.
Court (Part II)	S 24(1)	See Matrimonial Causes Act 1973, s 52(1): (except where the context otherwise requires) means the High Court or, where a county court has jurisdiction by virtue of Matrimonial and Family Proceedings Act 1984, Part V, a county court.
Court (Part IV)	S 57	The High Court, a county court or a magistrates' court. See para 14.1.

Glossary of terms—*contd*

Court (Sch 5)	Sch 5 para 1	The High Court or a county court. See para 10.6.
Court (Sch 7)	Sch 7 para 1	Does not include a magistrates' court. See para 13.4.
Development	S 63(1)	Physical, intellectual, emotional, social or behavioural development; see Children Act 1989 s 31(9). See para 8.26.
Divorce order	S 2(1)(a)	An order which dissolves a marriage. See para 3.4
Divorce proceedings	S 20(3)(b)	An application for a divorce order that has not been withdrawn. See para 2.2.
Dwelling-house	S 63(1), (4)	Includes any building or part of a building which is occupied as a dwelling, any caravan, house-boat or structure which is occupied as a dwelling, and any yard, garden, garage or outhouse belonging to it and occupied with it. See paras 7.2, 12.5.
Entitled applicant	S 33(1)	Person who is entitled to occupy a dwelling-house by virtue of a beneficial estate or interest or contract or statute or who has matrimonial home rights in the dwelling-house; and the dwelling-house is or was the home of the entitled person and of another associated person or is the former, existing or intended matrimonial home of the parties. See para 8.2.
Ex parte order	S 45(1)	An occupation order or a non-molestation order made even though the respondent has not been given such notice as would otherwise be required by rules of court. See Ch 11.
Family proceedings	S 63(1), (2)	Any proceedings under the inherent jurisdiction of the High Court in relation to children and Family Law Act 1996, Parts II or IV, Matrimonial Causes Act 1973, Adoption Act 1976, Domestic Proceedings and Magistrates' Court Act 1978, Matrimonial and Family Proceedings Act 1984, Part III, Children Act 1989, Parts I, II and IV, and Human Fertilisation and Embryology Act 1990, s 30. See para 6.25.
Financial arrangements	S 9, Sch 1 para 6	See Matrimonial Causes Act, s 34(2). Provisions governing the rights and liabilities towards one another when living separately of the parties to a marriage (including a marriage which has been dissolved or annulled) in respect of the making or securing of payments or the disposition or use of any property, including such rights and liabilities with respect to the maintenance or education of any child, whether or not a child of the family. See para 4.2
Former cohabitants	S 62(1)(b)	Persons who were cohabitants, but not those who have subsequently married each other. See para 6.7.
Full hearing	S 45(5)	A hearing of which notice has been given to all the parties in accordance with rules of court at which the respondent must have the opportunity to make representations relating to an ex parte order. See para 11.3.

Harm (in relation to an adult)	S 63(1)	Ill-treatment or the impairment of health. See para 8.26.
Harm (in relation to a child)	S 63(1)	Ill-treatment or the impairment of health or development; see Children Act 1989, s 31(9). See para 8.26.
Health	S 63(1)	Includes physical or mental health; see Children Act 1989, s 31(9). See para 8.26.
Ill-treatment	S 63(1)	Includes forms of ill-treatment which are physical and, in relation to a child, includes sexual abuse; see Children Act 1989, s 31(9). See para 8.26.
Information meeting	S 8(6)	A meeting organised for the purpose— (a) of providing relevant information to the party or parties attending about matters which may arise in connection with the provisions of Parts II and III; and (b) of giving the party or parties attending the opportunity of having a meeting with a marriage counsellor and of encouraging that party or parties to attend that meeting. See paras 2.7, 3.23–3.27.
Initial order	S 45(5)	An occupation order, made ex parte by virtue of s 45(1). See para 11.3.
Landlord	Sch 7 para 1	Includes (a) any person from time to time deriving title under the original landlord; and (b) in relation to a dwelling-house any person other than the tenant who is, or (but for Rent Act 1977, Part VII, or Rent (Agriculture) Act 1976, Part II) would be, entitled to possession of the dwelling-house. See para 13.11.
Marital proceedings	S 20	Divorce proceedings and separation proceedings. See para 2.3
Matrimonial home rights	S 30	Rights enjoyed by a spouse who has no other right to occupy the matrimonial home. See Ch 7.
Mortgage	S 63(1)	See Law of Property Act 1925, s 205(1)(xvi). Includes any charge or lien on any property for securing money or money's worth.
Mortgagee	S 63(1)	See Law of Property Act 1925, s 205(1)(xvi). Includes a chargee by way of legal mortgage and any person from time to time deriving title under the original mortgagee.
Mortgage payments	S 59(1)	Any payments which, under the terms of the mortgage, the mortgagor is required to make to any person. See para 8.35.
Mortgagor	S 63(1)	See Law of Property Act 1925, s 205(1)(xvi). Includes any person from time to time deriving title under the original mortgagor or entitled to redeem a mortgage according to his estate interest or right in the mortgaged property.

Glossary of terms—*contd*

Non-entitled former spouse	S 35(1)	A former spouse who has no entitlement to occupy the former, existing or intended matrimonial home by virtue of a beneficial estate or interest or contract or statute. See para 8.3.
Non-molestation order	S 42(1)	An order prohibiting a person from molesting an associated person and/or a relevant child. See Ch 9.
Occupation order	S 39	An order under s 33, 35, 36, 37 or 38. See Ch 8.
Order preventing divorce	S 10(1)	An order that a marriage is not to be dissolved. See paras 2.4, 4.10–4.20.
Parental responsibility	S 63(1)	See Children Act 1989, s 3; all the rights, duties, powers, responsibilities and authority which by law a parent of a child has in relation to the child and his property. See paras 6.22, 6.23.
Party	S 24(1)	In relation to a marriage, means one of the parties to a marriage.
Period for reflection and consideration	S 7	A period for the parties to reflect on whether their marriage can be saved and to consider what arrangements should be made for the future. See paras 2.5, 3.18–3.20.
Power of arrest	S 47	Power attached to one or more provisions of an occupation order or a non-molestation order whereby a constable may arrest without a warrant a person who he has reasonable cause for suspecting to be in breach of any such provisions. See Ch 10.
Relatives	S 63(1)	See para 6.16.
Relevant child	S 62(2)	(a) any child who is living with or might reasonably be expected to live with either party to the proceedings, (b) any child in relation to whom an order under Adoption Act 1976 or Children Act 1989 is in question in the proceedings, (c) any other child whose interests the court considers relevant. See paras 6.27–6.28.
Relevant judicial authority	S 63(1)	Where an order was made by the High Court, a judge of that court; Where the order was made by a county court, a judge or district judge of that or any other county court; Where the order was made by a magistrates' court, any magistrates' court. See para 10.6.

Relevant tenancy	Sch 7 para 1	(a) a protected or statutory tenancy within the meaning of Rent Act 1977; (b) a statutory tenancy within the meaning of Rent (Agriculture) Act 1976; (c) a secure tenancy within the meaning of Housing Act 1985, s 79; (d) an assured tenancy or assured agricultural occupancy within the meaning of Housing Act 1988, Part I. See para 13.5.
Representative	S 60(1)	A prescribed person or any person in a prescribed category authorised to act on behalf of another in relation to proceedings to which Part IV applies. See para 14.4.
Separation order	S 2(1)(b)	An order which provides for the separation of the parties to a marriage. See para 3.4.
Separation proceedings	S 20(3)(a)	An application for separation order that has not been withdrawn. See para 2.2.
Significant harm	S 63(3)	Where the question of whether harm suffered by a child is significant turns on the child's health or development, his health or development shall be compared with that which could reasonably be expected of a similar child; see Children Act 1989, s 31(10). See paras 8.26–8.28.
Specified period	S 5(3)(b)	A period of one year from the end of the period for reflection and consideration. See paras 3.10–3.12.
Statement of marital breakdown	S 6(1)	A statement under s 5(1)(a) which complies with the requirements of s 6 and regulations. See paras 2.6, 3.13.

Index